CHARACTERS AND SCENES
STUDIES IN CHARLOTTE M. YONGE

Charlotte Mary Yonge
Aet. about 35
From a photograph taken by the Rev. Duke Yonge.

CHARACTERS & SCENES
Studies in
Charlotte M. Yonge

EDITED BY

Julia Courtney & Clemence Schultze

CONTRIBUTORS

John Alves

Cecilia Bass

Hilary Clare

Julia Courtney

Amy de Gruchy

Barbara Dennis

Barbara J. Dunlap

Wendy Forrester

Maria Poggi Johnson

Clemence Schultze

June Sturrock

BEECHCROFT
BOOKS

2007

Copyright © 2007 by The Charlotte M. Yonge Fellowship

Published by Beechcroft Books
Blunsden
Faringdon Road
Abingdon
Berkshire OX14 1BQ

Beechcroft Books is the publishing name of The Charlotte M. Yonge Fellowship

Designed by Clemence Schultze and Joy Wotton
Set in Perpetua
Printed by CPI Antony Rowe, Eastbourne

ISBN 978-0-9557096-0-9

CONTENTS

LIST OF ILLUSTRATIONS

CONTRIBUTORS

JOHN ALVES (1922-2005) read PPE at New College, Oxford and served in Intelligence from 1942 to 1945. He had a distinguished career at the Bank of England and with the International Monetary Fund. In retirement he pursued his varied interests: history, railways, and Yonge's works. He was a frequent contributor to the Charlotte M. Yonge Fellowship's *Review* and *Journal*.

CECILIA BASS read English at Oxford and later taught at Winchester County High School. She wrote an MPhil thesis on Charlotte Yonge's narrative methods and her literary sources. More recently she has developed an interest in contemporary criticism of Yonge's work and changes in critical practice in nineteenth-century periodical literature. She edited the *Journal* of the Charlotte M. Yonge Fellowship from 1995 to 2005.

HILARY CLARE is a freelance genealogist and researcher but also writes about children's literature, particularly girls' books, and is co-author of *The Encyclopaedia of Girls' School Stories* (2000, 2nd revised edition impending). She has a life-long interest in Charlotte M. Yonge, and has contributed articles on her to *Children's Literature in Education* and to the *Review* of the CMYF.

JULIA COURTNEY is an Associate Lecturer with the Open University, tutoring on undergraduate and postgraduate literature courses. Born and educated in Winchester, local interest drew her to Yonge's novels, and her PhD focused on Yonge's influence on younger women novelists, Church workers and teachers. She has also published on Flaubert and Stevenson.

AMY DE GRUCHY taught English at the Dorset Institute of Higher Education until retirement. For her higher degree she researched *The Monthly Packet*, the magazine edited by Yonge. She contributes to the Charlotte M. Yonge Fellowship *Review* and *Journal*, writes summaries of Yonge's works for the CMYF website, and has published articles on her in historical periodicals.

BARBARA DENNIS recently retired as Professor from the English Department at the University of Wales, Lampeter, where she was Head of Victorian Studies. Her published work on Yonge includes articles, an edition of *The Heir of Redclyffe* (World's Classics), the 'Introduction' to *The Daisy Chain* (Virago) and a monograph: *Charlotte Yonge, Novelist of the Oxford Movement* (1992).

BARBARA J. DUNLAP is Professor Emerita and retired head of Archives and Special Collections of the City College of the City University of New York. She has published articles on Yonge and on Barbara Pym, including 'Reading

Charlotte Yonge into the Novels of Barbara Pym' in *"All This Reading": The Literary World of Barbara Pym* (Fairleigh Dickinson University Press, 2003).

WENDY FORRESTER is a retired journalist who worked on *Woman's Weekly* for thirty-five years. She published *Great-Grandmama's Weekly*, an appreciation of the Victorian years of the *Girl's Own Paper*; and *Anna Buchan and O. Douglas* (Maitland Press, 1995) a biography of the Scottish novelist Anna Buchan (sister of John Buchan) who wrote under the pseudonym 'O. Douglas'.

MARIA POGGI JOHNSON read English at Oxford and is now a Professor in the Theology Department of the University of Scranton, in Pennsylvania. Her doctoral work at the University of Virginia was on Keble, Yonge and the Christian moral life; and her research interests include the interaction between Christianity and culture, in particular art and literature, especially in Victorian England.

CLEMENCE SCHULTZE read Greats at St Hilda's College, Oxford; she is a Roman republican historian, and Lecturer in Classics and Ancient History at Durham. Her research interests lie in ancient historiography and in the reception of the classical world in nineteenth-century Britain and France. She has published on Yonge's version, in *My Young Alcides*, of the myth of Hercules.

JUNE STURROCK is an Emeritus Professor in the Department of English at Simon Fraser University in British Columbia. She has published widely on the Romantics (particularly Blake), Jane Austen (including editing the Broadview Texts of *Mansfield Park*), and Charlotte Yonge, including *"Heaven and Home": Charlotte Yonge's Domestic Fiction and the Victorian Debate over Women* (University of Victoria, 1995).

ACKNOWLEDGEMENTS

The Editors thank the Charlotte M. Yonge Society for allowing the reproduction of the genealogical tables from *A Chaplet for Charlotte Yonge*, ed. G. Battiscombe and M. Laski (1965). Maria Poggi Johnson's article appears by kind permission of the Editorial Board of *Clio*.

Grateful thanks are due to all those who kindly helped in many ways: Margaret Birch for much work on the original typescript; Joy Wotton for the cover and for invaluable guidance about production and marketing; Gyles Glover and Martin Rush for help in preparing text and illustrations; Dave Cradduck for indexing; and the staff of Antony Rowe Ltd for technical assistance. The late Professor Philip Drazin's unpublished Yonge bibliography was exceptionally useful. Past and present members of the Committee of the Charlotte M. Yonge Fellowship are thanked for constant support and advice.

INTRODUCTION

Julia Courtney and Clemence Schultze

On the morning of Palm Sunday, 31 March 1901, two days after
Charlotte Mary Yonge had been interred at the foot of the Keble
Memorial in Otterbourne churchyard, the eminent Anglican
theologian Robert Campbell Moberly entered the pulpit of the little
Hampshire church so closely associated with the Yonge family.
Moberly had known Charlotte Yonge all his life, as had most of the
congregation: 'without [Miss Charlotte Yonge]', he claimed, 'there is
no one, I suppose, now living who can at all remember the village of
Otterbourne.'[1] Today, more than a century later, all those gathered to
'reverently miss and mourn' the novelist, teacher, editor and historian
have also passed into memory; but those qualities of 'life-giving
imagination' celebrated by Moberly's Funeral Sermon have ensured
consistent, if never extensive, readership for Charlotte Yonge's works,
especially her novels.

In the Centenary Year of her death, members of the Charlotte M.
Yonge Fellowship resolved to mark the anniversary by collecting a
number of essays on her work. The Fellowship was founded in 1996
by Jean Shell and Janet Clarke with the main aim of promoting the
dissemination and study of Charlotte Yonge's writing and includes
scholars, book collectors and general readers amongst its members, a
combination which informs this volume. Our one hundred and fifty
members meet twice each year for day conferences of lectures,
presentations, visits and discussions; we have a *Journal* and a twice-
yearly newsletter, the *Review*, and we also keep in touch through a
network of friendships and scholarly collaboration. Our contributions
to this book reflect not only the current range of Yonge studies, but

1

also celebrate the character of the Charlotte M. Yonge Fellowship, with its diversity of interests and approaches.

Moberly's sermon sited Charlotte Yonge firmly within the Tractarian theology of fiction, which gave the novelist the sacramental function of 'setting forth [. . .] essential truth through fiction [. . .] preaching righteousness and truth [. . .] under the shifting forms which human experience suggests'. The ten essays in *Characters and Scenes: Studies in Charlotte M. Yonge* are similarly aware of both Charlotte Yonge's commitment to a set of universal religious and social values and the changing ways in which she was able to mediate those values as (in Moberly's words) 'fascinatingly interesting' and 'all alert with living power'.

Barbara Dennis' essay clearly presents Charlotte Yonge's relationship with the Oxford Movement as central to any understanding of the novelist's work. Using the late *The Carbonels* (1895) as a paradigm of the interaction between the novels and successive stages of the Movement, and progressing to detailed analysis of *The Castle Builders* (1854), *Hopes and Fears* (1860) and a range of subsequent novels, this essay illustrates the extent to which 'the history of the movement is Charlotte Yonge's discourse'.

Amy de Gruchy furthers this enquiry by taking issue with both contemporary and more recent descriptions of Charlotte Yonge as inflexible and unable to relate to social change. Her essay charts movement and progression as well as continuity in the thematic concerns of the novels, exploring her subject with particular reference to *Heartsease* (1854), *The Daisy Chain* (1856), *Friarswood Post Office* (1860), *Dynevor Terrace* (1857), *Hopes and Fears* (1860), *The Young Stepmother* (1861), *The Clever Woman of the Family* (1865) and *My Young Alcides* (1875).

Another plea for reconsideration of received attitudes to Charlotte Yonge comes when Wendy Forrester compares *The Heir of Redclyffe* (1853) with *Dynevor Terrace* (1857), arguing against Georgina Battiscombe's dismissal of the latter as 'a plagiarism of *The Heir*' and recommending it to a new generation of readers.

Reactions of nineteenth-century reviewers to the novels as they appeared is the focus of 'Charlotte Yonge and the Critics' by Cecilia Bass. Offering an extensive survey of Victorian periodicals, this essay notes that 'to read contemporary criticism of Charlotte Yonge's novels is a reminder of how familiar yet how strange was her world'.

While one might expect comparisons with Jane Austen and George Eliot, it is stimulating to find Yonge described as a social realist along the lines of Balzac, Flaubert and Zola.

Particularly towards the end of Yonge's career many reviewers noted her largely female readership, and 'an intense if conflicted interest in women's ambitions and the proper use of women's energies' is shown as integral to Charlotte Yonge's project in June Sturrock's essay 'Women's Work, Money and the Everyday – the Novels of the 1870s'. Using three of the contemporary novels: *The Pillars of the House* (1873), *The Three Brides* (1876) and *Magnum Bonum* (1879), Sturrock presents Charlotte Yonge as 'increasingly engaged with the economic aspects of women's work' and thus with mundane and quotidian details. The essay suggests that this 'everyday' focus on continuity conveys the incomplete nature of experienced reality in almost Modernist terms.

In 'Charlotte Yonge: Embodying the Domestic Fiction' Barbara J. Dunlap also examines Yonge's relationship with the real, in this case through her dramatic re-presentation of the physical body 'in motion which advances the narrative', acting as 'a vital factor in the reader's belief in the world she creates'. Again, a selection of the domestic, contemporary novels is analysed, in particular *The Daisy Chain*, *The Heir of Redclyffe* and *The Pillars of the House*.

Since all the essays noted so far rely on the contemporary, linked novels, the updating and clarification of the genealogies originally prepared by members of the Charlotte M. Yonge Society will be especially welcome. This is the joint work of the late John Alves and Hilary Clare. Their acknowledgement underlines the Fellowship's debt to the earlier Society and notes that our present essay collection is the successor to the Society's *A Chaplet for Charlotte Yonge* (1965).

The three remaining essays site Charlotte Yonge's contemporary concerns within a wider cultural context. Maria Poggi Johnson offers a valuable addition to the small body of criticism of Charlotte Yonge's historical novels with her analysis of *The Armourer's Prentices* of 1884. In this novel, set in the Evil May Day riots of 1517, Charlotte Yonge portrays the Reformation as 'a struggle between systems of meaning' symbolised by the two rival places of trade, Dragon Court and Warwick Court. The *via media* of Anglicanism is daringly personified by a Morisco swordsmith whose faith links the newly emergent Church of England to 'the ancient Semitic roots of Christianity'.

Clemence Schultze's survey of 'Charlotte Yonge and the Classics' takes as its starting-point 'the all-pervasiveness of classical culture in Yonge's own milieu' and proceeds to demonstrate 'how the shared and assumed background [. . .] can foreground conflict and ambiguity'. This essay touches on Yonge's non-fiction to confirm 'that she envisaged classical material at an appropriate level as being available to all age groups and classes' and then focuses on *My Young Alcides* (1875) as an example of how fiction with a classical theme enables discussion of sensitive religious issues. Lastly, classical learning is seen to function as 'a touchstone of right behaviour' beyond its accepted signifiers of class and gender.

Finally, Julia Courtney's essay returns to the theme of critical reception by looking at Charlotte Yonge's followers, women novelists such as Christabel Coleridge, Frances Peard and Mary Bramston whose work was explicitly informed by, yet moves beyond, Charlotte Yonge's immediate concerns. Using Elaine Showalter's notable definition of 'a literature of their own' she attempts to show a female line of wit culminating in Ivy Compton-Burnett, whose novels invert and subvert the Tractarian metaphor outlined by Moberly in his Funeral Sermon.

The writers of these essays hope that their work will interest a range of readers: scholars in the field of nineteenth-century literature and Victorian culture, members of the Fellowship, and also readers coming to the novels for the first time. Sadly, few Yonge novels are currently in print, but second-hand copies can still be found and the Fellowship is an effective means of locating these.

The Charlotte M. Yonge Fellowship can be contacted through its website, the URL of which is: **www.cmyf.org.uk**

---

1 Robert Campbell Moberly, *Funeral Sermon for Charlotte Mary Yonge* (Eastleigh, Hants: The Eastleigh Printing Works, 1901). This is reprinted on pp. 213-18 of the present volume.

CHARLOTTE YONGE, NOVELIST OF THE OXFORD MOVEMENT

Barbara Dennis

Charlotte Yonge was on the verge of her tenth birthday when John Keble preached his sermon on 'National Apostasy' in July 1833, and at the even more impressionable age of twelve when he finally came to be vicar of Hursley. When he arrived in the parish in early 1836 the Oxford Movement was under full steam, and in parishes far distant from Oxford the influence of the *Tracts for the Times* was perceptible. In his own he found a nucleus of parishioners for whom the message from Oxford was no startling novelty, but the confirmation of a familiar tradition which went back to the Non-Jurors of the seventeenth century; and they were fertile ground for what the Tracts were urging. In Hursley and the neighbouring village of Otterbourne the young squire and patron of the living, Sir William Heathcote, and his friend William Yonge belonged to the old High Church tradition, and welcomed the new school which Keble represented. George Moberly, the new headmaster of Winchester, and who was to become a distinguished theologian, was another, and made up the complement of the circle round Keble. There was never a time, in fact, when Charlotte Yonge, then little more than a precociously intelligent child, was not familiar with the old religion, and on Keble's arrival she eagerly embraced the new emphases. She grew to be, in the course of Keble's own lifetime, almost as significant a figure in the Movement as her master.

Keble brought to her not so much new doctrines as new attitudes to them. The awesome number of novels she published (written, she famously said, 'Pro Ecclesia Dei') all promoted in fictional form the ideals of the Oxford Movement, though never explicitly: 'reserve' was a key word for the Tractarians (Isaac Williams, Newman's curate and Keble's potential successor as Professor of Poetry at Oxford, had written a notorious tract on 'Reserve in Communicating Religious Knowledge'), and all her teaching must be inferred from the narrative and characters.

Yet in a career that covered nearly sixty years she chronicled every stage of the Oxford Movement, and recorded aspects that characterised each. She is an invaluable witness as to how the revolution that convulsed the church in 1833 was experienced by society at large, and of the marks it left on the community; and she always thought of herself, in her own phrase, as 'a sort of instrument for popularising church views'.

She began her career as a novelist in the first stage of the Oxford Movement, which was concerned primarily with doctrine and what was set out in the rubrics, Articles and Homilies of the Book of Common Prayer – all of which had been, the Oxford reformers roundly declared, so carelessly disregarded by the church in the previous 150 years as to have fallen out of all common usage. The situation as it stood, they declared, was critical ('Speak I must;' Newman had avowed passionately in the opening Tract, 'for the times are very evil'), and tract after tract appeared impressing on the clergy duties such as confession and absolution, the daily saying of Morning and Evening Prayer, the significance of a priesthood ordained by Apostolic Succession, and so on, which were enjoined on them in the Prayer Book. Most of all they were reminded of the prime importance of the ordinances and the sacraments of Baptism and the Eucharist. This first stage lasted for the duration of the publication of the Tracts, for the years between 1833 and 1841, and for the final reception of Newman into the Roman Catholic Church in 1845.

The second stage of the Movement grew from the first. It was as much concerned with the externals of religion as with doctrine, and starts to become obvious in the 1850s and 1860s, at the time when Charlotte Yonge had established herself as a mature and confident novelist and was producing her best work. It is the period of the Ritualists and their work in the inner cities, and what Scott Holland called 'the recovery of the slums by the Oxford Movement'[1] and Charlotte Yonge makes it her material in a significant number of her most impressive novels.

In her later work she faithfully transcribes the period in the Oxford Movement that takes us to the end of the century, when the excesses which had sometimes characterised the middle phase had generally abated or had been absorbed, and the Movement had become an accepted part of church history. The reforms so urgently called for in the 1830s were now to a recognisable extent in place, and the church was a very different institution from the one called to account by the Tracts. The representations of church life and clergy in the last novels suggest the effectiveness of the Tractarian mission.

One novel to represent this progression almost as a paradigm is *The Carbonels* (1895), a retrospective tale for National School children, which covers the period of Charlotte Yonge's own life, and is full of autobiographical detail: early in the 1820s the newly wed Carbonels arrive (like William and Fanny Yonge) to find their parish (as Keble had described Hursley) 'rather settled on its lees'; and the church itself, with its box-pews and dilapidated fabric, is a model of pre-Ecclesiological abuses. It is in the hands of a non-resident vicar, younger son of the squire 'who had been made to take Holy Orders without any special fitness for it and with no idea of the duties of his vocation'[2] and an incompetent curate. But new clergy, straight from Oxford and fired with new reforms, institute proceedings more in line with the rubrics of the Prayer Book. Daily services are adopted, communions and communicants are increased; and under the paternalistic supervision of Edmund Carbonel, full of Tractarian zeal, a village school is established, while his wife takes charge of a new Sunday school. At the end of the novel the authorial voice reflects 'The church is beautiful now, not only to look at, nor merely in the well-performed music of the services, but in the number and devotion of the worshippers and communicants'.[3]

But *The Carbonels* is a sketchy and unsophisticated overview almost at the end of Charlotte Yonge's career, which recalls in general terms the experience of a previous generation, with an easy assumption of a job well done. Much more interesting are the novels written when she was moving to the height of her powers, and which record less consciously but more valuably what was happening to the contemporary church in the early and middle years of the Oxford Movement.

THE EARLY OXFORD MOVEMENT

Two novels in particular identify the early concerns of the Tractarians, *The Castle Builders* (1854) and *The Daisy Chain* (1856), and both take the Prayer Book as a constant source of reference. The Tractarians had stressed the sacramental side of religion, and the importance of ordinances and the services of the Prayer Book; and the subtitle of *The Castle Builders*, *The Deferred Confirmation*, is a pointer to the subtext, the importance of obedience to the rules established by the church. Emmeline and Kate Berners acknowledge what they come to see as their wilful irresponsibility, for instance, in delaying their chance for confirmation when their stepbrother, Frank, who is also their guide and mentor, dies in a tragic accident: his last words to them are to secure their promise to be confirmed.

Frank is the very embodiment of the ideal young Anglican as defined by the Tractarians. He attends Morning and Evening Prayer daily, he is at the weekly Eucharist where this is available, he has the highest concept of the priestly vocation, to which he feels himself strongly drawn, he rules his life by the precepts of the Catechism. At the end, as death by drowning is imminent, he draws comfort from the Prayer Book and the Prayer to be Used at Sea ('[. . .] hear us, calling out of the depth of misery, and the jaws of this death which is ready now to swallow us up'). But he is fortified by the early communion in which he has taken part before the ill-fated expedition, and as he encounters death 'the sunlight seemed to have bathed his countenance and hair, as he sat with his face turned westward, looking intently [. . .] as if he saw something far beyond the horizon-line of pale glimmering light'.[4]

The same lesson is driven home in *The Heir of Redclyffe* (1853), published only a few months before *The Castle Builders*, but less rigidly based on the Book of Common Prayer. Guy Morville is a precursor of Frank and his religious life is that defined by the Tractarians: the Daily Service (even on one's honeymoon) and a keen appreciation of those sacraments 'generally necessary to salvation', Baptism and the Eucharist. Guy's rejoinder to the old woman who has ensured his baptism at birth is well known – 'I have to thank you for more than all the world besides!'[5] – and an alert reader will remember his search for a church celebrating a Communion Sunday when his fortunes seem at their lowest ebb during his exile at Moorworth.

The Tractarian veneration of the priesthood is a significant element in *The Castle Builders*. Frank dies before he is able to fulfil his vocation (and is thus spared a threatened clash of principle, for obedience to lawful authority was something else stressed in the Catechism – and Frank's worldly father has quite other ambitions for his son than a humble parish), but the ideal parish priest is represented in the novel by Lord Herbert Somerville. We watch his devotional life in the slum parish of Dearport, where he is the pattern priest with his daily routine of services, sick-visiting, catechising, etc. Moreover his wife (soon to become his widow), as idealised a figure as he, is the founder of a new Sisterhood in Dearport, an early and at that date recent manifestation of Oxford Movement influence (Pusey and Keble had been discussing the idea of Sisterhoods as early as 1838, and Pusey's community at Park Village had been founded in 1845). But it is an important point that none of these characteristics is an object of comment in the text: the details appear as incidentals in the narrative. The significance is implicit and must be inferred. The same is true of another notable novel of the 1850s, *The Daisy Chain* (1856). It is as strongly marked by the signs of the early Oxford Movement as *The Castle Builders*, but only an informed and observant reader will be aware of it – Charlotte Yonge is as reticent about liturgy and doctrine as the Tracts demanded in their insistence on 'reserve'. The May family, whose history we follow, provides the material for the lessons of the Tracts. The eldest, Richard, becomes in the course of the novel an exemplar of the ideal parish priest, transformed by ordination from the rather dull-witted butt of his cleverer brothers and sisters to the rock-solid embodiment of Tractarian teaching as the incumbent of a slum parish. Baptism is a point in the narrative when the youngest child, Gertrude, is born days before her mother's death; and confirmation becomes a significant issue when Harry May, an engaging young scapegrace about to leave home on his first voyage as a midshipman, is detected in an outrageous prank and is accordingly threatened with the withdrawal of his 'ticket'. The Eucharist is never mentioned directly, but there are covert references throughout the novel ('don't you remember last Sunday?' says Meta. 'I felt myself so vain and petted a thing! as if I had no share in the Cup of suffering').[6]

These are all novels of her most impressionable period (*Heartsease* is another) where we read most explicitly the lessons of the Tracts, and the teaching of the Catechism. The Catechism is firm, of course, about the duty of obedience – to 'governors, teachers, spiritual pastors and masters', or any other rightfully constituted authority, a list which includes parents – and this is a theme that runs through all the early novels. It is most notorious in *The Heir of Redclyffe* where the question of Laura's secret and unauthorised understanding with Philip has bothered every later reader to whom the Catechism means nothing (and even her contemporary public sometimes felt that Charlotte Yonge was interpreting her text rather narrowly). But it is a theme forcefully expressed in all the novels of the 1840s and 1850s when she was most consciously promoting the Catechism and the teachings of the Oxford Movement: honour and obey all who are put in (rightful) authority. So in *Abbeychurch*, *Scenes and Characters*, and *Heartsease*, too, the rightful claim of authority to obedience is a pivotal theme in the narrative.

THE LATER OXFORD MOVEMENT

The second stage of the Oxford Movement, when the Tracts had come to an end and Newman had left the church, was as much concerned with the externals of religion, and its practical effects in society as with the academic reading of the liturgy. The early leaders of the Movement – Newman, Keble, Pusey – were not particularly interested in the ceremonial and elaborate devotions which came to be associated with the Movement, though they promoted vigorously its other manifestations, in forms like education, the mission field, and the work of the church in what we now call the inner cities.

Charlotte Yonge records them all. The High Church commitment to education had been there from the beginning, and all her early novels chronicle the responsibility ideally felt by the better-born to educate their poorer neighbours. As early as 1811 the National Society had tried to instil church teaching in the schools it established, but all elementary teaching was rather random, and largely in the hands of individual parishes. Charlotte Yonge taught in the village school (founded by her father before she was born) all her life, and the heroines of her novels, especially those written before the Education Act of 1870, look on teaching as quite as much part of their duty and routine as the Daily Service. (And the lawful authority here which requires it, and to which they owe obedience, is, of course, the church: when Rachel Curtis attempts to organise a school without 'clerical interference' in *The Clever Woman of the Family* (1865), under the supervision of a smooth, unscrupulous, fast-talking layman, the results are disastrous. Ethel's school in the deprived hamlet of Cocksmoor in *The Daisy Chain*, run first under Cherry Elwood and later under the auspices of the curate and then vicar, Richard, produces 'clean faces instead of dirty, shining hair instead of wild elf-locks, orderly children instead of little savages'.)[7]

'The battle of the Church', as W. J. Butler foresaw in 1847, 'would be fought in the schools':[8] the schools themselves were a permanent reminder of the work of the Movement, and as the influence of Tractarian teaching began to be felt not only in country parishes but in the inner cities, new churches appeared, and with them educational establishments where the teaching of the church could be continued. It became the early mission of the slum-priests to establish orphanages and schools simultaneously with churches: schools, first for boys and then girls, were a regular part of the foundation endowed by benefactors. Famous monuments of the Movement like All Saints, Margaret Street; All Saints, Boyne Hill; St Barnabas', Pimlico; St Peter's, Vauxhall; St Peter's, London Docks, etc., all have schools among the buildings adjacent to the church. Some schools came to offer more than just elementary education as choir-schools were established as part of the foundation, and occasionally they became Clergy-Orphan schools from which boys could proceed to the professions or the universities. And for the middle classes the church organised public school education with schools like Hurstpierpoint and Lancing. Charlotte Yonge chronicles them all in her fiction.

A large number of novels written from the 1860s on are witness to these developments in the Movement, but two are pre-eminent, *Hopes and Fears* (1860) and *Pillars of the House* (1873). By the time she came to write *Hopes and Fears* the church was moving to a stage which included what became known as 'Ritualism', a phase much associated with the Movement's mission to the slums. Evidence of High Church involvement here can be seen in the East End of London and in other poor parts of the city where, as Ollard tells us, it changed both the face and the life of the district,[9] and similar results can be seen in most other Victorian city centres in Britain. The clergy, with their encouragement of ceremonial and insistence on the less familiar ordinances and rites of the Book of Common Prayer, were often targets of the rabble (the hostility throughout the 1840s and 1850s to

Bryan King at St George-in-the-East, to W. J. E. Bennett at St Barnabas, Pimlico, and to J. M. Neale at East Grinstead, is notorious; and there are other examples), but their permanent monuments are the churches, and associated buildings, which are the obvious witness to this phase of the movement. The most famous, perhaps, is All Saints, Margaret Street, designed by Butterfield and consecrated in 1859. Butterfield designed not only the church but also schools, a clergy-house, a choir-school and an orphanage. The same was true, in many details, of his other London churches, St Matthias', Stoke Newington (1850), and St Alban's, Holborn (1859), all surrounded by the same complex of buildings. St Paul's, Knightsbridge, and St Mary's, Paddington, are others founded at this time to promote the ideals of the Oxford Movement, and are all part of the same pattern of Tractarian life. Further afield the pattern was repeated in churches like All Saints, Boyne Hill, and St German's, Cardiff.

Charlotte Yonge was very conscious of this development: in her own circle, nephews and cousins, and the husbands of various female family members, had served their curacies in industrial parishes, and Sir William Heathcote's son had been the target of a hostile mob for his Ritualistic practices in a northern cure. And on her own visits to London to stay with her philanthropist friends, the Gibbses (benefactors of Keble's memorial in Oxford, Keble College), she was a regular worshipper at W. J. E. Bennett's St Paul's, Knightsbridge.

HOPES AND FEARS

So it is not surprising that *Hopes and Fears* (1860) is, in many respects, almost a transcript of this area of church history. Robert Fulmort, though not the only one, is certainly the most interesting of her clerical portraits of this period, and the one she explored in most detail. Previously she had worked on different representations in Richard May and Lord Herbert Somerville, but Robert Fulmort is a much more detailed, thoughtful version, and virtually the embodiment of the Tractarian ideal – the more interesting in that as a character he does not enjoy unqualified authorial approval; the young priest with whom he shares duty in the district 'wished his liking for the young deacon were in better proportion to his esteem' when Robert answers the summons to a baptism 'with an alacrity which sometimes almost irritated his fellows'.[10] Charlotte Yonge's models for Robert are W. J. E. Bennett, Charles Lowder, Alexander Mackonochie and Edward Stuart, all famous slum priests of the time and known to her (Mackonochie had been curate to her friend W. J. Butler, for instance, and several of them were visitors to Hursley). Like Stuart, Lowder and others, Robert comes from a wealthy family, and determines to pledge his part of the family fortune to this mission to the poor: like others, he resists the career and lifestyle proposed for him by his family to become a curate among them. As Edward Stuart had founded and built St Mary Magdalene, Paddington, Robert builds St Matthew's, Whittingtonia, complete with schools, clergy-house, orphanage, and so on. And having witnessed the appalling poverty of the area, and holding his own family, rich on the profits of a gin distillery, responsible for the degradation, he forswears shares in the business and becomes a clergyman. He cites

> [. . .] appalling instances of the effects of the multiplicity of gin-palaces, things that well nigh broke his heart to witness [. . .], never able to divest himself of a sense of being a sharer in guilt and ruin. (p. 256)

Charlotte Yonge describes the results of Robert's plan for the 'festering masses of corruption' (p. 126) in Whittingtonia through his proposals for the mission:

> There was to be a range of buildings round a court, consisting of day-schools, a home for orphans, a crèche for infants, a reading room for adults, and apartments for the clergy of the Church which was to form one side of the quadrangle. (p. 256)

Robert alone was answerable for the cost of all this. St Matthew's, Whittingtonia, takes shape, and the church, in Robert's words, comes to the people. One result for him, as for Lowder, Mackonochie and many others, is persecution from the mob, in Robert's case incited by a vestry notoriously under the influence of the Fulmort firm whose interest was to promote the vice he came to withstand – 'their violence against his attacks on their vicious practices being veiled by a furious party outcry against his religious sentiments' (p. 342).

Charlotte Yonge does not pursue the question of the Oxford Movement and the slums further here, though we learn from a later narrative (*The Long Vacation*, 1895) that St Matthew's has been threatened by a prosecution for ritualism; but in *Hopes and Fears* the triumph of Robert's mission – and the church's – is represented by the festival of 2,000 children and young people drawn from the parish schools, the orphanage, the Young Women's Association, the choir school, etc. It becomes an emblem of the reconciliation between Robert and his previously sceptical brother, and is triumphantly organised on the country estate of Mervyn Fulmort, Esq.

THE PILLARS OF THE HOUSE

Hopes and Fears ends with the triumph of the Oxford Movement (as seen by Charlotte Yonge) in the inner cities, and *Pillars of the House* (1873) shows how the urban church begins to assimilate it. *The Pillars of the House*[11] is set in a small industrial town near a large trading port, Dearport. It opens in the early 1850s (more or less the date of *Hopes and Fears*) with an advertisement from ten years before, which shows how far the church had advanced even then, for an assistant curate of 'Catholic opinions' who would be required to assist in the 'Daily Prayers. Choral Service on Sundays and Holy-days. Weekly Communion', and where a 'rubrical war' has been fought out by the last incumbent (vol. 1, p. 3). Mr Underwood, the impeccably Tractarian priest who is appointed, and his large family, are Charlotte Yonge's demonstration of the reforms in the church. St Oswald's, Bexley, (though she had expressed reservations about the practices implied, through the conservative Honor in *Hopes and Fears*) is now her model of the ideal contemporary church, with its revised liturgy, its surpliced choir, its 'principled' architecture and sensitive restoration.

But after the death of their parents the Underwood family is split up: the boys leave the aggressively secular grammar school, and Clement goes to what is now the Clergy-Orphan School at St Matthew's, Whittingtonia, and thence later to Cambridge and ordination. Lance goes to a parallel institution, the recently reformed cathedral choir-school where, after 'a period of decay [. . .] an excellent Precentor had been just appointed' (vol. 1, p. 140). The younger girls are transferred to a Fulmort school run by one of Robert's sisters, where 'girls of small means might be prepared for becoming first-rate governesses' (vol. 1, p. 240). All the children of the right age, in fact, are the inheritors of what Charlotte Yonge sees as Oxford Movement ideals in education (Bernard, one of the younger Underwoods, joins in due course one of the earliest undergraduate cohorts at Keble College), and in *Pillars of the House* we see how what were novelties in *Hopes and Fears* have become absorbed into society and are now the norm. As in *Hopes and Fears* Yonge uses a social gathering, this time a Choral Festival at the cathedral, as an indicator of how far liturgical reforms in the church, and reforms in the institutions attached to the church, are due to Tractarian influence. The surpliced choirs which flock from all over the diocese, and the music they sing, are in stark contrast to the choirs of fifty years earlier, portrayed in *The Carbonels*.

THE FINE ARTS

The Underwood children are witnesses to other areas in which Charlotte Yonge wishes to show the influence of the reformed church. The fine arts is one such area. As Ollard was to point out in his *History*, 'A natural channel for the Oxford Movement's energies lay in those of the fine arts which more directly serve the worship of God – architecture, painting, and music' (Ollard, p. 222). Architecture in the form of churchbuilding had always been an obsession with Charlotte Yonge (it was the main theme of the first novel, *Abbeychurch*, and a very significant element in *The Daisy Chain*). The early years of her career as a novelist had seen the foundation of the Cambridge Camden Society, quickly re-named the Ecclesiological Society, and closely linked with the Oxford Movement, and the 'principled' architecture of the Ecclesiologists dominated churchbuilding throughout the middle decades of the century. Charlotte Yonge is less concerned with the features of the church than its function, and gently mocks one fervent ecclesiologist in *Pillars of the House* for his misguided enthusiasm – 'I'm afraid he minds his ecclesiology more than his ecclesia' (vol. 2, p. 270), says Clement sniffily – while applauding the eager restoration work which accompanied churchbuilding. When Felix takes repossession of Vale Leston, for instance, and Clement finally agrees to become the vicar, they find the magnificent church much neglected by the last incumbent (a representative of much pre-Tractarian abuse), and they set about the restoration forthwith. The church is transformed from the kind of building found in *The Carbonels*, with its triple-decker pulpit, its choir-gallery, and chancelful of tall family pews, to one rather more in line with the teaching of the Ecclesiological Society:

> As to the church, now brought to all the glory that reverent hands, careful taste, and well-judged expenditure could give it, the contrast was not small from the dreary bepewed building, and all its native beauties were unobscured or renovated. (vol. 2, p. 457)

Painting is another of the 'fine arts [. . .] that serve God', and in Ollard's *History* of the Movement it figures prominently. It makes a greater appearance in *Pillars of the House* than in any other novel, and confirms Ollard's view about Tractarian use of art in promulgating the message. The second phase of the Oxford Movement coincides with the movement in English painting which looked to the early Italians for techniques, the Pre-Raphaelite Brotherhood, and one of their early patrons was the wealthy Anglo-Catholic, Thomas Combe. The PRB was not in itself a religious group, though several of its members and associates were sympathisers with the Movement, and all were interested; and their use of religious topics, and their obsession with symbolism, provoked suspicion in hostile areas of the public that they were 'Romanists' and 'Puseyites'. Some of them (Millais and Charles Allston Collins) were living at Thomas Combe's house in Oxford, and others (like Holman Hunt) were known to be his friends. William Dyce, who had decorated the House of Lords and All Saints, Margaret Street, was a regular worshipper at Butterfield's church. Ruskin, of course, was a well-known defender of the PRB, and had written famous letters to *The Times* endorsing their principles and discounting their 'Romanist' leanings.

All the same, sufficient numbers of the PRB and their circle were known for their sympathetic inclination to the Movement for Ollard to include the Brotherhood as a 'result' of its work and two above all (Dyce and Collins) he selects for particular comment. Charlotte Yonge had recognised their significance many years earlier in *Pillars of the House* (1873): the most obvious representation of the Pre-Raphaelite contribution to the Movement is Geraldine Underwood and – in a different way – her brother Edgar. Geraldine, brought up on Ruskin, expresses her ideals throughout in art, using the symbolism endorsed by the PRB and the Ecclesiologists. Her 'Waves of this Troublesome World' represents 'the sea of life' in which 'all are making for the golden light of Heaven, and the star of faith guiding them' (vol. 1, p. 180), while her 'Phantom Host that Beleaguered the

Walls of Prague' contains a portrait of a young man 'watching his armour the night before he was baptized', which is based on an episode in the novel. She has chosen to represent him allegorically, a mode recognised by her young sister, a child 'to whom allegory seems a natural element, with which they have more affinity than with the material world' (vol. 1, p. 180). Her most significant and celebrated picture, though, is the watercolour of 'The Faithful Acolyte', exhibited at the Academy, which is full of the brilliant, naturalistic detail and 'strength of colouring' beloved of the Brotherhood:

> The Church was in a brown dim shade, within which [. . .] its perspective vaultings, arches, and tracery, were perfectly drawn, knowing where they were going and what they meant, yet not obtruded; and the Altar hangings, richly patterned in olive green and brown gold, were kept back in spite of all their detail, throwing out the 'flake of fire' and the glitter reflected on the gold ornaments [. . .] while in the fragments of the east window, just seen above, glittered a few jewels of stained glass touched by the rising sun [. . .].' (vol. 2, p. 109)

The Acolyte of the picture has 'touched the Altar tapers / With a flake of fire'[12] both subject and symbolism are Pre-Raphaelite in conception, and very reminiscent of Collins' 'Convent Thoughts', which must have been familiar to Charlotte Yonge.

Edgar's picture, on the other hand, an ambitious painting of the pagan Brynhild, which appears in the same exhibition, is, by comparison, a disaster. Edgar has apparently tried to combine the naturalistic detail of the Pre-Raphaelites with the impressionism of Turner to convey 'a wild scene of terror in the world of mists' (vol. 2, p. 108), and the attempt satisfies nobody, neither friends nor critics. It is, of course, predictable: while Geraldine embodies in her life every aspect of Tractarian teaching, Edgar's religion is known to be insecure. Art reflects the character of the artist, as Ruskin was teaching, and Edgar's art is as flawed as his morals.

DOUBT

Edgar has reacted against the teaching of home to follow the dubious influence of a schoolmaster, and he is an example of what some experienced as the negative effects of the Oxford Movement. Owen

Sandbrook in *Hopes and Fears* perhaps makes the point even more clearly, that there were those who felt that Tractarian teaching was indoctrination, and whose response as a result was total rejection of religion. One commentator, J. A. Froude (who as Hurrell Froude's younger brother had been through it all), observed:

> By their attempts to identify Christianity with the Catholic system, they provoked doubts, in those whom they failed to persuade, about Christianity itself [. . .] By their perverse alternative, either the Church or nothing, they forced honest men to say, Let it be nothing, then, rather than what we know to be a lie.[13]

Oxford, the home for some of spiritual revival and a new appreciation of the truth, proves for others (especially after Newman's secession in 1845) merely the testing ground of their faith, and one source of the scepticism which marked the 1840s and 1850s. Oxford represents all that is dangerous in terms of the intellect, and in a series of novels Charlotte Yonge urges in narrative form the way to resist this temptation – 'Don't argue. Live and act' (*Hopes and Fears*, p. 433). It is an imperative acknowledged by a line of potential victims of the Oxford threat to the intellect. Norman May in *The Daisy Chain*, his faith dangerously threatened by the currents of Oxford thinking, takes himself off to the mission-field and 'the simplest, hardest work, beginning from the rudiments, and forgetting subtle arguments' (p. 461); and David Ogilvie in *Magnum Bonum*, the prey at the university of 'daring talkers, who thought themselves daring thinkers' (p. 220), finds the answer in a demanding job. Owen Sandbrook, too, becomes at the university 'one of the youths on whom the spirit of the day had most influence, one of the most adventurous thinkers and boldest talkers: wild in habits, not merely from ebullition of spirits, but from want of faith in the restraining power' (*Hopes and Fears*, p. 155).

Owen emerges from Oxford with his opinions unsettled – 'It was more' the author comments, 'uncertainty than denial, rather dislike to technical dogma than positive unbelief' (p. 299). The directives of the Tractarian regime, under which he has been brought up by his guardian Honor, prove an irksome curb to his independence at the post-Tractarian university. He explains it to Honor once the crisis is finally past:

'After believing more than enough, the transition is easy to doubting what is worthy of credit at all [. . .] overdoing articles of faith and observances, while the mind and conscience are young and tender, brings a dangerous reaction when liberty and independent reflection begin.' (p. 557)

This negative quality of the Oxford Movement, which could turn men to doubt, had its parallel effect in the positive results which followed from the examples of those engaged in promulgating the faith: Charlotte Yonge gives examples. Fernan Travis, for instance, in *Pillars of the House*, is a young pagan, half-Mexican, who has led a 'roving, godless life' in the US, and has 'never been inside [a church] in his life' (vol. 1, p. 102); but when he comes to live among the Underwoods the teaching they embody, particularly Felix and Lance, and the example of Mr Audley, the curate, work on him, and he is soon received into the church with Baptism and Confirmation. Fernan has never been an 'infidel' by choice, but only through ignorance.

Another sceptic in *Hopes and Fears*, Miss Fennimore, represents what Charlotte Yonge sees as a much more dangerous threat to society, the intellectual doubter. Miss Fennimore is moral, intelligent, thoughtful, one who thinks herself 'above creeds'. Her religion is 'all aspiration to the God of nature', and 'what she thought reasonable – Christianity, modified by the world's progress' (p. 363).

The unsatisfactoriness of her undefined belief – 'Jehovah, Jove, or Lord' – is challenged by her failure with her pupil Bertha, who, unchecked by the rules of the church, leads a life of total disorder, and attempts at fifteen to elope with a scoundrel. Miss Fennimore witnesses the pattern Christian life of her other pupil, Phoebe Fulmort – 'my living lesson' – and the priestly ideal represented by her brother Robert, and comes to accept that her system is inadequate 'You cannot argue – you can only act', she reflects. She adds

'When I see a young man, brought up as your brother has been, throwing himself with such energy, self-denial, and courage into a task so laborious and obscure, I must own that, such is the construction of the human mind, I am led to reconsider the train of reasoning that has led to such results.' (p. 342)

Nor can her admiration of Robert be ascribed only to his personal magnetism, for he is not personally popular at St Matthew's or with the rest of the society in which he moves, and he is always reluctant to impose his views on her when she is his sisters' governess. (He dismisses her briskly at one point (p. 101) as a 'nasty latitudinarian piece of machinery'.) Her acceptance of the faith has less to do with 'Robert's powers of controversy' (p. 433) or his personality, in fact, than the example of his life. The Tracts had stressed the importance of personal holiness and the example of a godly life, and Robert is an interesting example of the precept in practice.

Charlotte Yonge lived through every stage of the Oxford Movement, and recorded each. In her last novels (like *Beechcroft at Rockstone*, 1888, *The Long Vacation*, 1895, and *Modern Broods*, 1900) she is a witness as to how the initial impact of the Movement was absorbed by the church, and how reforms, so startling in the early days, had become almost the norm. In *The Three Brides* (1876), for instance, Cecil Charnock, the bride of the eldest son, is a not unsympathetic character but a conservative who looks back; she regards her own old home as perfection, because 'the clergyman always does as *we* tell him'. She comments with dismay on the liturgy practised by her clerical brother-in-law: 'What's all this? So many services – four on Sunday, two every day, three on Wednesdays and Fridays! We never had anything like this at Dunstone.'[14]

Deeply conservative as she is herself, Charlotte Yonge was never comfortable with the later excesses of Ritualism, or with the latest forms of Tractarian thinking at the end of the century. The Reverend Augustine Flight in *Beechcroft at Rockstone* is her ironic representation of what she deplored as the unnecessary ceremonial of Ritualism – his church is 'oppressed with ornament', so 'there seemed not an inch devoid of colour or carving'; and the liturgy at St Kenelm's includes 'a very musical service, in the course of which it was discovered to be the Feast of St. Remigius, for after the Lesson a short discourse was given on the Conversion of Clovis, not forgetting the sacred ampulla'.[15] The latest forms of Tractarian thinking were expressed by the essays by various members of the movement in *Lux Mundi* in 1889, which Charlotte Yonge read seriously but with some dismay. *Lux Mundi* was an 'attempt to put the Catholic faith into its right relation to modern intellectual and moral problems', and was written for 'Christians perplexed by the new knowledge [. . .] scientific, historical and critical'.[16] 'Religion interprets', it declared, 'and is interpreted by science.' Charlotte Yonge, though personally bewildered, was prepared to listen sympathetically to younger friends (Robert Moberly was a contributor) who found no contradiction in the new teaching. So in *The Long Vacation* Gerald Underwood, Edgar's son, is a representative of the new ideals, part of the liberal school of theology which has superseded early Tractarian thinking at Oxford. Charlotte Yonge, like Gerald's aunt Geraldine, is puzzled and fearful, and presents the changes, as she herself tells us, not as a younger writer would 'with inner sympathy, but from the outside' (p. vi).

But present them she does. They are the latest manifestations of the movement begun some seventy years before, and she is consistent in her record. The history of the movement is her discourse from first to last, and provides an invaluable record of how it was received and experienced by society.

1   Henry Scott Holland, *A Bundle of Memories* (London: Wells Gardner, Darton, 1915) p. 956.

2   C. M. Yonge, *The Carbonels*, 1895 (London: National Society, 1895) p. 46.

3   *The Carbonels*, p. 269.

4   C. M. Yonge, *The Castle Builders*, 1854 (London: Mozley, Smith, Masters & Son, 1859) p. 152 (= London: Innes, 1896, p. 144).

5   C. M. Yonge, *The Heir of Redclyffe*, 1853 (London: Macmillan, 1889) p. 226.

6   C. M. Yonge, *The Daisy Chain*, 1856 (London: Macmillan, 1894) p. 253.

7   *The Daisy Chain*, p. 277.

8   A. J. Butler, ed., *Life and Letters of William J. Butler* (London: Macmillan, 1897) p. 128.

9   S. L. Ollard, *A Short History of the Oxford Movement* (London: Mowbray, 1915).

10   C. M. Yonge, *Hopes and Fears*, 1860 (London: Macmillan, 1899) p. 260.

11   C. M. Yonge, *The Pillars of the House*, 1873 (London: Macmillan, 1893) 2 vols.

12   Sabine Baring-Gould, 'The Three Crowns', *The Silver Store*, 1868 (London: Skeffington, 1898) p. 146.

13   James Anthony Froude, 'The Oxford Counter-Reformation', *Short Studies on Great Subjects* (4th Series, London: Longmans, Green, 1883) p. 177.

14   C. M. Yonge, *The Three Brides*, 1876 (London: Macmillan, 1888) p. 11, p. 30.

15   C. M. Yonge, *Beechcroft at Rockstone*, 1888 (London: Macmillan, 1892) p. 20, p. 46.

16   Charles Gore, ed., *Lux Mundi* (London: John Murray, 1890) p. x, p. xi.

CONTINUITY AND DEVELOPMENT IN THE FICTION OF CHARLOTTE YONGE

Amy de Gruchy

Charlotte Yonge's own life showed a remarkable degree of continuity. She spent it in the Hampshire village of Otterbourne where she was born, leaving it only to visit friends or relatives. Her days followed a quiet routine of attending church services, giving lessons in the village school, and writing, varied on Sundays by teaching in Sunday School. She never experienced economic insecurity. She came from an authoritarian background and adopted without question the beliefs of her elders, whose dictates she obeyed throughout her life. Her closest relationships were with her immediate and extended family, and with her clerical guides; she belonged to a like-minded circle of friends. John Keble, one of the early leaders of the Oxford Movement or Tractarians, influenced her directly as her religious teacher and indirectly through her friends and relatives who shared or had imbibed his views. Keble, like her own family, sprang from the old High Church party, which has been described as 'revering Charles I, distrusting religious enthusiasm, stern Tories in politics'.[1] To Geoffrey Rowell, 'Keble's sacramental doctrine of the Church is linked to the Tory reverence for the order and hierarchy of established institutions in society.'[2] The early Tractarian idea was that in the eternal pattern God was the Father, the Church the Mother, and the laity of the human race the children. In society the pattern was, or should be, repeated. The monarch was at the head, the aristocracy and gentry were immediately below, and everyone else was subject to these powers. In the family the same hierarchical structure was supposed to pertain. These views were promulgated in the Tractarian novels and Tory periodicals that were Charlotte Yonge's reading in youth.[3]

The chief aim of Charlotte Yonge's life, which never altered, was to be useful, to serve the Church by disseminating the principles in which she had been reared. In an article published in 1894 she recalled how her father had questioned her motives for publishing her first novel, *Abbeychurch* (1844). 'I answered, with tears, that I really hoped I had written with the purpose of being useful to young girls like myself.'[4] (It is worth noting that at the age of twenty-one she was still in tutelage to her father and identifying herself with young girls who in her fiction are in their teens.)

In the preface to *The Two Guardians*, written in 1852 after the serialisation of the book in 1850-52, Charlotte Yonge claimed that each of her previous tales had been written to 'illustrate some principle which may be called the key note'. In *Scenes and Characters* (1847), for example, the keynote is 'the effects of being guided by mere feeling in contrast with strict adherence to duty', in *Henrietta's Wish* (1849-50) 'the opposition is between wilfulness and submission' and in *The Castle Builders* (1851-53) 'the instability and dissatisfaction of mind occasioned by the want of a practical, obedient course of daily life'.[5] All these are, in effect, failures of obedience to authority, whether that of the Church or the family, on the part of the chief characters. The result is a group of very well-constructed tales, rigidly controlled by the need to point the moral. The Preface signalled the abandonment of her earlier theory, that the best way of conveying moral teaching was to present a picture of real life from which many lessons might be drawn, in favour of that of her cousin who preferred what was, in effect, the keynote method. Both agreed, however, that the purpose of fiction was to offer moral teaching.

Nevertheless other motives influenced Charlotte Yonge's writing. In the 1894 article she named them.

> History never failed to have great power over my imagination. This, and the desire to supply good tales to my school children, and the pleasure of living, as it were, with large families, were three separate fields of delight in which my mind could expatiate.[6]

These are closely linked to her primary aim. She loved the romance of history for its own sake, but she used it to propagate Tractarian views on obedience, subjection and the sin of rebellion. The good tales for her schoolchildren contained moral lessons suited to their situation in life, as did the tales of large families in a higher one.

But the 'pleasure of living, as it were, with large families' had another source. It arose from her enjoyment of her childhood holidays with her Yonge cousins in the West Country, and her sense of loss when these ceased when she was thirteen and remained at home with an only brother six years younger than herself. Her 'solitude and longing for young companions' caused her to invent tales of large families, one of which, *Le Château de Melville* (1847) was published in French when she was only fifteen and sold to family and friends to raise funds for the village school.

> The curious thing is that the *dramatis personae* have been more or less my companions through life. I took them up again, much modified, with some names changed, six or eight years after in *Scenes and Characters*, and again in the *Two Sides of the Shield*.[7]

This family, the Mohuns, with their descendants, appear in four other novels, including Charlotte Yonge's last, *Modern Broods*, published in 1900. According to Christabel Coleridge, Charlotte Yonge's official biographer, the characters 'grew up and grew old with their creator, and all through life were expressions of herself'.[8]

The Mohuns represent a strong element of continuity in Charlotte Yonge's life. They reveal two forms of nostalgia, a longing to be part of a large family, the joyous experience of her childhood, and a desire to return to the world of her childhood itself, where the authoritarian but loving parental rule in the various branches of the Yonge family was seen as a microcosm of society at large and the Church in particular. Lilias, the chief of the Mohun characters, shares Charlotte Yonge's romantic view of the past and when she marries a stern authoritarian soldier supports her husband's determination to rear their large brood in the traditional ways. Beechcroft Court, the ancestral home of the Mohuns, remains in a kind of time-warp. Bessie Merrifield, Lilias' niece by marriage, considered that her own home was 'behind the world, and thus a haven of rest; but it was nothing to Beechcroft Court'.[9]

Three things are very noticeable about the Mohun family. They and their relatives enjoy unchanged social status and financial security throughout their lives. Although the middle-aged Jane Mohun is an active supporter of the Girls' Friendly Society, an organisation set up by the Church of England for the benefit of working girls, the Mohuns are never social reformers. In the three novels in which they are the chief characters, the theme is the duty of obedience. In *Scenes and Characters* Lilias sets up her own rule against that of her elder sister, in *Two Sides of the Shield* (1885) her niece Dolores Mohun rejects the authority of Lilias herself, whose own daughter Gillian rejects that of her aunt Jane in *Beechcroft at Rockstone*. In the works which the Mohuns share with characters from other novels this obedience theme either plays only a minor part, or does not concern the Mohuns.

In 1857 *The Saturday Review* published a lengthy article which, along with some praise, accused Charlotte Yonge of promoting snobbery, introspection and a false view of society.

> She loves a lord dearly [. . .] She has her ideal of life, and it is an ideal which suits the taste of very many readers. There is to be a grand ancestral mansion with a squire and his daughters, and a neglected parish entirely dependent for the first lessons of Christianity upon the young ladies of the Hall. They are to be assisted spiritually by a stern curate, and cheered temporally by a lively young nobleman. This we take to be the dream [. . .] of the authoress and many of the good girls who admire her. Nothing could be pleasanter than to trip along under the shade of ancient oaks, conscious of several wrong tendencies calling for self-analysis [. . .].'[10]

This suggests the Tory and Tractarian ideal of a static, hierarchical, rural society. It is a composite picture that does not fit any of Charlotte Yonge's works exactly, but the one that most resembles it is *Scenes and Characters*. It may have been the world of Charlotte Yonge's sheltered childhood and its imaginings but it bore little resemblance to real conditions in Britain during most of her lifetime.

If Charlotte Yonge had really been writing in the way described in 1857, why were her works reviewed in periodicals aimed at an intellectual and educated readership such as *The Saturday Review*? The answer is the success of *The Heir of Redclyffe* (1853). Charlotte Yonge was given the idea for this novel by her friend, the minor author, Marianne Dyson, and discussed it with her at every stage of writing. It marked a great advance on the previous keynote tales, but it was more than a return to her earlier preference for a picture of real life. In it she allowed her imagination full rein, and the book was an immediate best-seller. Had it failed, no doubt Charlotte Yonge would have reverted to writing moral tales for the young. Instead, a new field of usefulness was opened to her, providing the opportunity to influence adults as well as youth, males as well as females and non-Anglicans as well as fellow Tractarians. She developed new methods of imparting her teaching. The keynote was not entirely abandoned, but became a major theme surrounded by minor ones. It and they are treated in a less simplistic and schematic manner. For adults it was neither necessary nor desirable to hammer home the moral. The longer time-span and greater length of the novels allowed characters to grow up and face the complexities of adult life, leaving behind them the self-absorption, idealism and mistakes of adolescence, which Charlotte Yonge had so faithfully portrayed in her earlier fiction.

It is fair to say that *The Saturday Review*'s picture of the world that Charlotte Yonge drew in the 1850s was more inaccurate than the world she portrayed in her earliest works. Somehow, though, she became labelled as a writer of moral tales for youthful readers, set in an ideal world, peacefully static, where everyone knew their place and kept to it. This is not true, for she altered her early views and, because of the greater freedom she allowed herself after the success of *The Heir of Redclyffe*, it is possible to trace her development by following through successive novels the way in which she explored and modified certain ideas.

The Mohuns themselves illustrate this. Though they are rooted in the past they show varying degrees of acceptance of the present. When Jane and Lilias discuss the changes that have taken place since their youth, Jane's realism contrasts with her sister's romanticism. That Charlotte Yonge can put both points of view fairly in a discussion shows how far she has come from *Scenes and Characters* and the other keynote tales. Even more striking is the marriage of Adeline, the youngest sister, to a person unimaginable in the earlier tale, a workman who has risen to become a wealthy businessman, which occurs in *Beechcroft at Rockstone*.

'She loves a lord dearly', complained the writer in *The Saturday Review*. Her early works might justify the criticism. In these, members of the peerage are well-drawn minor characters whose overt function is to advise and assist the major ones to whom they are related by birth or marriage. As they could equally well do this without titles, it must be assumed that their rank serves other purposes. One might be to enhance the status of the principal characters in the eyes of the readers, as is suggested in *The Saturday Review*. Another purpose would be to place the aristocracy and the gentry on the same footing, and to reinforce the idea of a two-class society, stable, ordered, built on historic foundations and ruled wisely and benevolently from above.

Charlotte Yonge certainly seems to have had some illusions about the peerage, and its innate qualities of leadership. In *The Castle Builders* a family connection offers the Reverend Lord Herbert Somerville the incumbency of Dearport, a decayed seaside town with much poverty and Dissent, and a divided and neglected parish. His experience hardly seemed adequate. A successful Oxford career had been followed by a curacy in a congenial country parish with a docile population. Even this is too much for his fragile health, and he has to spend a year abroad to make a partial recovery. He seems to have had no previous acquaintance with the urban poor, the middle classes or Dissenters, no experience of working in, much less running, a large parish, or of dealing with conflict. He accepts the post, merely stipulating that his Oxford tutor should serve as his curate, carrying out the normal parish duties while he himself acts as a manager. Apparently this gentleman is prepared to sacrifice status and salary in order to serve under his titled erstwhile student. Equally improbable is the incident in *Heartsease* (1854) when Lord St Erme, brought belatedly to a sense of his duties, goes to inspect his neglected coal mines, whereupon the roof promptly caves in. Though badly injured, he calms and rallies the trapped miners, so that all are brought to safety. To describe Chartist miners as accepting the leadership of a long-haired aesthete – who had never seen the inside of a mine-shaft before – simply because he was a lord, argues a very great faith in the hereditary principle.

However, this did not last. Charlotte Yonge made partial amends for these errors in following works. Indeed, her apparent correction of what she seems to have come to regard as mistakes is a marked feature of her writing, and may be regarded as further evidence of her powers of development. In *Dynevor Terrace* (1857) Lord Louis Fitzjocelyn, the hero, decides to show leadership and set an example to the lower orders by taking part in a militia review when he is ill. His father and commanding officer disapprove. When he uses his influence to gain a post for his cousin, for which the latter is unsuited, he shows even worse judgement. In *The Daisy Chain* (1856) the town council offers the incumbency of Stoneborough to Richard May, the son of the respected local physician. Like Dearport it is a difficult parish, and, like Lord Herbert, Richard is in his first curacy. He is, however, in good health, was born, brought up and educated in the town, is well aware of its problems and has very good judgement. His father refuses the post for him on the grounds of his youth and lack of experience, and Richard is happy to serve as curate under the new clergyman. Though Charlotte Yonge never suggests that the Dearport appointment was a mistake, the later novels describe Lord Herbert's difficulties in a way that imply that this was the case.

Indeed, after 1854 Charlotte Yonge's view of the peerage becomes more realistic. The lords of that period, though well-intentioned, seem rather in need of guidance and support than qualified to offer it, much less rule their country. In the 1860s and 1870s there is a further decline in the standards of her aristocracy, which affects the baronetcy as well. These are mainly older men who would have grown up under the Regency or during the reign of George IV, when morals were notoriously lax. Charlotte Yonge's historical sense was coming to the fore. In the later novels only lords reared in the High Church or Tractarian tradition are shown as worthy characters, serving their country or managing their estates to the best of their ability, and not all peers reached their standard. In the last novel, *Modern Broods*, a middle-aged roué, the heir to a dukedom, is considered to be too bad even for the low-born, mercenary girl he marries. Charlotte Yonge may once have had illusions about lords, but they did not last.

Even in her earliest works Charlotte Yonge suggested that the social fabric was under threat, and could only be maintained by vigilance and determination. In *Abbeychurch* the threat is from the local Mechanics' Institute, which teaches poor adults, and spreads the ideas of those whom Charlotte Yonge described as 'so-called reformer[s] (though destroyer[s] would be a better word) in both Church and State'.[11] Later she accepted that changes were occurring, and even that in some situations they were desirable. A feature of her writing is that certain topics or ideas recur in successive works, are then abandoned and taken up again at intervals. This is particularly true of the topic of social concern where characters are shown trying to amend a situation they see as harmful to those less fortunate than themselves. It appears in nearly every work of fiction Charlotte Yonge wrote between 1854 and 1860 as well as in several later works. Her concentrated use of this topic coincided with the publication in her magazine *The Monthly Packet* of the two serials, *The Daisy Chain* (1853-55) and *The Young Stepmother* (1856-60) in both of which it is a major theme. Thus ideas presented in one tale are developed or modified in others, possibly written or devised at the same time. It is sometimes a major, sometimes a minor theme, and she explores it from many different angles.

It occupies only a small place in *Heartsease* where Lord St Erme's building of a church and reading room where he delivers lectures is seen as proof of his reform. It illustrates the duties of a land-owner, not the needs of his work-force. Those situations where Charlotte Yonge or those close to her had personal experience are given much more prominence in her fiction and are treated with realism, an abundance of detail and, in general, a greater concern for the unfortunate.

The Daisy Chain is the first of this type. For many years John Keble had taken services in a cottage at an outlying hamlet called Pitt. Charlotte Yonge provided a schoolroom and later endowed a church there.[12] *Friarswood Post Office* (1860) was based on a real incident in Charlotte Yonge's village, where the villagers helped a boy from the infamous Andover workhouse.[13] In *The Clever Woman of the Family* (1865) the detailed knowledge of conditions in the lace industry may have been gained from Charlotte Yonge's friend and relative Mary Coleridge who lived near a centre of lace-making and wrote a short story about it. In all these works concern for the unfortunate is a major or the major theme. The unfortunate themselves are viewed sympathetically, their plight shown in some detail, and some are individualised. Indeed, the workhouse boy in *Friarswood Post Office* is a major character. The difficulty of solving the problems and the solutions themselves are realistically shown. In contrast, where Charlotte Yonge had little direct knowledge of a situation the theme is usually a minor one, there is less detail, and less concern for the unfortunate, who are generally anonymous, and frequently a lack of realism in the solution.

In *The Daisy Chain* fifteen-year-old Ethel May, shocked at the wildness of the people of Cocksmoor, an outlying quarry village, proposes to build a church for them, to make them orderly and religious. Instead, the May family start a part-time school there, in which they themselves teach. Later they are given funds to start a full-time school with a servant girl as teacher, and later still a large bequest enables the church to be built. The results are not dramatic. After eight years of effort on the part of the Mays there is still poverty, but not of 'reckless destitution' or 'hopeless neglect', and the people are less indifferent to religion or education. This, and not the alleviation of poverty, was the aim of the Mays. At every stage they are shown as attempting what might be expected of their years and experience, and no more.

Dynevor Terrace, like *The Young Stepmother*, introduces a new development: the voice of the social protester, and the assignment of guilt. The indignant eloquence of the hero Louis informs the readers that his grandfather had moved his villagers to a desolate and unhealthy heath three miles from their work and church, because their homes spoilt his view. As a result the people had become lawless. The situation is essentially the same as in *The Daisy Chain*, but while the Mays' solution has been to take church and school to the people, benefiting all alike, Louis returns the respectable members of the Marksedge community to the original village, rehousing them in model cottages he has built on his own land. This is a realistic, if half-hearted solution. No-one would want the lawless characters any nearer.

The Young Stepmother (1861) contains another new idea, that of retribution for past neglect or wrongdoing. A slum-based epidemic has killed the first wife and favourite son of Mr Kendal, who has inherited a life-interest in the tenements. A visiting clergyman sees this as retribution for Kendal neglect, but this is never followed up.[14] In this complex novel the social concern theme partakes of the general ambiguity, with Charlotte Yonge apparently trying to balance the rights of property and the needs of the poor. In the novel's early part the needs take precedence and the poor are portrayed sympathetically. In the later part they become anonymous crowds, drunken and violent rioters, and the difficulties of clearing the slums are emphasised. Charlotte Yonge's conclusion may have been that of the heroine:

> [. . .] how much easier it is for women and boys to make schemes, than for men to bring them to effect, and how rash it is hastily to condemn those who tolerate abuses.[15]

It is the first time Charlotte Yonge has dealt with purely secular problems, those of bad housing and bad drainage. She sets out credible situations, and shows but does not comment on the insensitive luxury of the Kendal family. Indeed, her concern seems to be to justify them. The reader is left wondering whether this is due to her ability to see both sides of a question or a failure to think clearly about the evidence she herself has presented.

In *Hopes and Fears* (1860) a new question arises: that of the proper reaction of those who benefit from a social abuse. The wealth of the Fulmort family derives from Mr Fulmort's gin distilleries and gin palaces. His second son Robert tells his younger sister Phoebe

> 'You and I, and all of us, have eaten and drunk, been taught more than we could learn, lived in a fine house, and been made into ladies and gentlemen, all by battening on the vice and misery of this wretched population.'[16]

His reaction is to withdraw completely from the business. He then uses his personal fortune from another source to buy a site his father wanted for a new gin palace and build on it a church, clergyhouse, orphanage, schools, reading rooms and soup kitchens, thus providing for the spiritual, intellectual and physical needs of the local people. Phoebe is initially horrified, and contrasts the fine new clothes she has just bought with the rags of the squalid children of the gin-drinkers. However the impression has gone by the next morning and for the rest of the novel she enjoys the advantages of her wealth in peace of mind. Her author endorses her position by claiming that 'fortunately, sins, committed neither by ourselves, nor by those for whom we are responsible, have not a lasting power of paining' (p. 144). This sidesteps the question of what action would have been appropriate on Phoebe's part while casting doubt on Robert's act of restitution, but Charlotte Yonge seems not to have recognised this. She shows no interest in the gin trade in general, and the solution as to what should be done with the Fulmorts' part of it seems half-hearted. Robert acknowledges his elder brother's view that the business cannot be closed down because 'you can't annihilate property without damage to other folks', and accepts with delight a scheme 'for gradually contracting the most objectionable traffic' (p. 416).

In *Friarswood Post Office* and *The Clever Woman of the Family* Charlotte Yonge seems to see both sides of the question. In the latter sympathy is expressed for the child lace-makers working in sweatshop conditions, but also for their employer, a fisherman's widow, trying to make a living for herself and her children by her trade. In *Friarswood Post Office* the generosity of the village folk is clearly shown, but the good intentions of the various authority figures who try to hinder them are stressed as well. Nevertheless she seems to go too far, and indeed contradicts herself when defending the workhouse system.

After a lapse of three years Charlotte Yonge returned to the subject of social concern in *The Clever Woman of the Family*. The evils of the lace industry, however, are given less prominence than the ill-effects of female philanthropy when uncontrolled by male authority. This is also stressed in *The Three Brides* (1876). This novel and *My Young Alcides* (1875) mark a very considerable development in Charlotte Yonge's thinking, amounting to a repudiation of much of what she had previously accepted or commended.

In *The Young Stepmother* Mr Kendal's tolerance of abuse is condoned. His decision to take his family on an extended holiday on the Continent and thus avoid the danger from the foul drains he has exposed when clearing the slums is not criticised, though he leaves his fellow townsmen to face the possible epidemic. In *The Three Brides* the town drains are in a very dangerous condition, but a good-hearted townsman who deals with his own at the instance of a female philanthropist simply starts an outbreak of fever. The local MP is aware of the state of the drainage system, but does not speak out for fear of alienating public opinion. He saves his seat but loses his life in the epidemic, while the female philanthropist heroically nurses the sick. Charlotte Yonge thus seems to have changed her attitude as to the toleration of evils and the proper treatment for drains.

Mrs Duncombe, the philanthropist, is also allowed to criticise the building of model cottages, as practised in *Dynevor Terrace*:

> 'The poor are to be fitly housed, as a matter of right, and from their own sense of self-respect [. . .] not a few favourites, who will endure dictation, picked out for the model cottage.'[17]

In *My Young Alcides* (1875) the criticism is even stronger. The novel is set in the 1850s, the time when Charlotte Yonge wrote most of her social concern fiction. It depends largely on events of the 1830s, and is sharply critical of the attitudes of the gentry of both periods. Mid-century England is seen through the eyes of the Australian hero whose father had been transported for taking part in the agricultural riots a quarter of a century earlier. The heroine at first rejects and then accepts his view.

> I was somewhat hurt at his way of viewing what had always seemed to me perfection, at least all that could be reasonably

expected for the poor – our pet school, our old women, our civil dependants in tidy cottages [. . .].[18]

He is equally dismissive of her accounts of the ragged schools set up to help the London poor, seeing them as inadequate responses to such misery. It is as if Charlotte Yonge herself is seeing the recent past with new eyes.

One further development occurs as late as 1889. In *The Cunning Woman's Grandson* the social concern of Hannah More is shown entirely from the viewpoint of those she comes to help, the poor of Cheddar.

The question may be asked, did Charlotte Yonge depict social evils because she was concerned about them, or was she more interested in the effect they have on the characters of the victims or those who try to help them? The answer would seem to be that she was sincerely concerned about two topics, religion and education, and seems to have been little concerned about others. In almost all the fiction there is an emphasis on the effect on the characters of those performing good deeds rather than those benefiting from them. This is most marked in *The Stokesley Secret* (1861) where the different responses of the children to the challenge of saving their pocket money to buy a poor widow a pig are more important than her need, but it occurs in almost all the others. In *My Young Alcides* the hero's good works are tailored not to illustrate his character development, or existing wrongs, but the labours of Hercules. Charlotte Yonge could not have shown more clearly her detachment from good causes in general.

Why then did she choose this subject and use it so often? The hamlet of Pitt gains little attention from Charlotte Yonge's early biographers, but the setting up of a school and the building of the church there must have taken much of her time as well as her money over a period of several years. From this sprang the idea of *The Daisy Chain*. In this she combined character development with a matter of social concern about which she felt strongly. The popular success of the book encouraged her to go more widely and at times more deeply into the subject of social reform, though she was limited by the assumptions she derived from her background. The change of stance noted in her later works on the subject may be attributed to the influence of her own magazine *The Monthly Packet*, at least in part. From the 1860s onwards articles describe the miseries of the poorest members of society in graphic detail, as well as the attempts of the churches to alleviate them. This would have opened her eyes to a state of affairs unknown in her quiet village home. However, though her sympathy was real, her principal concern was with the shaping of the character of individuals, rather than with the reform of any particular aspect of society.

According to Lettice Cooper, Charlotte Yonge's themes are almost always a task or a reconciliation.[19] This is true in the widest sense, for there can be many different kinds of reconciliation. An individual can be reconciled to another person, to their family, group or society, to their situation or their God. In Charlotte Yonge's keynote stories the reconciliation is always between the individual and her society, sometimes mediated by another individual who represents the values of that society. Later, most of the reconciliations take place between individuals, usually of the same family. She explores this theme, treating it with more depth and developing variations on it throughout her career. The need for a reconciliation also changes. In *Heartsease* and *The Heir of Redclyffe* jealousy is the cause of hostility on the part of one person which requires a reconciliation. In most of the other novels the cause is a difference of temperaments. In general, as in *Heartsease* and its predecessor, a gentle open character is oppressed by a stern, forceful and reserved one.

This is not the case in *The Daisy Chain*. Here, the need for a reconciliation arises naturally from the characters involved, but plays only a very small part in the novel, while the relationships that develop seem improbable. Dr May is a loving parent, but he is impulsive and impatient, and is unjust and unkind to two of his sons, dull steady Richard and reserved intellectual Tom. After the accident in which Mrs May is killed, Richard shows himself to be so practical and reliable that he becomes his father's friend and confidant for life. The doctor is similarly won over in the book's sequel, *The Trial* (1864), when he realises that Tom is not, as he had supposed, selfish and cold-hearted. Yet Richard's deliberation would surely have continued to exasperate his excitable parent as much as the doctor's erratic ways would have irritated the precise and orderly Tom.

Dynevor Terrace shows a great advance in that blame is more evenly distributed, and the later relationship is realistic. On the surface, Louis, gentle, open, affectionate and devout, is the victim, his stern, reserved ambitious father is the aggressor. At another level, Louis, who knows how much his unreliability and recklessness disappoint his father, but makes no effort to amend his faults, is the real aggressor. But the faults on both sides spring from their relationship in Louis' childhood, and there the severe and over-critical father is to blame. Their reconciliation occurs as a result of Louis' dangerous illness, and is followed by a brief period of strong affection and mutual illusion. The latter soon passes and the problem of widely differing temperaments and principles remains to be solved. Time sobers the son and makes the father more appreciative of his merits, a realistic solution. However, *Hopes and Fears* shows that there are some personalities that will always jar on each other. After years of rebellion on Lucilla's part, and unconscious hostility on Honor's, they come together in an emotional reconciliation scene, but the relationship that follows is satisfactory to neither, and they separate for life.

In *The Young Stepmother* and in *Countess Kate* (1862) Charlotte Yonge shows that reconciliations can be imperfect or impossible because of a lack of trust. Mr Kendal's early severity has made his timid son Gilbert untruthful, and he is easily led astray by more forceful companions. Though he does well as an army officer, and becomes a hero in the Crimea, his father can never feel sure that he will not relapse. When Gilbert dies, his father is 'more at rest about his son than he had been for many a year'.[20] Their final reconciliation is therefore conditional on its being a deathbed one. In *Countess Kate* stern Aunt Barbara dislikes and distrusts honest heedless Kate, and will not do her justice. Kate is removed from her charge, as she is clearly unfit for the task.

Variations on the theme of reconciliation and the ensuing relationship occur in these novels and several later ones. One notable one is the reconciliation of a debauched gentleman of the court of Charles II and his puritanical wife in *The Danvers Papers* (1867), and those between Dolores and Gillian and their respective aunts in *The Two Sides of the Shield* (1885) and *Beechcroft at Rockstone* (1888). However, the theme of reconciliation between individuals is given most prominence in the 1850s.

This may have had some connection with the emergence of a particular type of character, a father or authority figure, sometimes but not always connected with the reconciliation theme, who makes his appearance at about the same time. In Charlotte Yonge's fiction certain character types do recur, but none so frequently as this one, which is found in both the contemporary and historical novels and tales. These characters share certain good qualities, determination, benevolence and a concern for justice, but they are also grave, stern taskmasters, who are often misunderstood and unloved outside a very small circle, because of their reserve, severity and apparent coldness. The proper attitude towards them is to revere them, strive unceasingly for their slowly given regard, and rejoice in their rare commendation.

One example is the father of Berenger in *The Chaplet of Pearls* (1868), a minor character who dies early in the novel. The boy's relationship with his father is described:

> He loved his father exceedingly; but the Baron, while ever just towards him, was grave and strict to a degree [. . .] His son was always under rule, often blamed, and scarcely ever praised; but it was a hardy vigorous nature, and respectful love throve under the system that would have crushed or alienated a different disposition.[21]

A similar character is Prince Edward in *The Prince and the Page* (1866). He is, as his page discovers, 'a strict, cold, grave disciplinarian, ever just, though on the side of severity, and stern towards the slightest neglect or breach of observance.' If he had been 'gay, open-hearted and careless' he would never have gained the reputation of a 'hard, cruel tyrant', earned by being unconciliatory even when most merciful and generous. At the same time the novel stresses his loving relationship with his immediate family and the 'warm deep heart' behind his reserve.[22]

Mr Kendal in *The Young Stepmother* has many of the same characteristics. The townspeople regard him as a tyrant and '[h]ad he been more free spoken, real oppression would have been better endured than benefits against people's will'. He was 'past acquiring the winning considerate manner that softens so much', while showing tenderness and sweetness at times to his nearest relations.[23]

Lord Ormersfield in *Dynevor Terrace* has elements of the same character, being just and honourable, though severe and reserved. Colonel Umfraville in *Countess Kate* is another of the same type, as is John of Lancaster in *The Caged Lion*, the stern reserved warrior whose tenderness had almost as much effect on the prospective nun, Esclairmonde, as did that of General Sir Jasper Merrifield on Lilias Mohun. Her sister recalls how 'her stately warrior came, and made her day dreams earnest [. . .] I don't think his severity ever dismayed her [. . .] there was always such sweetness in it'.[24]

In 1895 Charlotte Yonge published *The Carbonels*. Captain Carbonel is shown as just and upright but unpopular outside his immediate circle, due to his apparent severity. The novel is based on the early life of her parents, and Captain Carbonel is a portrait of her father.

In 1877 she wrote her autobiography. In it she describes her father:

> He was grave, and external observers feared him, and thought him stern, but oh, how tender he could be, how deeply and keenly he felt! His great characteristic was thoroughness. He could not bear to do anything, or see anything done by halves.[25]

He often reduced her to tears, but she was never afraid though much in awe of him. She loved him dearly. He was her teacher in childhood and youth and the close companion of her literary labours. He shared many of the characteristics of the stern authority figures already mentioned, including the military background of most of them. He died suddenly at a comparatively early age in 1854.

As an adolescent Charlotte Yonge had reconciled herself to the loss of her young companions by creating imaginary families. Perhaps she tried to reconcile herself to the loss of her father by creating a succession of characters who resembled him.

There is another possible explanation. In *The Daisy Chain*, in a chapter written after Mr Yonge's death, the May family are visited by Harry's commanding officer, whose 'short peremptory manner' reduces the lively youth to silence.

> 'And yet,' said Margaret, 'Harry will not hear a single word in dispraise of him. I do believe he loves him with all his heart.'
>
> 'I think,' said Ethel, 'that in a strong character, there is an exulting fear in looking up to a superior, in whose justice there is perfect reliance. It is a germ of the higher feeling.'[26]

Thus Harry's feeling for his strict captain is seen as a microcosm of what people should feel about the ultimate authority figure, God. It is possible that Charlotte Yonge felt that God had been severe to her in taking away the father whom she loved so dearly. She may have tried through her writing to reconcile herself to His decrees and to understand His nature by relating them to earthly authority figures, just, stern but loving, who resembled her earthly father. The reconciliation that she shows taking place between the wayward child and the stern parent, and the relationship of mutual love and trust that follows perhaps symbolised her own spiritual progress.

Certainly the religious views expressed in her fiction undergo a change during the 1850s. In *Womankind*, written long afterwards, she describes different types of religious experience.

> The original meaning of the word Religion is "rule." Therefore the religious are those who order their lives by the rule of God's Law, and live as in His sight [. . .] There are, in fact, three classes: those who have attained to happy personal love of God; those who act from strong sense of duty; and those who are absolutely careless [. . .].[27]

In many of the early novels the rule aspect is emphasised. Religion is shown as obedience to the teaching of the Prayer Book and a strict attention to duty. Baptism, confirmation and subsequent communion are essential for entry to Heaven, and give valuable aid in the performance of duty, which is also a requirement. Most of the characters in the keynote tales seem unconscious that there could be any other dimension to the religious life.

In the later novels of the 1850s Charlotte Yonge recognises this dimension. It appears in all the novels, and most clearly in *Hopes and Fears*, when Honor finds spiritual peace.

> He whom she 'had not seen' had become her rest and her reliance, and in her year of loneliness and darkness, a trust, a support, a confiding joy had sprung up, such as she had before believed in, but never experienced. 'Her Best, her All;' those had been words of devotional aspiration before, they were realities at last. (p. 335)

With the recognition of the possibility of a personal relationship with the Divine Charlotte Yonge shows a new tolerance towards those who seek it by non-Tractarian paths, such as Evangelicals, Roman Catholics and Non-conformists. In *A Modern Telemachus* (1886) she suggests that the Scottish renegade can go to Heaven, possibly without baptism and certainly without other Christian rites, on the strength of his dying belief, and even shows respect for the Muslim faith whose tenets have made him sober, honest and charitable.

She is also more critical of the faults and failings to be found in her own branch of the faith. In *The Pillars of the House* (1873) Clement Underwood is censured for his introspection and concern for the outward forms of religion, while the orthodox clergyman is shown to have hastened the death of Clement's father Edward by his selfishness and weakness.

Several factors may have contributed to these developments. As Tractarian tenets became widely accepted in the Church of England, it was no longer necessary to defend them at every point. In the face of the growing scepticism and increasing secularism in society, the different branches of Christianity were drawing closer together. It is also possible that Charlotte Yonge's personal religious experience played a part.

Dispossession is a theme which appears frequently in Charlotte Yonge's fiction during the 1870s. From the 1880s onward one of the principal themes is that of the outsider, one who rejects or is rejected by society, although examples do appear much earlier. In her first works society was always right, and if it and an individual were at odds, the individual had to change to meet its requirements. In the novels of the middle and later 1850s and many later ones, she shows that both individuals and society are imperfect, and reform and mutual adjustment are necessary. However, as time goes on, she takes a more critical view of society and a greater understanding and tolerance of those who reject or are rejected by it.

The earliest of those who reject their society is Henry de Montfort, Earl of Leicester, who appears in *The Prince and the Page* (1866). Blinded, maimed and left for dead on the battlefield of Tewkesbury, he becomes a professional beggar and beggar leader. He subsequently declines the offer of his cousin Prince Edward of a place at court as his friend and adviser, preferring to retain his independence. He is a compelling character who at the end of the tale, as the father-in-law of Sir John Mohun and ancestor of the Mohun family, speaks a moving obituary to his royal kinsman.

Another outright rebel is Angela Underwood of *The Pillars of the House* who continues her defiant course over many years before finding peace and a heroic death in *Modern Broods*. Charlotte Yonge also shows sympathy and understanding for the autistic child in *A Reputed Changeling* (1889) and the renegade Scot in *A Modern Telemachus*. If they have rejected their societies they are shown to have every excuse.

Although not wholly excused, Dolores Mohun, an only child from a very quiet home, is given some sympathy in *The Two Sides of the Shield* when she is plunged into the hurly-burly of a large family. Society is shown to be deeply at fault in a number of other cases. The mediaeval country folk treat the heroine of *Grisly Grisell* (1893) as a witch because of her facial disfigurement. In *The Armourer's Prentices* (1884) the jester has to conceal his occupation from friends and neighbours. In *My Young Alcides* the gross prejudice of the gentry of the district where the action takes place is stressed. In *Beechcroft at Rockstone* the White family, whose father had risen from the ranks to become a commissioned officer, are scorned by those who consider themselves to be of higher standing, and persecuted by those who resent their superiority.

However, it is in her last novel, *Modern Broods*, that Charlotte Yonge makes her strongest case for the misfits, the outsiders, and against those who would force them into conformity. Lena Merrifield is an orphan child, backward, sickly and unprepossessing. The only person she loves and trusts is Angela Underwood, to whom she has been left by her father, an erring but penitent member of the family into which Lilias Mohun had married. The rest of the Merrifields had rejected and abandoned him, and in an ill-judged desire to atone for their harshness, insist on their right to the child, whom they propose to bring up as ruggedly as possible. They claim that she is not really ill, and that her heart-attack, which actually proves fatal, is hysteria. In all the previous fiction in which they appeared the Merrifields are shown as a wholly admirable family, with all the old-fashioned principles that Charlotte Yonge had valued, but here they are seen as hard, insensitive and obstinate.

The concern for misfits, and the disapproval of the societies in which they find themselves, may have arisen from a sense that Charlotte Yonge herself was becoming an outsider, and had been rejected by society. The reviews of her books in the major organs of the press suggest a decline in her popularity. *Heartsease* (1854) received eight, *Hopes and Fears* (1860) and *The Pillars of the House* (1873) five, but no later work of fiction by her had more than three, and many only two.[28] She was increasingly classed as a writer for the young, and dismissed as such, though she had long since parted with her youthful illusions, and come to terms with many of the changes in contemporary society. The rejection must have hurt all the more because over the years she had become an authority figure herself, whose words had been respectfully heeded. She was the masterful editor of *The Monthly Packet*, the magazine she had founded; she was Mother Goose to the Gosling Society, the group of young girls who wrote under her guidance in the 1860s. But after more than forty years as editor she was dismissed, as being too old-fashioned and out of touch. The Goslings grew up and flew away, some in directions of which she could not approve. Not surprisingly, she felt increasingly alienated from the society in which she found herself. She turned more and more to writing historical fiction, escaping into the past that she had always enjoyed.

In conclusion, it has been seen that Charlotte Yonge's writing shows both continuity and development. Some reasons for the development have already been suggested. Others, paradoxically, may have been the result of the very restricted background itself. She was deeply loyal to her beliefs, a lifelong Tory and a devoted member of that branch of the Anglican Church that had embraced the Oxford Movement. However, both these bodies changed considerably during her lifetime, and she dutifully followed their lead. Her close relationship with her own family included the younger generation, and she benefited by their wider experience of life. Her circle of friends came to include many of identical faith but differing backgrounds and life-style.

In her early years in an enclosed circle, many of whose members were older than herself, ideas held in common were simply accepted as unchanging truths, not analysed or questioned. Keble and Charlotte Yonge herself both refused to discuss their views or enter into argument. As they did not have to justify or defend them they remained vague. It was thus easy for Charlotte Yonge to slide from one position to another unconsciously. In the article of 1894, 'Lifelong Friends', she notes of *Abbeychurch*, her first tale,

> That the clerical family should discourage the Mechanics' Institute instead of taking the lead in the mental cultivation, is a curious memorial to the tone of mind at that period.[29]

It is as if she had not written the book herself. Her works often show a lack of clarity of thought. It was this lack of clarity that led her to be patronisingly classed as a writer for the young, and then almost forgotten for many years.

This would not have troubled her. She never modified her early belief that the aim of a writer was to be useful. In an article on *Authorship* she wrote:

> Woman can often speak with great effect to her own generation, even if her achievements do not obtain lasting fame, and this should be her aim.[30]

1   Owen Chadwick, *The Victorian Church* (London: A. C. Black, 1970) vol. 1, p. 65.

2   Geoffrey Rowell, *The Vision Glorious* (Oxford: Oxford University Press, 1983) p. 8.

3   Joseph Baker, *The Novel and the Oxford Movement* (Princeton: Princeton University Press, 1932) pp. 3-13; David Roberts, 'The Social Conscience of the Tory Periodicals' (*Victorian Periodicals Newsletter* 10.3, Sept. 1977) pp. 154-69.

4   C. M. Yonge, 'Lifelong Friends', *Monthly Packet*, new [fourth] series, 8 (Dec. 1894) pp. 694-97. Reprinted in *A Chaplet for Charlotte Yonge*, ed. Georgina Battiscombe and Marghanita Laski (London: Cresset Press, 1965) pp. 181-84. References here use the *Chaplet* pagination: p. 183.

5   C. M. Yonge, *The Two Guardians* (London: Masters, 1852) Preface.

6   'Lifelong Friends', p. 182.

7   'Lifelong Friends', p. 182.

8   Christabel Rose Coleridge, *Charlotte Mary Yonge: Her Life and Letters* (London: Macmillan, 1903) p. 124.

9   C. M. Yonge and C. R. Coleridge, *Strolling Players* (London: Macmillan, 1893) p. 270.

10   *Dynevor Terrace* in *Saturday Review* (18 April 1857) pp. 357-58.

11   C. M. Yonge, *Hints on Reading*, in *Monthly Packet*, first series, 2 (1851) p. 322-24 (passage quoted is from p. 322).

12   J. T. Coleridge, *Memoir of the Rev. John Keble* (Oxford: James Parker, 1869) p. 430.

13   C. R. Coleridge, p. 296.

14   C. M. Yonge, *The Young Stepmother*, 1861 (London: Macmillan, 1913) p. 122.

15   *The Young Stepmother*, p. 375.

16   C. M. Yonge, *Hopes and Fears*, 1860 (London: Macmillan, 1888) p. 143.

17   C. M. Yonge, *The Three Brides*, 1876 (London: Macmillan, 1892) p. 74.

18   C. M. Yonge, *My Young Alcides*, 1875 (London: Macmillan, 1888) p. 18.

19   Lettice Cooper, 'Charlotte Mary Yonge, dramatic novelist', in *A Chaplet for Charlotte Yonge*, pp. 31-40.

20   *The Young Stepmother*, p. 354.

21   C. M. Yonge, *The Chaplet of Pearls*, 1868 (London: Macmillan, 1898) p. 8.

22 C. M. Yonge, *The Prince and the Page*, 1866 (London: Macmillan, 1891) pp. 116, 155.

23 *The Young Stepmother*, p. 391; and in *Monthly Packet*, first series, 20 (1860) p. 385.

24 C. M. Yonge, *Beechcroft at Rockstone*, 1888 (London: Macmillan, 1889) p. 213.

25 C. R. Coleridge, p. 51.

26 C. M. Yonge, *The Daisy Chain*, 1856 (London: Macmillan, 1889) p. 494.

27 C. M. Yonge, *Womankind*, in *Monthly Packet*, new [second] series, 18 (1874) pp. 371-72 = *Womankind* (London: Mozley and Smith, 1876) pp. 73-4.

28 Collated from Lionel Madden, *J. B. Shorthouse and C. M. Yonge* (unpublished dissertation, University of London, 1964-65) pp. 130-50.

29 'Lifelong Friends', *Chaplet*, p. 183.

30 C. M. Yonge, 'Authorship', *Monthly Packet*, new [fourth] series], 4 (Sept. 1892) pp. 296-303. Reprinted in *A Chaplet for Charlotte Yonge*, ed. Georgina Battiscombe and Marghanita Laski (London: Cresset Press, 1965) pp. 185-92. References here use the *Chaplet* pagination: p. 189.

DYNEVOR TERRACE AND *THE HEIR OF REDCLYFFE*

Wendy Forrester

In her excellent biography *Charlotte Mary Yonge*, Georgina Battiscombe describes *Dynevor Terrace* as 'a plagiarism of *The Heir of Redclyffe*, with Louis Fitzjocelyn as Guy, James as Philip, and Mary Ponsonby a much less attractive Amy'.[1]

There are, of course, similarities between the books. Each has a pair of cousins, young men of very different dispositions, each has a pair of romances (*Dynevor Terrace* actually has three) and each has an aristocratic hero whose mother died at his birth. Perhaps the strongest similarity is the fact that hero and heroine are separated by self-denying obedience to her unreasonable father. However, the lovers in one book are little like those in the other and the plots are worked out very differently. Most important is the fact that the characters in *Dynevor Terrace* react on each other, grow and develop much more than those in *The Heir*.

The hero of *The Heir of Redclyffe*, Sir Guy Morville, is a lovable character, but might perhaps have been more so if he had not been already so far on the road to virtue at the age of seventeen, having no observable fault but a hot temper. Unpleasant though we may find such a temper in those we have dealings with in real life, it is often less disagreeable on paper than in flesh and blood, shared as it is by many of our childhood heroes and heroines. Guy's is, in any case, so well controlled that it is mostly seen only as a flashing eye or bitten lip, and then usually on behalf of an old schoolmaster, an ill-treated dog, or King Charles I. The only outburst on personal grounds is the one which separates him from Amy, the heroine, produced under the great provocation of a false accusation.

The hero of *Dynevor Terrace*, Louis Fitzjocelyn, motherless from birth like Guy, shares with him aristocracy, beauty, charm and religious faith, but there is never any fear of finding him too good to be true. 'So sincere, affectionate, and obliging, that not to love him was impossible; yet that love only made his faults more annoying.'[2]

Perhaps one should at this point face what may strike a modern reader as the worst thing about Louis. Out walking he sees a rosy-breasted pastor, a bird hardly ever seen in England. What does he do? Yes, alas, it must be said. He shoots it. Neither Charlotte Yonge nor anyone in Louis' company expresses any regret for the slaughter, both Louis' father and his author reserving their displeasure for the fact that it has made him late for an important dinner. However, it is hardly reasonable to blame a character for his attitude to nature study from the standpoint of a century and a half later, and Louis is after all kind to animals, lifting a farmer's little pigs over a gap 'as tender as if they were Christians'.[3]

Both Guy Morville and Viscount Fitzjocelyn have a shadowed heredity, Guy a line of Ruddigore-like bad baronets, and Louis, less dramatically, the mother who died at his birth and for whom he was named, sweet-natured and radiantly lovely, but silly and vain. Although Georgina Battiscombe said that none of Charlotte Yonge's characters is ever tempted to commit adultery,[4] it is hinted that death saved Louisa from something worse than silliness and vanity. Louis, with his mother's beauty and charm, has had a far sounder upbringing, and is neither vain nor silly, but the lack of 'bottom' which is his chief fault may have been inherited from her. 'Attempting everything, finishing nothing';[5] his belongings include 'half a poem on the Siege of Granada, three parts of an essay upon Spade Husbandry, the *dramatis personae* of a tragedy on Queen Brunehault'.[6] Asked by the Vicar to have a book bound and buy some church music, he buys lavish and unnecessary presents but forgets to perform what had been entrusted to him.

Louis' father, the Earl of Ormersfield, no doubt sees and dreads the resemblance to the charming, weak mother in the son, provoking his cousin Jem's complaint that he himself is considered the pattern young man while Louis can do nothing right. Even Louis' blameless conduct at university is an exasperation rather than a pleasure, seen as something near effeminacy. While his father would hardly have wanted the youthful Viscount to drink, gamble or womanise he says impatiently that '[t]here are faults that are the very indications of a manly spirit',[7] and he would have found Jem's hot temper less difficult to deal with than Louis' sweet but unstable nature.

Louis' near-deathbed scene comes, interestingly, not where such scenes are expected, near the end of the book, but near the beginning. 'Unstable, negligent, impetuous, and weak as he had been,' he repents of his errors: '"Everything purposed – nothing done!"'[8] His illness brings about a much more affectionate relationship between him and the Earl, each now seeking to please the other. In spite of their best endeavours, however, they often remain at cross-purposes, Louis' care to consult his father in everything resulting in irritation rather than pleasure.

Philip Morville is, of course, the villain rather than the secondary hero through most of *The Heir of Redclyffe*, although grief, shame and repentance break him and reset him differently. In the course of writing the book, Charlotte Yonge said she thought readers might begin by thinking him the good young man, but she signals her intentions as early as the second page, with the symbolic breaking of Amy's prize camellia through his officious helpfulness.

The two young men are temperamental opposites, the frigid gleam of Philip's character contrasting with the warm sparkle of Guy's. The author uses a quotation from Tennyson as a chapter heading, applied with merciless fitness to Philip.

> 'Himself unto himself he sold,
> Upon himself, himself did feed,
> Quiet, dispassionate, and cold,
> With chiselled features clear and sleek.'[9]

There is much to admire in Philip, including the fact that he has chosen his profession with a view to supporting his sisters rather than pleasing himself. He is temperate, hard-working, honest, and above all prudent, but his prudence is as repellent as his self-love, leading him into his unacknowledged romance with Amy's sister Laura. This seems less shocking to a present-day reader than it did to the author, but there is no question that Philip was acting wrongly according to his own lights when he involved a very young girl in deception, even though he managed to persuade himself that his course was one of perfect propriety.

Laura is one of Charlotte Yonge's rare examples of passionate love. Apart from her feelings for Philip she barely exists as a character. She apparently has intellectual interests, but since Philip is her mentor it is hard to say how seriously she would otherwise have taken them. Even if her love had not led her into allowing his chilly and cautious courtship without her parents' knowledge and blessing, her author would surely have felt it too passionate and partisan, without a firm spiritual ground; the lovers she approves of care for something even more than each other. As it is, Laura's consciousness of the need for concealment and her doubts about the future give her the air of being harassed beyond her years — 'harassed' is a word applied to her often. Even as a bride she is called 'poor thing', and the description of the cares of her blameless married life sound like a harsh punishment for the faults of her maidenhood.

'A much less attractive Amy'; true, Mary Ponsonby of *Dynevor Terrace* is not a particularly engaging heroine, but nor is she one of those one meets from time to time who, in spite of the stress laid on their charm, remain stubbornly less appealing to the reader than to the author. Mary is not meant to be charming. Although Amy Edmonstone is less beautiful than her sister Laura, she has glossy curls, a dainty figure and, in her teens, the pretty, caressing ways which call forth indulgence. Even at five Mary Ponsonby was not a kitten, earning the nickname 'Downright Dunstable'. Although a pleasing impression is left by the description of the adult Mary's clear eyes and sensible kindly mouth her appearance is an uncommon one for a heroine. They may be pale and slight, with irregular features, and possibly even a mouth too wide for beauty, but a broad face — and we may deduce the even less romantic attribute of a solid figure — is less usual. Heroines, too, often have a vein of poetry, a quick response to the beauties of nature, and a vivid emotional life of heights and depths, but Mary is prose and steadiness all through. Coming to England in early childhood she is brought up by a strict and religious aunt, returning to her parents in Peru at seventeen 'with a clear head, sound heart, and cramped mind.'[10] One of the most endearing things about her is the humility of her reaction when Jem Frost says indignantly of his cousin Louis Fitzjocelyn that if he were an ordinary, practical, commonplace block his father might value him. 'Mary knew that she was a commonplace block, and did not wonder at herself for not agreeing with James.'[11]

Guy's hot temper apart, he and Amy are very much like each other. Amy gains dignity and decision after her marriage, but marriage to any loving and well-principled husband would probably have had this result, even if he had been less exceptional than Guy. Mary Ponsonby and Louis Fitzjocelyn, on the other hand, are temperamental opposites, and while her influence on him is more noticeable than his on hers it is he who extends the narrow horizons of her imagination. When Louis is recovering Lord Ormersfield procures a rare book for him. Louis is delighted, but outrages his father by plunging into the middle. Attempting to please the Earl by starting at the beginning, but still weak from his illness, he soon gives up, until Mary begins to read regularly with him and 'came to be more interested than her mother had ever expected to see her in anything literary. It was amusing to see the two cousins unconsciously educating each other – the one learning expansion, the other concentration, of mind.'[12] Mary rounds Cape Horn three times as an adult, but the third voyage, unhappy as it is for her, is made with a mind now open to the mystery of the furrow of fire left in the ship's wake, the grandeur of a mighty, dazzling iceberg. We can feel, too, that her Peruvian exile, although it is her love for Louis which makes it exile, is enriched by what she has learned from association with him.

Philip Morville in *The Heir of Redclyffe* and James, or Jem, Frost in *Dynevor Terrace* are both guilty of the sin of pride, in very different ways. Philip's is gratification in his own self-control and contempt for his cousin Guy, whom he sees as a petulant boy with bad heredity, unjustly gifted with the rank and riches which Philip himself would use much more wisely, and all too likely to be led into gambling and debt. Jem Frost – no villain, but a true secondary hero – has none of Philip's prudence and self-command. His temper is as hot as the Heir of Redclyffe's, and unlike his it is by no means confined to flashing eye and bitten lip. Far from looking down on his cousin Louis, Lord Fitzjocelyn, he complains angrily that Louis's father does not appreciate him. '[...] browbeaten and contradicted every moment, and myself set up for a model. I may steal a horse, while he may not look over the wall!'[13] Self-love has little to do with Jem's pride; it is rather a corruption of self-respect, a 'lily that festers'. He and his younger sister have been brought up by their grandmother, the heiress of the Dynevors. Ruined by her husband's unwise speculation, she has supported herself and her orphaned grandchildren by keeping a school. Jem and his schoolgirl sister honour the noble simplicity of her life, but the pride which is dignity in her is perverted in them to a stubborn refusal to be beholden to anybody. Gawky tomboy Clara, slighted at the second-rate boarding-school which is all her brother can afford for her, glories in refusing to mask her poverty and concealing her aristocratic connections from her companions as much as possible. Her cousin Louis, who treats her more as a younger brother than a sister, remarks ruefully that his father would never dare to give her half a sovereign to improve her deplorable wardrobe. Jem, likewise, has a prickly alertness to refuse and resent anything which could be regarded as patronage. Like Philip Morville, Jem chooses his career rather to provide for his sister than to please himself. Philip picks the army, one of the vocations of which Charlotte Yonge seems to have thought most highly, instead of the university he had hoped for, and she honours him for his self-sacrifice. Jem chooses the one which she unquestionably believed to be the highest, and she thinks him wrong since his reason for seeking ordination is less a genuine vocation than a desire to provide independently for himself and Clara.

Both brother and sister learn the difference between self-respecting independence and self-regarding pride. Clara finds humility through the undesired – and fleeting – wealth with which her uncle burdens her; Jem through the poverty to which he brings his wife and children by his obstinate pride and the explosive temper which leads him to chastisement of his young pupils considered dangerous even by Victorian standards.

Isabel, the secondary heroine of *Dynevor Terrace*, Louis's cousin on his mother's side – it is as well that Charlotte Yonge provides a family tree – is a more typical example of her author's young women than the real heroine, Mary Ponsonby. Dreamy, devoted to chivalry, with literary ambitions, she has no doubts about her ability to face a life in straitened circumstances with Jem, and indeed is too high-minded to notice its inconveniences. 'She had married a vision of perfection, and entered on a romance of happy poverty, and she had no desire to awaken.'[14] Husband and guests, however, cannot help but notice that the queenly Isabel is a very poor housewife. The scene of Jem, blue with cold, sitting in his fireless study correcting school exercises with little Kitty asleep on his breast, while his wife works at her romance

The Chapel in the Valley is both comical and touching. Charlotte Yonge is much more merciful to Isabel than one expects. In another book she might have been shown by some infuriatingly wise person that her high-flown work was rubbish, dispatched to her distaff, and possibly, some years later, been allowed to publish something modest and domestic. It is a pleasant surprise that, after Isabel has become a better housewife and mother, *The Chapel in the Valley* actually makes a useful addition to the family income. Another agreeable surprise arrives when Jem's illness, which the reader assumes, like his cousin Louis, to be that old favourite brain fever, turns out to be something as unromantic as jaundice.

The romance between Louis and Mary begins comically, as another attempt by the Viscount to please his father. It is not surprising that Mary is tempted to accept the charmer, but following her mother's sensible advice not to take a man whose motive is filial duty rather than personal choice, she grits her teeth and turns him down. By his second proposal he has reached the point of really wanting Mary, but principally because he feels she can keep him steady; he is conscious that he has 'reached man's estate almost against his will'.[15]

Charlotte Yonge has been justly praised for her ability to show a character changing, through age or through grace or both, while still remaining recognisably himself or herself, and her reformations are not usually improbably sudden. When he recovers from his brush with death Louis does not at once become a sensible young man, but remains volatile and imprudent, making mistakes such as electioneering on behalf of his cousin Jem for a position in the local grammar school, resulting in a more suitable candidate losing the place. Only by slow degrees does he reach the degree of manliness and good sense which make him a fit husband for Mary.

The relationship between Louis and Mary is particularly interesting in view of the fact that the author's view of the superiority of the male sex is so entrenched. The eponymous heroine of *The Clever Woman of the Family* (1865) is put in her place in a way some readers find hard to bear: 'her old presumptions withered up to nothing when she measured her own powers with those of a highly educated man'.[16] Mary, neither as well-educated nor as naturally clever as Louis, improves him, not by her superior virtue – his being quite equal to hers – but by her superior strength of mind. When she refuses his second proposal, he tells her mother that Mary is the one person who can keep him steady. 'To be your husband, instead of your wife?' enquires Mrs Ponsonby dryly, calling on him to make a man of himself: 'You *can* do it; there is nothing that Grace cannot do,' and pointing out that his instability could make his father suppose religion is 'soft'.[17]

While Louis has gained stability, Mary's cramped mind has expanded through loving him. Charlotte Yonge had used the metaphor of expansion earlier, when the two young people were reading together, and later she writes that 'the intercourse and sympathy with him had opened and unfolded many a perception and quality in her, which had been as tightly and hardly cased up as leaf-buds in their gummy envelopes.'[18]

Dynevor Terrace appeared in 1864, fourteen years after *The Heir of Redclyffe*. The action begins in 1847 and closes in 1853, although by my calculations the author seems to have lost a year somewhere along the way. The book travels much further afield than most of Charlotte Yonge's 'contemporary' novels, Louis having adventures in Paris at the time of the 1848 riots, and Mary a voyage around Cape Horn and a climb by mule up the Andes to the silver mines of San Benito. However, for me the most interesting and appealing part of the book is the change in the four principals; stiffnecked and fiery Jem becoming humble and patient, dreamy Isabel practical, imagination unfolding in Mary, and Louis achieving firmness and energy.

Dynevor Terrace is nothing like as well-known as is *The Heir of Redclyffe*, but it well deserves to reach a new generation of readers.

---

1   Georgina Battiscombe, *Charlotte Mary Yonge: The Story of an Uneventful Life* (London: Constable, 1943) p. 117.

2   C. M. Yonge, *Dynevor Terrace*, 1857 (London: Macmillan, 1898) p. 42.

3   *Dynevor Terrace*, p. 86.

4   Battiscombe, p. 74.

5   *Dynevor Terrace*, p. 41-2.

6   *Dynevor Terrace*, p. 69.

7   *Dynevor Terrace*, p. 47.

8   *Dynevor Terrace*, p. 57; p. 56.

9   C. M. Yonge, *The Heir of Redclyffe*, 1853 (London: Macmillan, 1889) p. l96.

10   *Dynevor Terrace*, p. 28.

11   *Dynevor Terrace*, p. 63.

12   *Dynevor Terrace*, p. 83.

13   *Dynevor Terrace*, p. 9.

14   *Dynevor Terrace*, p. 338.

15   *Dynevor Terrace*, p. 183.

16   C. M. Yonge, *The Clever Woman of the Family*, 1865 (London: Macmillan, 1892) p. 337.

17   *Dynevor Terrace*, p. 196.

18   *Dynevor Terrace*, p. 281.

TRANSCRIPTION OF THE LETTER FROM CHARLOTTE YONGE TO MARY ANDERSON MORSHEAD, PRINTED ON THE FOLLOWING PAGE

Elderfield, March 17th 1888

My dear Mary

I am very glad you have this respite, it is so much better for you all. And you must be glad of time to put things in order, and see about Sister Sarah. I send the answer to the Feby question as no doubt you want to keep them all together. I have put in your apology and I can't put in the Jany class list now – as the printers must be early this month –, they tell me, and they were kept waiting by a mistake last time. I am just in from the Inspection, two days of it! Mr Brock's father is so ill that there is much fear of his being called away in Holy Week or before it.

I have a whole curious account of the skirmish on Clifton Moor in the '45 sent me which I would send you if you were likely to have time for it or mind.

Your affectionate C. M. Yonge

[At the top, in another hand] Addressed to her cousin Miss Anderson-Morshead

(addressed to her cousin
Miss Underwood-Markhead)

Oxford time
March 17
1882

My dear Mary

I am very glad you have this respite, it is so much better for you all. Then you must be glad of time to put things in order, and see about Sister Sarah. I send the answer

to the Febry question as no doubt you meant to keep them all together — I have put in your apology and I can't put in the Jany class list now — as the printers must be early this month they tell me, and they were kept waiting by

a mistake last time I am just in from the Inspection two days of it! Mr. Boock's father is so ill that there is much fear of his being called away in Holy Week or before it —

I have a whole curiat account of the Skirmish on

Clifton Avenue, in the '45 sent me which I would send you if you were likely to have time for it or mind

Your affectionate
C. M. Yonge

CHARLOTTE YONGE AND THE CRITICS

Cecilia Bass

In considering contemporary reviews of Charlotte Yonge's novels I shall concentrate on the periodicals, including quarterlies, such as the *Edinburgh*, *Modern*, *London Quarterly* and the *Quarterly* itself, which, though it ignored her novels, (as did the *Edinburgh*) nevertheless contributed a long and scholarly summary of her work as an obituary. The monthly magazines are especially important for their long and detailed reviews from the mid-fifties to 1861. These include the *Prospective* and *National*, edited in turn by R. H. Hutton, the *Dublin*, *North American*, *North British* and *Fraser's*, each of which noticed her work in long articles from 1854 to 1861, and the *Fortnightly*, (actually published monthly for most of its life) which was the first to abandon anonymous reviews. There are also interesting and detailed, though shorter, reviews in the periodicals of the last part of the century, the *Nineteenth Century* and *Academy*.

I shall also consider the weeklies, especially the *Athenaeum* and the *Spectator* and *Saturday Review*, each of which reviewed the novels at intervals from 1857 to 1883, though with increasing brevity, and in the case of the *Saturday Review*, increasing asperity. (The *Saturday Review* was noted for the savagery of its critics: 'Saturday Revilers', anti-feminist 'snarlers', 'scorpions, and 'scourgers'.[1]) These two periodicals were interested mainly in the fiction, but the *Athenaeum*, founded in 1828, reviewed not only the novels but also biographies, histories and children's books, both fiction and non-fiction, from 1854, when it reviewed *Heartsease*, to a brief paragraph on *Modern Broods* in 1900 (24 Nov. 1900, p. 680) missing only eight years of over fifty. This record is matched only by the fortnightly High Church *Literary Churchman*, also reviewing every branch of her work for most of its life – from 1855 to 1892. However, this magazine did not have the stature of the *Athenaeum* and may have supported Charlotte Yonge because she was a contributor and a friend of the editor.[2]

There were many reviews of her work in church magazines such as the High Church *Christian Remembrancer*, *Churchman's Companion* and *Penny Post* (with one paragraph on *The Castle Builders*). The *Church Times* was primarily interested in Charlotte Yonge's books on Sunday school teaching and, of the novels, reviewed only *The Pillars of the House*. I have given less attention to the Church magazines because of the difficulties of covering over fifty years of reviews of over 150 books,[3] and have also largely ignored periodicals, such as the *Reader* and *Literary Gazette*, which published brief occasional reviews, because they were chiefly informative rather than critical in their approach. For the same reason I have disregarded the biographical sketch, by 'Sybil', with photographs, in the *Girl's Realm Annual* of 1899.

I have included reviews from *The Times* although strictly speaking it is not a periodical, partly because Charlotte Yonge herself attached importance to it. The long-delayed review of *The Heir of Redclyffe*, published a year after the book, was of some consequence to her. 'I had to wait till morning in doubt whether it would be a knock-down one, and it was rather a relief that it was not all abuse.'[4] The opening of the review also offers us an explanation for the contemporary success of the novel which would escape the modern reader. It reminds us that it was published 'on the eve of great political contests and perhaps of contests still more terrible', from which, it is suggested, the novel offered some relief.

As regards the novels, some, most notably *The Heir of Redclyffe* and *Heartsease*, will be considered more fully because they attracted more critical attention than any others. I shall also refer in some detail to reviews of the family chronicles because of present-day interest in them, but I have had to pass by some novels, particularly *The Young Stepmother*, because, as far as I can discover, they were all but ignored by contemporary critics.

In general, to read contemporary criticism of Charlotte Yonge's novels is a reminder of how familiar yet how strange was her world. The very appearance of the articles is different. The monthly and quarterly periodicals commonly have reviews of eighteen to twenty pages, though it would appear from a letter of Charlotte Yonge[5] that the practice had changed by the 1890s. She regrets that the 'real review – not a mere notice – is so seldom to be seen in these days', because 'they teach one much'. However, it is more than possible that what Charlotte Yonge perceived as change was largely attributable to fading interest in her fiction rather than to a change in journalistic practice, since the review of her biography of John Coleridge Patteson runs to thirty-four pages in the *Quarterly Review* (Oct. 1874, pp. 458-92). The obituaries of her in *The Quarterly* and *Fortnightly* are also extensive.

Another striking difference in the reviews is the amount of space devoted to plot summary and long passages of quotation. These are no doubt used on occasion to pad out an article, but ostensibly they are meant to give the reader a flavour of the work under consideration – and sometimes more than a flavour. It is not uncommon, especially in the weeklies, to find the story told to the end as in the *Spectator* review of *The Daisy Chain* (29 Mar. 1856, p. 346). The proportion of commentary to quotation remains the same whether in the short, single-column articles in the weeklies or in the longer reviews of the weightier periodicals. Both normally devote about half the review to plot summary and quotation of extended passages. There are exceptions to this. In 'Religious Novels' in the *North British Review*, (Nov. 1856, pp. 209-27) *The Daisy Chain* is mentioned by name only in the title, nor are any details of plot or character given. The *Saturday* review of *Dynevor Terrace* gives details of the novel but fails to name a single character (18 Apr. 1857, pp. 357-58).

The long extracts are used in different ways, most commonly, as might be expected, to give the essence of a dramatic event such as the fire or the coal-mining accident in *Heartsease* (favourably compared with 'a striking scene of the same description in Mr Dickens'). Not surprisingly, considering Victorian enthusiasm for a 'good' death-bed scene, the death of Guy in *The Heir of Redclyffe* is quoted at length in four reviews to illustrate the pathos and beauty of the scene and the economy and effectiveness of the writing. The near-death of Violet in *Heartsease* is also quoted at length in *Fraser's Magazine* (Nov. 1854, pp. 489-503) and the *Spectator* (4 Nov. 1854, pp. 1157-58).

Extended passages of quotation are also used to illustrate felicities of characterisation, especially in dialogue. *Fraser's* quotes the introduction of Violet to her in-laws to show the contrast between her and Theodora, and a further extract from a dinner-party conversation illustrates Charlotte Yonge's skill in constructing 'clever, original conversation' for Percy Fotheringham. The editor and critic R. H. Hutton in 'The Author of *Heartsease* and Modern Schools of Fiction', in the *Prospective*, uses a passage focused on the same character, which 'inclines us to ascribe to our author no small share of the talent of Miss Austen' (Nov. 1854, pp. 460-82). Extracts are also used critically, most notably in Wilkie Collins' savage review of *The Heir of Redclyffe* in 'Dr Dulcamara', *Household Words* (18 Dec. 1858, pp. 50-51) where he quotes Guy's angry defence of King Charles and a passage from the Alpine idyll to demonstrate the grounds for his contempt for Charlotte Yonge's prose style.

There is, however, a different category of extended quotation, focusing not on narrative technique but on points of doctrine. Hutton, both in the *Prospective* review and in 'Ethical and Dogmatic Fiction: Miss Yonge' (*National Review*, Jan. 1861, pp. 211-30) is particularly interested in this approach – not surprisingly since he was trained in the Unitarian ministry. It is found elsewhere too, for instance in the Methodist *London Quarterly Review* (July 1858, pp. 484-513) and in 'Miss Sewell and Miss Yonge' in the Roman Catholic *Dublin Review* (Dec. 1858, pp. 313-28). Both the *Prospective* and *London Quarterly* use the same extract, concerning the baptism of Violet's baby, to deprecate what Hutton calls an 'absurd belief in sacerdotal conjuring' (p. 482) and the *London Quarterly* the 'Popish theory [...] of the doctrine of baptismal reclamation' (p. 500). The same technique is applied in 'Ethical and Dogmatic Fiction' to *Hopes and Fears*. Hutton quotes two long conversations focused on Miss Fennimore, the Unitarian governess, examining them 'not from a literary but a theological point of view'. The whole approach here is alien to the modern reader in its use of extended quotation in order to score theological points.

Other differences to be noted in the reviews concern the assumptions and attitudes current at the time. First, we are likely to be surprised by nineteenth-century assessments of writers, contemporary and others, whom we rate more or less highly than did Charlotte Yonge's generation. It is not too surprising to find, mid-century, R. H. Hutton rank Scott equal with Shakespeare, (*Prospective* 1854, p. 462) but the twenty-first-century reader of Jane Austen, who is used to a relatively sophisticated reading of her novels, may well be surprised to see her assigned to the second rank here and in *Fraser's* because of her 'poverty of conception and failure to 'grasp a great character'. (*Fraser's* actually sets her below Charlotte Yonge.) When Hutton, one of the great critics of his day, judges Thackeray's novels inferior to Charlotte Yonge's because, unlike her, 'he looks at everything through self-analysis', the effect is breath-taking.

'SACERDOTAL CONJURING': THE RELIGION OF PARTY

There is also a difference in the great importance attached to the religious and moral aspects of literature. The twenty-first-century reader may be startled to realise that to her contemporaries some of Charlotte Yonge's novels, especially *The Heir of Redclyffe*, were controversial, even dangerous. The Tractarian message underlying the fiction was seen at best as inappropriate, at worst as a serious threat. This is clear from nearly all the contemporary reviews. The author of 'Miss Sewell and Miss Yonge' expresses this most graphically when he warns that 'such novels as *The Heir of Redclyffe* have become a weapon in the hands of opposing parties, who rend and deafen England with their strife' (p. 315). The non-partisan *The Times* also voices objections to 'party catchwords' and 'the religion of party' in two articles (5 Jan. 1854, p. 9, and 28 Dec. 1854, p. 5). In the second review, of *Heartsease*, *The Times* is emphatic that 'it is quite needless, in the midst of the most affecting scene in the book, to thrust [at us] the doctrine of the author's party respecting the awful importance of the baptism to an infant'. The objection is partly aesthetic, that 'it creates a difference between the author and the ordinary reader', but there is also an implied criticism of the doctrine itself, and of 'the author's party'. Again, in 'Religious Novels' in the non-partisan[6] *North British Review*, though the reviewer praises the author's 'very remarkable power of delineating that kind of life with which she sympathizes' and though he carefully distances himself from controversy, he notes 'the narrowness of religious sympathy and what many of her opponents would regard as the moral and intellectual defects of the high Anglican school of writers' (Nov. 1856, p. 218).

Others, most notably Henry James briefly referring to Charlotte Yonge in 'Elizabeth Rundle Charles' (1865), a review of 'semi-developed novels',[7] have no quarrel with her religious views *per se* but instead blame the consequent narrowness of vision for the artistic limitations of novels such as *The Heir of Redclyffe*. James's argument is that 'where the meaning and the lesson are narrowed down to a special precept', the action of the writer's mind 'is restricted beforehand to the shortest gait and the smallest manners possible this side of the ridiculous'. This criticism is heard also in the weekly periodicals. For instance the *Saturday Review*, commenting on *The Daisy Chain* in a review of *Dynevor Terrace*, criticises the moral lesson of the book but objects 'much more to the mode in which the moral is worked out than to the haziness in which it is involved' (18 Apr. 1857, p. 357-58).

In the battle for men's souls and minds were ranged on one hand the High Church, high Tory magazines, the *Guardian*, *Churchman's Companion*, *Christian Remembrancer*, *Literary Churchman*, all likely to comment favourably on Charlotte Yonge's work, not least because she wrote for all of them, with the exception of *The Christian Remembrancer*.[8] It was the High Anglican magazines which first noticed her work. *The Christian Remembrancer*, attacked for its High Anglican stance in the *Dublin Review* of December 1854, devotes a quarter of a thirty-page article, 'Books for the Young', to *Abbeychurch* (Oct. 1845, pp. 386-91). In July 1853 it has a comprehensive and appreciative review, 'Miss Yonge's Novels' (pp. 33-63), probably written by her cousin.[9] Charlotte Yonge also receives early attention from the *Churchman's Companion*, (May 1851) which reviews *Kenneth* in a seven-page article in May 1851 (pp. 182-89). Of course she was well known to the magazine, since both *Henrietta's Wish* and *The Two Guardians* were serialised there, the latter still running when the review appeared. It was a High Church periodical, the *Guardian* (9 Feb. 1853 p. 95), which was one of only three periodicals of note to accord a review to *The Heir of Redclyffe* in the year of its publication. The others were the *Gentleman's Magazine*, (a single paragraph only: N.S. 40, p. 21) and the *Christian Remembrancer* already mentioned, which praised the novel as her best so far (July 1853, p. 47).

From 1853 until the 1880s a year rarely passes (except 1859) with no reviews of Charlotte Yonge's work in a Church of England periodical, whether it is the *Church of England Quarterly* commenting briefly on the *Monthly Packet* and *The Castle Builders* in process of serialisation there (Jan. 1852, p. 248), or the *Penny Post*, a magazine for the poorer members of the Church of England, with a short item on *The Castle Builders* (Dec. 1855, pp. 71-72), or the *Church Times* reviewing *The Pillars of the House* (3 Oct. 1873, pp. 442-43).

On the other side of the religious divide there are periodicals such as the *Dublin Review*, the Methodist *London Quarterly*, and the Unitarian *Prospective* and *National*, each of which takes issue with the Tractarian viewpoint – though they do also give careful consideration to the literary skills of the author. Indeed, it is her literary skills which in some eyes pose the greatest danger. The *London Quarterly* of 1858, though it praises the scenes of pathos, 'drawn with a master hand', warns against the enervating charm and dangerous 'Popish' teaching of the novels (July 1858, pp. 484-513). (Ironically, in the same year the *Dublin*, reviewing *The Heir of Redclyffe*, *Heartsease* and *Dynevor Terrace* in 'Miss Yonge and Miss Sewell', inveighs against the last novel for exactly the opposite reason, finding there what it calls 'Miss Yonge's *animus* against the faith'.)

However, after the 1850s, the fulminations against Charlotte Yonge's religious views decreased, perhaps because she became more circumspect in her choice of material – or as the *Spectator* would have it, 'has got over her besetting temptation to talk nonsense about "Church teaching" and self-discipline' (30 July 1864, pp. 880-81). Another reason may be that the religious controversy which had been an element in bringing her work into the wider public arena was no longer such a burning issue, either with the critics or with the general public. It is interesting that the *Saturday Review* referring to 'the two novels by which her fame was established', (that is *The Heir of Redclyffe* and *Heartsease*) assumes that the reader who 'confesses to Miss Sewell or Miss Yonge as her favourite novelist', is 'that type of young lady, fluent on the subject of church discipline and decoration' who was perhaps more in fashion ten years ago than now' (20 August 1864, pp. 249-50).

Linked with the preoccupation with religion is an equal obsession with personal morality. Continually we find critics assessing novels for their ability to do good or harm, especially to women and children. The *Guardian* commends *The Heir of Redclyffe* because 'it is eminently the book to send a man from the perusal better and wiser for the lessons hidden under the narrative' (9 Feb. 1853, p. 95). Five years later we find the *London Quarterly* saying that it is 'the great delicacy and refinement' of Charlotte Yonge's novels ('not a word that any lady might blush to read or write') which make them 'admissible to the female circle' (July 1858, p. 512). The moral climate has not changed by 1864 when the *Reader* (18 June 1864, p. 770) recommends *The Trial* solely on the grounds of its moral influence. 'Many a hasty man must have had cause to bless the day when he opened *The Heir of Redclyffe*, and many a wilful one will be softened and checked if he will read and inwardly digest its authoress's present work.'

The very vocabulary of literary criticism is influenced by this preoccupation with religion and morality. Over and over again we find terms such as 'pure', 'healthy', 'wholesome', as in *Fraser's* requirement that writers of fiction 'present us with truthful, noble, healthful histories' (Nov. 1854, p. 489). The terminology is still in evidence in reviews of the turn of the century. A late example is found in *Murray's* commendation of *Beechcroft at Rockstone* for its depiction of 'that pinnacle of home life which Miss Yonge invests with such wholesome glamour' (Mar. 1889, p. 432). *Murray's Magazine* (sub-title *A Home and Colonial Periodical for the General Public*) was a monthly with an eclectic range of contributions, including, in the one issue, an article on exotic birds by W. H. Hudson; 'The Evil of Scholarships' by Dorothea Beale; 'Twice Three' by Alma Tadema, and 'What is the Salvation Army?' by General Booth. Clearly it was not of itself narrowly moralistic, but the assumption is that a novel may be judged on its power to do good, like medicine or vitamins.

THE BEAUTY OF HOLINESS – *THE HEIR OF REDCLYFFE*

A variant of this attitude is seen in the frequent employment of a striking phrase, 'the beauty of holiness', used several times in the 1850s, usually of *The Heir of Redclyffe*. These words, which seem to assume that aesthetic and moral or religious criteria are one and the same, strike a modern reader oddly when he sees them used of a novel.

'Modern Novelists – Great and Small', published first in the *North American Review* (Apr. 1855, pp. 439-59) and later reprinted in *Blackwood's Magazine* (May 1855, pp. 554-68) is perhaps the best indicator of the mixture of religious excitement and aesthetic pleasure generated by *The Heir of Redclyffe* and expressed in the phrase 'beauty of holiness'. The style of the review is exclamatory, half-ironic, unusually personal in that the reviewer[10] refers to her own 'teardrenched' copy of the book – but it also captures something of the cultural climate of the early 1850s in its adulatory attitude to the hero. Sir Guy Morville is 'the glorious joyous boy, the brilliant, ardent, chivalrous child of genius and of fortune, crowned with the beauty of his early holiness'. (Since the last words here are taken from I *Chronicles* 16 v. 9, and are used in Psalm 29 v.2 and Psalm 96 v. 9, there is surely an overtone not just of adulation but of idolatry in their application to a fictional hero.)

The combination of aesthetic sentimentality and religious fervour, here melded into a kind of high-minded hero-worship, is found elsewhere. In February 1853, the *Guardian* uses the same words of the hero (9 Feb., p. 95). So does the *Christian Remembrancer* which describes Guy as 'utterly unconscious of his own beauty and holiness' (July 1853, p. 47). In November of the following year, *Fraser's*, though it has no specific religious commitment, expresses the same awe-struck sentiments when it describes Guy as 'a type of those heaven-commissioned messengers' to whose dying words 'we listen with reverence' (p. 501).

Even when the review is partially, even largely, critical, there is nevertheless a reverential response to the hero and especially to his death. The *London Quarterly Review*, despite its criticism of the privileged hero, praises the 'truthfulness and beauty' of the death-bed scene (July 1858, pp. 484-513). Similarly, *The Times* which also criticises the privileged hero, and other aspects of the narrative, cannot resist the mixture of purity and pathos in the characterisation of Guy. It finds fault with the plot· 'very little action [. . .] the one attempt at anything like complication of plot almost puerile'; the dialogue is 'heavy'; Philip and Mr Wellwood are created out of 'literary necessity'. Even the hero, 'pure and excellent creation' though he is, (as is Amabel) is also seen as a 'costly vessel of humanity' remote from the cares of ordinary men. The death-bed scene 'though it will live in all hearts', is seen as only just within the limits of what is acceptable, the pathos, 'pretty well exhausted, when we have had every step of it [. . .] detailed, drop by drop, without the relief of action'. Nevertheless, the same phrase recurs: 'Never, perhaps, did the beauty of holiness appear more beautiful or more winning than in this pure and excellent creation' (5 Jan. 1854, p. 9). Sentiments similar to these are expressed in the image 'that bright particular star' used of a hero, 'as exceptional in kind as well as in degree'. Such phrases are particularly indicative of the mood of the time because they are used in a review which is far from admiring of other aspects of the book.

What is interesting is that the critics too, despite their reservations about many technical aspects of the book, ultimately seem to have been swept along on the tide of popular sentiment. Various theories were advanced through the rest of the century to account for this. The *Edinburgh*, treating schoolroom classics in general (and *The Daisy Chain* in particular) makes a point that might equally apply to *The Heir of Redclyffe*: 'Judges are too much of their own day. There is an emotional communism belonging to certain periods of a century [. . .] common currents sway each seaweed on the sea surface, common influences bend each blade of the cornfield one way' (October 1901, p. 436).

However, the mood passed. Indeed, within months there was something of a modification in the attitude of the periodicals to Charlotte Yonge. Though reviews of *Heartsease* followed quickly upon those of *The Heir of Redclyffe* (*The Times* reviewing both in the same year), nevertheless, its heroine, Violet Martindale, does not on the whole inspire the same adulation, even though she rouses both pity and reverence in many reviewers. *The Times*, for instance, declares her to be 'a pale imitation of Guy [. . .] her unfolding will scarcely bear a critical eye', and has scant sympathy for her tribulations, 'which arise in great measure from her not having courage enough to tell her husband they are being cheated by the cook' (28 Dec. 1854, p. 5).

Even *Fraser's*, which is generally admiring of the novel, admits that 'there is no character in the present story which we can look upon as a counterpart to Guy Morville [. . .] Heaven commissioned messenger' (Nov. 1854, p. 503). The infant Johnnie, the other candidate for the position of 'heaven sent messenger', seems to have even less appeal. *The Times* goes so far as to wish that 'that most insufferably melodramatic infant' had not got over the croup. The *Athenaeum*, more moderately finds him 'pretty – but hardly probable' (18 Nov. 1854, p. 1396). Only *Fraser's*, which declares him to be 'one of those children who not only excite our tenderest love, but our deepest respect' finds him admirable (p. 498).

By 1858, Wilkie Collins, writing anonymously in *Household Words*[11] in 'Dr Dulcamara MP', is absolutely contemptuous of Guy Morville, whom he finds to be completely incredible, 'simply impossible'. At best he is a 'lifeless personification of the Pusey-stricken writer's fancies on religion and morals, literature and art', at worst he is a joke, 'going about the world in this present year of grace [. . .] with "the lion roused in him"'. He allows that the death-bed scene is 'tenderly and delicately written in some places', but has only mocking sympathy for 'the young lady who reads for five minutes, and goes upstairs to fetch a dry pocket handkerchief; comes down again, and reads for another five minutes' (18 Dec. 1858, p. 50). The article is actually a disguised attack on M. Guizot, the French statesman, and so cannot be said to be a truly impartial or detached judgment of the book. In 1854 the *Spectator* dismisses the hero in a word. He is simply ridiculous: 'absurd Sir Guy' (30 July, p. 880-81).

By the end of the century, when the controversial elements of the novel had sunk into the background, a review, *'The Heir of Redclyffe: An Inquiry'* in the *Academy* shows how the mood had changed yet again, from contempt to indifference. The reviewer, E.A.B., frankly admits that he opened the book only after reading Mackail's biography of William Morris, in order to discover how it had had such an influence on the Pre-Raphaelites. He is astonished that they could have been swayed by it. Though he admits to being genuinely moved by 'the simple and profound tragedy of the hero's death', he finds the whole book tedious and the hero incredible: 'He never existed, never could exist, save in the devout and serious vision of a girl untouched by the world'. Thus when the reviewer declares that: 'Apart from his temper the hero is not of earth', he means something very different from what earlier critics would have meant (22 July 1899, pp. 87-88).

Other exemplary characters – and deaths – in later novels seem to have had nothing like the impact of Sir Guy Morville. The martyred Minna in *The Trial*, for example, transcending time and space at the moment of her death to comfort her imprisoned brother, is ignored by the critics. So too is Felix, the near-saintly but work-a-day hero of *The Pillars of the House*. No other of her novels inspired the near-reverential encomia awarded to Guy Morville.

DUTCH PAINTING, DAGUERREOTYPE AND 'THE TRUE REALISTIC CHIQUE'

A third preoccupation of the periodicals, which is seen in reviews of Charlotte Yonge in the mid-years of the century, was what Henry James in 'Elizabeth Rundle Charles' terms 'the true realistic *chique*'[12] The importance of the question of realism is suggested by the fact that three major monthly periodicals, the *Prospective*, *Fraser's* and the *National*, all devote time to discussion of the realistic method in relation to Charlotte Yonge's novels. The first two discuss *Heartsease*, the third considers five novels: *The Heir of Redclyffe*, *Heartsease*, *The Daisy Chain*, *Dynevor Terrace* and *Hopes and Fears*. The two articles in the *Prospective* (Nov. 1854, pp. 460-82) and *National* (Jan. 1861, pp. 211-30) both by R. H. Hutton, would have been regarded by Charlotte Yonge's contemporaries as two of the most important reviews of her work to appear in her lifetime.

Different terms are used to denote what constitutes the slippery idea of realism. For instance, 'true-looking' is used in the *Athenaeum*, which praises *Heartsease* as 'the most true-looking story we have read for a long time' because 'the interest lies in the details of daily life and the daily trials of the different characters' (18 Nov. 1854, pp. 1396-97). Here the realistic method seems to be equated with the faithful reproduction of the details of everyday life, but when the *Spectator* judges that 'the strong air of reality characterizes the whole [novel]', 'reality' here does not refer to daily life as it is experienced by the novel's readers, for though the critic goes on to praise the characters 'because they have a strong appearance of reality about them', he adds a rider: 'though the persons are not very likely to be encountered in life' (4 Nov. 1854, pp. 1157-58).

In order to elucidate how the method works in Charlotte Yonge's novels, the critics refer to painters, for instance to Teniers and the Pre-Raffaelites [sic], also to other writers, particularly to Jane Austen, but also to Trollope and Thackeray, whose 'brilliant daguerreotypes of superficial life alternating with heathen passion form the staple of those writers' work'. This extraordinary opinion is voiced by R. H. Hutton in the opening paragraph of 'Ethical and Dogmatic Fiction: Miss Yonge' in the *National* (p. 211). Henry James compares Charlotte Yonge's deployment of 'the true realistic *chique*' in *The Daisy Chain* to 'the works of MM. Flaubert and Gérôme'. Unfortunately, James gives no detailed explanation of what he means by 'the so-called principle of realism' beyond noting that in France it is associated with 'the research of local colour'.

Elsewhere the critics allude to daguerreotype, photography and Dutch painting,[13] but the terms are not defined with any precision and are used with different connotations. When *The Times*, reviewing *Heartsease* complains that 'the author seems to cultivate to excess a taste for Dutch painting' it is criticising 'the unnecessary inclusion of immaterial details apparently to produce a sense of reality'; the reviewer also criticises the author's 'over-indulgence in dialogue' which, 'though natural has the great demerit of being pointless and terribly diffuse' (28 Dec. 1854, p. 5). In the same year, the *Prospective* uses 'Dutch painting' in yet another way to describe the writer who is interested in verisimilitude rather than the depiction of 'fine elements of character'. 'Daguerreotype' is also used to mean verisimilitude in the *Saturday* reviewing *The Daisy Chain*, where the critic complains that it is 'a bad daguerreotype' because 'the painting is not from life' (22 Mar. 1856, pp. 416-18). Presumably, if the review had found the book to be true to life, it would then have been admired as a good daguerreotype. When the image is used by R. H. Hutton in the *Prospective* it again means 'true to life', as it does in the *Saturday*, but it is also used to describe a form of narration which reproduces 'with calm fidelity' the slow pace as well as the uneventful details of daily life.

Ten years later, the *Spectator*, reviewing *The Trial* and looking back at *The Daisy Chain*, combines the images of photography and Dutch painting in a lengthy analysis which illuminates both Charlotte Yonge's narrative method and the reviewer's own ambivalent feelings about it. He defines 'that kind of realism which is Miss Yonge's strength' as 'not Dutch painting so much as careful but inartistic photography'. By this he means firstly that 'she always introduces the facts of life which novelists forget, and keeps the income of her heroes and heroines before you'; secondly that she makes her characters' behaviour consistent with their natures – 'she makes their acts square to them as they do everywhere out of novels'; thirdly that she makes their conversation reflect their physical well-being – 'she tells you about their health, and makes their conversation headachy or rheumatic accordingly'; and lastly that she 'never lets her children think and feel as only grown-up people have the self-restraint to do'. This point is illustrated by a passage from *The Trial* where the little Wards want Mary to dress their dolls even while their parents' coffins are being borne across the threshold. The reviewer comments: 'Very thin that appears, only it was just what children would do, and what inferior artists would insist on making them a good deal too good to attempt doing' (30 July 1864, pp. 880-81).

At this point the reviewer seems to be in two minds as to whether or not to admire Charlotte Yonge's technique: 'The details are horribly tiresome sometimes but they are true.' He appears to be uncertain how to assess the dialogue. Indeed, he seems somewhat baffled as to how it works. 'There are scores of pages of dialogue [. . .] which on any one of the principles usually guiding writers or readers are insufferable, the speakers saying just the dreary, pointless things they would say if they were alive and placed in those circumstances. But when they have said them you understand nearly as much about them as you would if the words were uttered in your hearing on your lawn or in a dining-room.' This praise for her characterisation is reiterated many years later in the *Athenaeum* which actually compares Charlotte Yonge to Balzac in her 'power of giving life-likeness to her characters and to the scenes in which they live and move' (27 Sep. 1873, pp. 392-94). The *Spectator's* final judgment is that despite the tedium of the realistic process, we see in Charlotte Yonge's ability 'to describe every-day life just *so* [. . .] a genuine and very scarce power'.

A more idealistic and romantic view of realism is seen in *Fraser's* review of *Heartsease*: 'Now, we become conscious that there is a hidden poetry, a beautiful romance, even in the most outwardly common-place existence, lying *perdu* [sic] until brought to light at the command of some subtle magician'. The critic is convinced that he has found in *Heartsease* the epic poem of the age. 'Only a woman with a poet's soul could have conceived a character so lovely and so true to nature as Violet Martindale, one of the loveliest, sweetest, and most attractive creations that ever sprang to life at the poet's bidding.' To this reviewer Charlotte Yonge is a great artist because in *Heartsease* she gives us 'not only a faithful likeness' of actuality but 'that likeness idealised'. It is because of this ability to create 'likeness idealised' that Charlotte Yonge is declared to be not only like but superior to Miss Austin [sic] (Nov. 1854, pp. 489-503).

Of all the reviews which discuss Charlotte Yonge's narrative method, Hutton's 'The Author of *Heartsease* and Modern Schools of Fiction' in the *Prospective* (1854) and 'Ethical and Dogmatic Fiction: Miss Yonge' in the *National* (1861) are particularly interesting because they not only describe and evaluate the realistic narrative but also attempt to set it in the context of the whole fictional canon. In the first review, Hutton begins by noting the coolness of Charlotte Yonge's art, her pleasure in 'pure white-light delineations of life', as contrasted with 'that painting of characters seen under the warm tints of special sentiments which so strongly marks the allied schools of religious fiction instituted by Miss Sewell and Lady Fullerton'.

To him not only the narrative but the reader's response to the narrative is almost like experiencing life itself: 'To read her last two novels, *The Heir of Redclyffe* and *Heartsease*, especially the latter, is like living for a few years *at least* [sic], with a well-conducted family, and it takes up almost as much time. You have all the small life as well as the eventful; you sit down to nearly every breakfast, you are admitted every day to almost every room. When we laid down *Heartsease* to look back upon the tale, it seemed less like a review of a story than the memory of a few years of ordinary life, with all its casual observations and slow intervals as well as its shining eras. The strict impartiality of the Daguerreotype process has seldom been carried so fully into fiction. What the little Johnnie did on Thursday and what he did on Friday and what he said to his aunt, and what to his mother, and what to his sister, is told with the same calm fidelity and the same skill with which the not very vehement affections and passions of the principal characters in the narrative are delineated, in their most critical moments.'

However, like many other critics, Hutton is in two minds about the value of the realistic method. On the one hand he sees in those who, like Charlotte Yonge, 'paint that which they see, and just as they see it' some 'hope of the fertility of genius'. On the other hand, he notes the disadvantage of the method, as it is used in *Heartsease*, that it fails in the first requirement of fiction, that is 'to delineate humanity in movement' Hutton finds that 'the tale has no momentum [. . .] You go on for a chapter or two rather leisurely, and then you sit down and rest. What you see while you rest is generally very real and excellent, – perhaps a well-drawn nursemaid walking out with a few children, – still it is far from exciting vehement interest. There is no rapid unfolding of the view, no eager anxiety as to the next glance.'

It is in fact an over-simplification to speak of *Heartsease* in terms of realism or of Dutch art, and Hutton understands this: 'the author does not indeed, exactly belong to the Dutch school of literary painting, because her own taste obliges her to select fine elements of character.' This to him is a virtue because he thinks that the simple rendition of reality is far from high art, which should reveal 'the deeper aspects and finer capacities of men'.

Seven years later, Hutton returns to the theme of realism in 'Ethical and Dogmatic Fiction: Miss Yonge'. Here he compares Charlotte Yonge to Chaucer, Shakespeare and Scott (*National Review*, Jan. 1861, p. 212) because, he says, like them she is both realist and idealist, her novels combining 'pure ideal enthusiasm and strong moral convictions' with 'a real grappling with the problems of life' together with 'artistic power in reproducing them' (p. 214). The novels in question are *The Daisy Chain*, *The Heir of Redclyffe*, *Heartsease* and *Dynevor Terrace*. He praises her 'appreciation of the light and humorous aspects of character which enable her to paint life with much felicity', but regretfully concludes that although he values these works as 'the best of Miss Yonge's for their truthful and inspiriting delineations of life from an affirmative and spiritual point of view', they do not equal the works of the great masters, because 'she gives us little beyond the ordinary routine of life' (p. 216). At this time he may well have been influenced by George Eliot's comparison of her narrative method in *Adam Bede* to the truthful rendition of 'monotonous homely existence' found in Dutch masters'. His final word on Charlotte Yonge's (and possibly George Eliot's) narrative method, then, is of qualified approval.

An article in the *Saturday Review*, although not written from the specifically doctrinal point of view held by the Unitarian Hutton, nevertheless reached a similar conclusion in reviewing *Dynevor Terrace*. Whilst acknowledging Charlotte Yonge's pre-eminence in 'stories of domestic detail', the reviewer finds that 'there is a certain pettiness in the whole thing' ... 'We miss the free elastic air of great moral teaching' (18 Apr. 1857, pp. 357-58). Some years later, the *Athenaeum* reviewing *The Clever Woman of the Family* also complains about 'an over minuteness to which we must apply the epithet "niggling"' (8 Apr. 1865, pp. 489-90). Here, however, the criticism is only of the narrative method, not of her didactic purpose. A more serious criticism of the novel is expressed in acid form by the *Saturday* which pours scorn simultaneously on the author's narrow vision and on the programmed nature of the narrative, in which the characters are no more than puppets or lay figures, set up by the author 'merely for the pleasure of knocking them down again [. . .] the whole thing a sort of intellectual Aunt Sally, only the novelist has an amiable fancy that the grotesque figure whose pipe she is endeavouring to put out is a living creature, and the representative of a class'. Here the argument is that 'despite a good deal of carefully written dialogue', the novel cannot be considered in any way realistic because verisimilitude is destroyed by 'an authoress who labours under a sense of mission' (8 Apr. 1865, pp. 419-20).

Yet another criticism of Charlotte Yonge, linked with criticisms of her religious stance already noted, derives from an interpretation of the realistic method which argues that a fiction which restricts its scope to the privileged members of the upper classes, however faithful the characterisation, is necessarily a glamourised version of reality as it is experienced by the common man and thus offers not truth but escapism. This view is put by the *Dublin Review* which finds 'an air of strong unreality' about *The Heir of Redclyffe* (Dec. 1858, p. 318), also by the *London Quarterly* and in two reviews by *The Times* in 1854, the first of *The Heir of Redclyffe*, the second of *Heartsease*. *The Times* complains that in *Heartsease* (as in *The Heir of Redclyffe*), 'the whole party belong to the number of those who live by the sweat of another man's brow. To personal and intellectual gifts are added to the gifts of wealth. The miseries of failure and contempt no more intrude into this charmed circle than the miseries of the overtasked hand and brain. If the hill of virtue is steep to these people, they go up it in a carriage and four' (28 Dec. 1854, p. 5). The *London Quarterly*, in an article which considered the same novels plus *Dynevor Terrace*, expresses strong disapproval of the dangerously beguiling charms of the 'country mansion which is peopled by people of superior endowments, intellectual and moral as well as pecuniary', and asks the question, 'How much of reality [. . .] is there in such representations?' (1858, p. 492). In 1857, the *Saturday*, also reviewing *Dynevor Terrace*, derides its hero as 'a young nobleman on his way to heaven' and finds that the whole fiction represents an ideal which is no more than 'a dream which not only floats before the eyes of the authoress, but before those of many of the good girls who admire her' (18 Apr. 1857, pp. 357-58).

Of these reviews it is probable that Charlotte Yonge would have read *The Times*; possible though not very likely that she would have read the *London Quarterly*, but certain, since we know she sent it to a Mrs D., that she read the *Saturday* on *Dynevor Terrace*.[14] Whether or not they influenced her it is impossible to say, but the fact is that apart from *Countess Kate* and the historical novels, after *Dynevor Terrace* she never selected her protagonists from the ranks of the aristocracy.

THE FAMILY CHRONICLES – 'NEITHER DEFINITE BEGINNING NOR
ENDING AND NO PLOT IN PARTICULAR'[15]

Following publication of *The Daisy Chain* the criticism most commonly
made of domestic fictions is that they are without discernible
structure, the *London Quarterly* for instance dismissing the novel as 'a
series of conversations upon things in general' (July 1858, p. 498).
The *Spectator* even more summarily condemns it in a single paragraph
review where it is contrasted unfavourably with the 'carefully
constructed story' of *Heartsease*. It is described as 'the most faulty
work that has appeared from her pen. The story, such as it is, is
overlaid by scenes of which it is nothing to say that they continually
impede its march; for if the incidents, characters, and dialogue of a
scene have interest, the want of connexion [sic] is merely a critical
defect. In *The Daisy Chain*, the subject of the scene is so flat or
commonplace, the persons are so numerous, their sayings and doings
often so confused and weak, and the whole is so overlaid by words,
that the result is mere tediousness.' (29 Mar. 1856, p. 346). In a later
review, of *The Trial*, but looking back to *The Daisy Chain*, the critic
reiterates the complaint, saying that it has 'no end, and so no story,
and no particular plot, no very able writing and an endless quantity of
exceedingly tiresome conversation' (30 July 1864, pp. 880-81).

At one level, the criticism is simply of Charlotte Yonge's failure to
control an over-elaborate plot, as in a *Spectator* review of *Dynevor
Terrace* which can find no good either in the story, 'complex to a
degree, and attended by minor stories, that further complicate the
complicated', or in her management of the narrative. Haste is blamed
for the fact that 'all the higher qualities of distinctness and coherence
of plot, cogency or weight of thought, and closeness of style are
naturally overlooked' (18 Apr. 1857, p. 422). However, this view of
the novel is not universal. The *Saturday* is more charitable. Though it
criticises Charlotte Yonge's inclination to present everything from the
viewpoint of 'the territorial but untitled grandees of an English
county', it finds 'much skill shown in the constant change of scene; in
the variety of persons woven together' and in the control of the
threads of the narrative (18 Apr. 1857, pp. 357-58).

That contemporary reviewers had continuing difficulty in evaluating
Charlotte Yonge's plot construction is clear in *The Times* where the
critic, reviewing *The Three Brides*, is dismayed by its apparent lack of
excitement or structure yet finds an unexpected and scarcely definable

pleasure in its meandering narrative. 'Once launched on the book, you feel yourself much in the position of a tourist who has embarked on the Rhine at Cologne for Rotterdam. You are in for a rather tedious voyage; and yet if you make up your mind to enjoy yourself you are pretty sure not to be disappointed. There is nothing that is highly picturesque or sensational, until at the last you are landed in the midst of a fearfully destructive epidemic. Yet you are constantly coming upon scenes and incidents which arrest the attention and even excite you, while the current of the story is so smooth and agreeable that it is easy to give yourself up to drift with it.' Nevertheless, despite this qualified praise, his initial assertion, that '*The Three Brides* can scarcely be called a novel' remains unmodified (29 Aug. 1876, p. 4).

In some reviews the lack of focus and excitement is linked, directly or indirectly, with 'realism', as in the *Saturday Review* of *The Daisy Chain* (22 Mar. 1856, pp. 416-18). Here, although the critic praises Charlotte Yonge's skill in the delineation of character, particularly of Ethel, Harry and Tom, he goes on: 'Unfortunately there is no great interest in the circumstances in which [the characters] are placed, and no central unity of design around which their deeds, their characters and their fortunes are ranged. Perhaps this may be in real life; but real life is often dull and its stories are not worth telling.' Four years later, the *Saturday* is still making more or less the same point in a review of *Hopes and Fears*, where the reviewer refers to 'this substitution of a domestic ledger for a plot' (10 Nov. 1860, p. 593).

R. H. Hutton in the *National* is also severely critical of the same novel, which he says is 'sadly spun out, and in every way inferior to her other tales, even to *Dynevor Terrace*, which was decidedly not equal to its predecessors' (Jan. 1861, p. 220). The *Spectator* critic too, finds many technical faults: 'the book has 'little or no story [. . .] the scenes change often [. . .] the characters multiply [. . .] it evinces no striking narrative power; no descriptive faculty; no bent for vivid dramatic presentment or exhibition of passion'. However, he concedes that, in a novel whose sub-title is *Scenes from the Life of a Spinster*, 'probably some of these elements would scarcely be in place' (27 Oct. 1860, pp. 1029-30).

The Trial fares rather better, both with the *Saturday* and the *Spectator*. Though the *Saturday* is not without misgiving at the prospect of meeting 'the interminable May family' once again, it allows that 'Miss Yonge understands how to work the machinery of the large family — to show how the different members act and react on each other — in a probable and calculable manner'. It praises the representation of Leonard's lassitude and confusion when he is released from prison as having an 'air of truth' in contrast to the 'startling effect and intense joy portrayed 'on the boards'' (20 Aug. 1864, pp. 249-50). The *Spectator* praises the addition of the Leonard story because it 'makes a good centre to all the family activities, which in the *Daisy Chain* rather wanted a pivot'. The review concludes: 'If she would give her readers a few more incidents, widen her range of characters a little, and study to produce a hero who should be something different from an ill-tempered girl in a white choker and black trousers, we see not why she should not occupy the same shelf as Miss Austen. Higher praise it is not given to this generation to bestow.' (30 July 1864, pp. 880-81).

The implausibility of *The Trial* is what most concerns the *Athenaeum* (13 Aug. 1864, p. 209). It asks why Leonard and Dr May did not set the police on the track of the real murderer, since they both know his identity and Leonard saw him. Secondly it cannot see on what grounds Leonard's life was spared and presumes that he serves three years to show 'how a young High Churchman ought to suffer for conscience' sake'. Edith Sichel in 'Charlotte Yonge as a Chronicler' in the *Monthly Review* points out the even more glaring anomaly that 'for three years the escaped villain keeps in his pocket the only document that can inculpate him' (May 1901, pp. 88-96). At the same time she notes that in *The Clever Woman of the Family* 'the deceptions practised by the robber and forger are such that a baby-thief would not attempt' (p. 94). *The Times* finds 'strange improbabilities' in the plot of *Heartsease* (28 Dec. 1854, p. 5), and more than one critic complains about the unlikeliness of Guy's monetary transactions.

The simplest criticism of the family chronicle novels is that they are too long. This point is made more than once, but is expressed most animatedly in an entertaining — but careless — review of *The Pillars of the House* by the *Saturday*. Turning self-defence into attack, (for, 'to make a clean breast of it, we have never been able to get within even a long distance of the end of the work') the critic does nothing more than compose variations on the theme of the excessive length of the novel. Yet even he acknowledges that if he were to 'daub out at least three fourths of what she has written' (in particular the petty details and petty talk) he 'would undertake to make Miss Yonge's story a very good book indeed'. Nor would he 'turn Herod and begin by a massacre of the babes' (27 Sep. 1873, pp. 415-16). However, for all the entertainment afforded by the sprightly style, this review cannot be taken seriously. The fact is that the critic had not read beyond the first few chapters, as is made clear in his prophecy that Theodore, early established as severely retarded, would be at college by the time the novel ended.

The only review that makes a serious and determined attempt to understand the narrative method of the family novels is found in the *Athenaeum*, where the critic examines the relationship in *The Pillars of the House* between what he calls 'the life-likeness' of the scenes and characters, and the narrative form. He asserts that it is 'the intimate realization of her own characters as living people' (and in this he compares her to Balzac) 'that gives to Miss Yonge's stories, in spite of their want of construction, a tendency to one point which we sometimes miss in novels more ambitiously composed, and involving an obvious and avowed "plot"' (27 Sep. 1873, pp. 392-93). As in real life, he says, 'everything depends upon everything else, so no incident however apparently unnecessary at the moment, is without its result, and no episode could well be omitted without injuring in some way the sequence of events, and depriving some subsequent effect of its cause, either remote or immediate'. Further, he sees what no other critic of the time observes – the skill entailed in managing fictional time and events in a serialised fiction, so that, as he says, Charlotte Yonge found 'exactly the right amount for everybody to do, in order that the time required by the supposed events might end simultaneously with the time occupied in telling the story'. He adds to this a commendation of the complete 'effacement' of the author, so that her '*dramatis personae* have the reality which others seek in vain'. Some doubts are voiced about her inclusion of characters from earlier fictions who confuse the uninitiated reader; also her style is found to be 'rather slipshod, even to the verge of questionable grammar', but the conclusion is that 'she will hereafter take her place, and no mean one among the English authoresses, even in an age which has produced *Adam Bede* and *Old Kensington*'. (This never-to-be-forgotten masterpiece is by Anne Isabella Thackeray.) The concluding sentence is most telling in that it suggests that in the estimation of the *Athenaeum*, it is not until *The Pillars of the House* that Charlotte Yonge qualifies to take her place among the great writers. The review as a whole is perhaps the most subtle, comprehensive and appreciative analysis of her narrative method.

As a last word, it must be said that at the turn of the century, Edith Sichel's 'Charlotte Yonge as Chronicler', first published in the *Eclectic Magazine*, reprinted in the *Monthly Review*, (May 1901, pp. 88-97) and again in the American periodical *Littell's Living Age* (22 June 1901, pp. 783-88) shows that there was still some interest in some aspects of Charlotte Yonge's work. The article is an 'Appreciation', the approach more sentimental than that of the *Athenaeum* or *Saturday Review* in that it consists chiefly of fond recollections of favourite scenes and characters. Edith Sichel does, however, offer two striking comparisons. She asserts firstly that *The Daisy Chain* is an epic, 'the *Iliad* of the schoolroom – and should hold its place as a moral classic'. Secondly, she says, 'If we are to make a preposterous analogy, Miss Yonge is, on the whole, more like Zola than Homer in her methods. Both she and the French novelist take an enormous canvas and, with prodigious industry, work out the experience of each of their characters, both writers have the same courage in the face of tediousness, and the same faults – overgrown conscience and prolixity'. What Charlotte Yonge would say to this comparison makes entertaining food for thought! Edith Sichel does admit that 'their themes are very different'. The fact that the review was twice reprinted and on both sides of the Atlantic suggests that despite their structural faults, Charlotte Yonge's novels were still capable of rousing some critical interest, even though literary fashion had swung in another direction.

'THE LOWER FIFTH FORM OF THE PROVINCIAL GRAMMAR SCHOOL DOES NOT ADMIRE MISS YONGE'S LIFE WORK'

By the turn of the century, Charlotte Yonge's reputation was probably at its lowest point, at least among the critics of the popular press – and, by inference, among the general public too. The decline in her influence and popularity, accelerating through the 1880s and 1890s, and the change in literary fashion which caused that decline are summed up in a heated defence of her work mounted in an obituary, 'Charlotte Mary Yonge', in the *Fortnightly* (May 1901, pp. 852-58). E. H. Cooper was prompted to this defence when, he says, 'I took up a dozen papers and read one contemptuous criticism after another on work which generations of English folk have loved and reverenced since they could spell'. He then cites some of the criticisms. First he quotes 'the witless young journalist trying to be smart' who dismisses Charlotte Yonge as 'an oldfashioned nonentity, a writer for the Parish Library'. Second, he quotes another of the breed, 'who did indeed graciously allow that "there is something in her books besides sanctified twaddle"', from which Cooper gathers that 'the Lower Fifth Form of the provincial Grammar School does not admire Miss Yonge's life work'. Cooper does not, he says, take such remarks very seriously, but they do indicate a sea-change in the general perception of Charlotte Yonge from the days when the *London Quarterly* feared for the children of England because of the popularity of *The Heir of Redclyffe*. Clearly, if she is regarded merely as 'a writer for the Parish Library' she is no longer in the main stream of literary life.

Cooper cites two other reviews which voice more or less the same opinion as that offered by the 'witless young'. First he quotes a sweeping generalisation in *Literature*: 'There probably never was a trained critic who ranked Miss Yonge's work very high or derived any acute pleasure from its perusal.' This is particularly interesting not only because it shows a contemporary reaction to Charlotte Yonge but also because it shows the rise of the professional critic (presumably represented by the *Literature* reviewer) superseding the gentleman amateur, indignantly represented here by Edward Cooper.

He quotes another review which offers some explanation of the change in attitude to Charlotte Yonge from the early days of adulation and respect: 'The kind of incidents which she thought attractive and interesting', says a very kindly critic in the *Daily Telegraph*, 'the gentler and more affectionate psychological analysis to which she was wedded, make her seem old-fashioned to those who have been trained in the work of George Egerton, Iota, and Sarah Grand.' With this is coupled some censure on her lack of humour, prolixity, and historical inaccuracy.

Fashion has gone round again from the hey-day of George Egerton and company but there is no doubt that in the period between the publication of *The Pillars of The House* and 1901 there seemed to be a marked decline in Charlotte Yonge's appeal except to Sunday School teachers and children. This is clear from the reviews of the 1880s and 1890s. The august *Edinburgh* in 'Schoolroom Classics in Fiction – A Survey' (Oct. 1901, pp. 414-37) remarks of *The Daisy Chain* that 'the demand, if not extinct by any means, has suffered eclipse, and with it the fame of Miss Yonge and her fellow authors' (p. 436).

In some ways it makes sad reading to go through the reviews of the 1880s and 1890s. There are long gaps when her novels, except for those composed for Sunday School pupils, are ignored. It is her works for the National Society's Depository and the various history books intended for the schoolroom which attract critical attention, so in one sense the 'witless young' were right. It is certainly true that material for the Sunday Schools formed a large part of Charlotte Yonge's publications from the early 1880s onwards, the *Church Times*, *Church Quarterly* and *Literary Churchman* reviewing for example, *Scripture Readings for Schools and Families*, *Questions on the Psalms* and *How to Teach the New Testament*.

Such reviews as do concern themselves with non-Sunday School fiction are usually short, usually squeezed into a paragraph in 'Novels of the Week', and are composed of summaries of the plot with a sentence or two of vague praise or tired criticism. As we have seen, *The Three Brides* was received with modified rapture by *The Times; Nuttie's Father* was reviewed only in the *Athenaeum*. *Murray's Magazine* gives *Beechcroft at Rockstone* a paragraph of vague praise for the author's 'accustomed skill in marshalling a family which baffles all counting' (Mar. 1889, p. 432). *The Long Vacation* and *Modern Broods* merited no more than a couple of sentences in any periodical. In addition the *Athenaeum* and the *Literary Churchman* looked at the reissues of *Scenes and Characters* and *Henrietta's Wish*. In the 1880s, the *Literary Churchman* reviewed the children's stories centred on Langley School and Village. No serious or lengthy evaluation, however, was accorded to these domestic fictions.

What did attract the attention of the critics at this period were the historical novels. In 1880 and 1882, for instance, there were five articles on *Love and Life* and four on *Unknown to History*. Both were reviewed in the *Academy* and *The Times*, and noticed in the *British Quarterly*. The former was also reviewed in the *Athenaeum* and *Spectator*, the latter in the *Saturday*. Similarly, there were four reviews each for *Chantry House* and *A Modern Telemachus* in 1886 and 1887, the *Academy*, *Athenaeum* and *Dublin* reviewing both. However, by and large, the standard of critical appraisal of these novels was superficial. The *Saturday* on *Stray Pearls*, for example, has one sentence commending the book 'taken as a whole [. . .] the story is very pleasant reading', and two columns of plot summary (5 May 1883, p. 568). This is more cursory than some reviews of the period but by no means untypical. *The Times*, for instance, has three sentences of critical comment on *Love and Life* in half a column of plot summary (2 Nov. 1881, p. 11). It approves the graphic descriptions of period detail but has doubts about the sensational elements of the plot. Its review of *Unknown to History* (9 Sep. 1882, p. 4) offers the same proportion of commentary to summary – and more or less the same criticisms.

Especially in the 1890s, there are also many reviews of her 'improving' historical novels for children, usually in Church of England magazines, occasionally in others, such as the *Athenaeum*, which reviewed *The Slaves of Sabinus* (22 Nov. 1890); *Two Penniless Princesses* (17 Jan. 1891); *Strolling Players* and *Grisly Grisell* (20 May and 22 July 1893); and *The Pilgrimage of the Ben Beriah* (1 May 1897). However, these reviews are neither lengthy nor deeply considered. The *Athenaeum*, for example, is merely polite about *The Slaves of Sabinus:* 'On the whole the tale does credit to Miss Yonge's historical imagination [. . .] it is told in [her] usual attractive manner' (22 Nov. 1890, p. 697).

If one looks back to the *Saturday* review of *The Lances of Lynwood*, where the critic is not afraid to use the word 'genius' and cannot decide 'whether to her domestic cabinet or to her historical sketches the palm ought to be assigned'(8 Dec. 1855, p. 103), or to Hutton's weighty deliberations on *The Little Duke* which he praises not merely as 'history finely reproduced in the artist's imagination' but as 'an alternative and possibly superior outlet for the writer's genius', (*Prospective*, Nov. 1854, p. 478), one is sadly aware of how far Charlotte Yonge had slipped in critical esteem.

However, in the 1880s and 1890s there was one periodical, the *Academy*, founded in 1869, which reviewed Charlotte Yonge carefully and consistently. There were a number of articles on her work in most years from 1876 until 1900, by named and relatively distinguished writers, among them George Saintsbury, the academic critic and literary historian who reviewed *Magnum Bonum* for the *Academy* in 1880. He found it disappointing, 'better than some which have recently proceeded from her pen' but 'inferior to its author's earlier works'. He complains about the 'want of central interest', the 'multitude of characters' and consequent 'looseness of texture and colourlessness of figure'. Nevertheless, and this, presumably, is why he reviews the novel at all, he acknowledges Charlotte Yonge's 'excellent faculties as a novelist' (Jan. 1880, p. 63).

The *Nineteenth Century*, founded in 1877 and noted for its impartiality and for the eclecticism of its contributors, took a different approach to the novels and to the question of her popularity. In 'What Girls Read' (Oct. 1886, pp. 515-29) the critic E. G. Salmon looks at Charlotte Yonge's novels among a number of girls' books, which he considers in order of popularity. Top of the list is Louisa Alcott's *Little Women*, which he says has yielded her £20,000 in twenty years. Charlotte Yonge by comparison has, he says fallen out of fashion because of a change in attitudes and expectations in 'the maiden of fifteen', who, he assumes, will be the reader of such a book as *The Heir of Redclyffe* or *The Daisy Chain*. Though commending her versatility and *The Heir of Redclyffe* ('a simple story told with equal simplicity and excellence'), he is not enthusiastic about *The Daisy Chain* ('spoiled as a book by the minuteness of the discussions of certain methods of learning') which he thinks 'not likely to secure much sympathetic enthusiasm' in girls whose favoured reading is Ouida and Miss Braddon (pp. 517-18).

However, and here is an innovation in critical response, almost as an after-thought Salmon ends with some statistics, gathered from a survey conducted by a Mr Charles Welsh into the reading habits of schoolchildren, which to some extent contradicts his previously expressed opinions. The survey, made in several boys' and girls' schools, elicited two or three thousand responses, of which about a thousand were from girls. It asked thirteen questions, of which Salmon considers replies to two only. These were: 'Who is your favourite author?' and 'Who is your favourite writer of fiction?' The results, he says, are not entirely reliable, being skewed by the fact that the survey was 'coloured by circumstance' so that girls wrote what they felt they ought to include, not what they really liked. This put C. M. Yonge joint third with Charles Kingsley with 91 votes each. Dickens came top with 330 votes out of 1000, Scott second with 226, and Shakespeare fifth, with 73 votes. Below him in descending order come Elizabeth Wetherall 54, Mrs Henry Wood 51, and George Eliot and Lord Lytton, tied with 41. Louisa Alcott has 12, Miss Braddon 11. ALOE (A Lady of England) has 30, one more than Hans Andersen.

These findings, which suggest that Charlotte Yonge was more popular than Salmon had supposed, are slightly backed up by his own anecdotal evidence of the little girl of his acquaintance who read *The Pillars of the House*, discovered that she had forgotten the name of one of the characters, so read it again, and immediately she had finished, started all over again. It is this anecdote which perhaps best indicates the reason for the continued popularity of the family chronicles into the twenty-first century, for it seems, again from anecdotal evidence, that it is the experience of the girl re-reading *The Pillars of the House* which most closely resembles that of the modern reader.

CONCLUSION

Of course, in considering the critics' view of Charlotte Yonge, the all-important question is: What did she think of them? What impact, if any, did they have on her ideas or narrative methods?

Her opinion of the value of reviews in general is made clear in an article 'Authorship' in *The Monthly Packet* (Sep. 1892).[16] It is plain that she felt that in the past she had benefited from them: 'They are not apt to be such as once they were – the fuller ones often valuable and instructive in the way of criticism, favourable or adverse.' She goes on with sage advice about how a writer should react to reviews, presumably based on her own experience. 'On one side, it is better not to be too eager for reviews, or to pin one's feeling on them as Charlotte Brontë did when she cried all night over what was said of *Jane Eyre*. On the other, it is not wholesome entirely to avoid the sight.' She quotes the example of George Eliot who, she says, lost chances of improvement because she was not allowed to see unfavourable criticisms.

This last opinion is later repeated in the second of several letters written to a Miss Christie,[17] following what Charlotte Yonge describes as her 'very kind and appreciative notice of my books'. (Christabel Coleridge says this appeared in the *Guardian*, presumably not long before the first of the letters, which was written in December 1896.) In this second letter, of December 10, she repeats her criticism of George Eliot's failure to benefit from reviews 'because', she says, 'they teach one much'. However, the first of the letters suggests that it was not the periodicals but the 'good men and women' among whom she grew up, who most influenced her work. She says that is 'to their influence, and, in earlier times, their actual criticism all that is best in my work is owing'. In the second letter she gives more details of how what she called the 'external influence' of her father and friends 'in merry discussion of the characters' shaped 'developments'. She does not comment here on press reviews except to refer briefly to 'the only thoroughly spiteful review that ever befell me, in *Household Words*, written I imagine by some blindly jealous admirer of Dickens'. (She refers to the Wilkie Collins article. Miss Yonge herself delivers a pretty fair put-down here.)

Nevertheless, despite these suggestions that Charlotte Yonge felt that reviews could be beneficial and instructive, there is no direct evidence that she at any time changed her narrative method because of a review. It might be possible to make a case for saying that in the family chronicles she altered her chosen arena for fiction from the domains of Sir Guy Morville, Lord Martindale and the Earl of Ormersfield after reading *The Times* and *Saturday Review* (and possibly the *London Quarterly*) on the subject of 'her taste for high life', as the *Saturday* reviewing *Dynevor Terrace*, cruelly put it (18 Apr. 1857, p. 358). But it is equally possible to say firstly, that the Mays, Wards and Underwoods were simply developments of her 'lifelong' imaginary 'companions' and secondly, that they were fictional equivalents to the envisaged readers of the *Monthly Packet*.

At a stretch it might be argued that she turned to historical fiction following R. H. Hutton's suggestion that her talent might best be served by developing the talent revealed in *The Little Duke*. But again, her pleasure in history and historical romance was already well-established by the time she wrote *The Little Duke*, so that later historical novels would merely be evidence of her following a natural bent rather than well-intentioned advice. One might also say that the method of using long passages of self-analysis and dogmatic discussion in the *Daisy Chain* was modified in later novels as a result of strongly voiced complaints from almost every periodical which was not High Church. Charlotte Yonge herself says of *The Daisy Chain*[18] that when she re-read it and *The Pillars of the House*', 'I found myself preferring the latter, as brighter, and on the whole less pedantic than is the effect of Ethel in parts, and with more of hope throughout'. However, at no point does she make a connection between the influence of the critics and the different techniques in the two novels, which are, after all, twenty years apart. Indeed, Charlotte Yonge was known by her friends to be notoriously resistant to advice. Certainly, although complaints about her prolixity and slackness of style were voiced continuously and with increasing irritation by almost all periodicals from the appearance of *Heartsease* onwards, she seems to have ignored these criticisms entirely.

On balance then, it seems likely that, if her narrative methods changed, they were as likely to be influenced by the passage of years, changing tastes, her own predilections and interests as by articles in periodicals. It seems likely that although she probably read many reviews, of her own and others' work, and although, as she said in 1873, 'one likes to be approved of – when one writes a fresh thing to know it is not a falling off',[19] nevertheless it seems unlikely that she was swayed by them. No doubt she was stung by some, really delighted by others, such as the *Guardian* review by Miss Christie, for which she wrote to thank the editor, but being a soldier's daughter brought up with military discipline, she would neither flee the reviews, like George Eliot, nor weep all night over them, like Charlotte Brontë.

Of all the reviews it is possible that she would concur most heartily with the concluding passage of A. J. Butler's review in the *Quarterly* (May 1901, pp. 520-38). This was both obituary and over-view of the great body of her work. It sums up well her achievement and the temper of her mind and of the age which bred her. His conclusion was this:

> Miss Yonge belonged to an earlier school. The generation which was in its prime during the first quarter of the nineteenth century regarded life – and it is no wonder – both seriously and strenuously, and brought up its children to do the same. It had, no doubt, the faults natural to a military age, but it had the virtues also; and not least among these was a strong and operative sense of duty. Nelson's last signal was no new invention, it was merely a reminder of what was always present to the thought of his contemporaries. It would be interesting, if this were the place, to consider how far this habit of mind contributed to shape the special form of piety, austere yet practical, which distinguished the early Tractarians. Miss Yonge, at any rate, as the daughter of an old Peninsula and Waterloo officer, grew up under its full influence. Duty and discipline were ever before her eyes, and the stamp of them is upon every line she wrote.

This review, with its stern reminder of the ideals which prompted her work, offers also an explanation of why she seems to have remained relatively unmoved by the critics, neither greatly fearing their strictures nor courting their approval.

My thanks go to the late Professor Philip Drazin for the invaluable help afforded by his 'Publications about Charlotte Yonge and her Works', Part 5 of his bibliography of Charlotte Yonge's works.

---

1   Valerie Sanders, *Eve's Renegades: Victorian Anti-Feminist Women Novelists* (Basingstoke and London: Macmillan Press, 1996), p. 128.

2   Charlotte Yonge, letter to Sir William Heathcote, 28 February 1869, quoted in Christabel Coleridge, *Charlotte Mary Yonge: Her Life and Letters* (London: Macmillan, 1903), p. 299.

3   P. J. Drazin, 'Publications about Charlotte Yonge and her Works', unpublished Bibliography, 1999, pp. 72-82.

4   Charlotte Yonge, letter to Miss Barnett, undated, quoted in Ethel Romanes, *Charlotte Mary Yonge: An Appreciation* (London and Oxford: A. R. Mowbray, 1908), p. 69.

5   Charlotte Yonge, letter to the *Guardian* critic, Miss M. E. Christie, 10 December 1896, quoted in Coleridge, p. 340.

6   The *North British Review* 1844-71 is described as 'liberal in politics and Christian in tone [. . .] religious articles were not to advocate the peculiarities of any particular sect', *Wellesley Index to Victorian Periodicals 1824-1900*, ed. W. E. Houghton (Toronto: University of Toronto Press, 1966-89) vol. 1, p. 663.

7   Henry James, 'Elizabeth Rundle Charles', *The Nation*, (28 September 1865) pp. 409-10.

8   Charlotte Yonge, letter to Sir William Heathcote, 28 February 1869, Coleridge, p. 299.

9   Amy de Gruchy (in a personal communication) has suggested that the article is by John Coleridge, a cousin of Charlotte Yonge.

10 Margaret Oliphant identified as the author, *Wellesley Index* 1, p. 99.

11 Wilkie Collins identified as the author in *Household Words: A Weekly Journal 1850-1858, conducted by Charles Dickens. A Table of Contributors and their Contributions, based on the "Household Words Office Book" in the Morris L Parrish Collection of Victorian Novels in Princeton University Library*, compiled by Anne Lohrli, (Toronto and Buffalo: University of Toronto Press, 1973). See 18 Dec. 1858.

12   The noun 'le chique' (or 'le chiqué') has the meaning of 'affectation' in the mid-nineteenth century. Whether Henry James intended this or 'fashion' is not clear from the context.

13   'Dutch painting' was used by George Eliot in *Adam Bede*, (ch. 17) 1859, to describe a form of art without heroic subject or style: 'It is for this rare, precious quality of truthfulness that I delight in many Dutch paintings [. . .] these faithful pictures of a monotonous homely existence.'

14   Romanes quotes Mrs Dyson as saying in 1857: 'Charlotte sent us the *Saturday Review* of her [*Dynevor Terrace*]. It is clever enough, and the praise just, we think. But the reviewer would never enter into her principles, and evidently wants her to undertake the great social questions, such as Mrs Gaskell and suchlike writers. Why she may not take her own line, instead of imitating them or trying to compete with Shakespeare, one cannot comprehend.' Romanes, p. 177.

15   *The Times* on *The Three Brides*, 29 Aug. 1876, p. 4.

16   C. M. Yonge, 'Authorship', *Monthly Packet*, new [fourth] series, 4 (Sept. 1892) pp. 296-303. Reprinted in *A Chaplet for Charlotte Yonge*, ed. Georgina Battiscombe and Marghanita Laski (London: Cresset Press, 1965) pp. 185-92. References here use the *Chaplet* pagination: pp. 191-92.

17   Charlotte Yonge, letters to Miss Christie, 8 Dec., 10 Dec., 15 Dec. 1896; 19 Nov. 1897, Coleridge, pp. 338-41.

18   Charlotte Yonge, letter to Miss Christie, 8 Dec. 1896, Coleridge, p. 338.

19   From Elizabeth Wordsworth's reminiscences of Yonge, quoted in Romanes, p. 156.

P. 267.

GUY AT THE WRECK.

WOMEN'S WORK, MONEY AND THE EVERYDAY – THE NOVELS OF THE 1870S

June Sturrock

For most of her professional life, both as novelist and as editor of *The Monthly Packet*, Charlotte Yonge manifested an intense if conflicted interest in women's ambitions and the proper use of women's energies. She was, of course, by no means alone in this concern. 'Work', the well-known painting (1852-65) by Ford Madox Brown, with its detailed depiction of a wide range of human employments, epitomises an important contemporary preoccupation of its period. This preoccupation with work combined with demographic anxieties and the evident problems facing women in search of employment directed mid-Victorian attention to the more specific question of women's work. Periodicals and books alike provided lengthy and various commentaries on related questions. Women activists, from the late 1850s onwards, campaigned to extend the variety of occupations open to women. *The Clever Woman of the Family* (1865) is probably Yonge's most notable contribution to this debate, but the three subsequent novels of contemporary life, *The Pillars of the House* (1873), *The Three Brides* (1876) and *Magnum Bonum* (1879), are all also engaged with this issue, though in very different ways.[1] This essay began life as an account of Yonge's treatment of women's work in these novels. The other two terms of my title – money and the everyday – indicate the outcome of a closer examination. In the 1870s – a decade in which she herself began to feel the need for money – Yonge becomes increasingly engaged with the economic aspects of women's work.[2] Moreover, in writing about women's work, she exploits the great strength of her fiction, her close concern as a novelist with the details of everyday life, a subject explored in the last section of the essay.

A grateful correspondent wrote to *The Monthly Packet* in 1869: 'Your pages have kindly been thrown open for the discussion of 'Woman's Work'.'[3] Indeed the pages of *The Monthly Packet*, especially at this period, were full of items relating to this subject – articles, book-reviews, translations, correspondence, and, above all, fiction.[4] Serial after serial from various writers, including Yonge herself, deals with the issue of how women use their time and their powers. All the same, *The Monthly Packet* gives very limited coverage to the related economic questions concerning the necessity and practicability of paid employment for impoverished women.[5] Most of the items relating to women's work focus rather on the frustration suffered by young middle-class women with inadequate outlets for their ambitions and energies – women like Rachel Curtis in *The Clever Woman of the Family*. They are represented as wanting *A Vantage Ground for Doing Good* or *An Object in Life*, to quote the titles of two of these serials.[6] Most, though certainly not all, of *The Monthly Packet*'s discussions of women's work move toward the conclusion that appropriate work for able and intelligent women can and should be found in ordinary domestic life, submitting to traditional authorities as 'gentle sisters, dutiful daughters'.[7] In complete contrast, economic concerns drive the plots of both *The Pillars of the House* and *Magnum Bonum*, which show women making a vital social and economic contribution to the survival of the family through both traditional and non-traditional forms of work. In the present essay I look at how women's economic contribution is treated in these two novels from the beginning and the end of the decade. The very different treatment of gender in the filling in the sandwich – *The Three Brides* – complicates my argument. The negatives in *The Three Brides* counterbalance the positives in the other two novels; its more ambitious scope highlights the qualities of the less assuming family chronicles.

I

'Quiet narratives, however true and skilful, rarely soar above the average [in sales], and are generally below it', claimed *The Quarterly Review* in 1859 ('Cheap Literature', p. 325). *The Pillars of the House* is just such a 'quiet narrative', being, like *The Daisy Chain*, a 'family chronicle', and spanning eighteen years in the lives of the Underwood family. The market value of such fiction probably declined during the 1860s, the 'sensation decade', when reviewers and reading public alike were more interested in stories of bigamy and murder – 'sensation fiction' such as Ellen Wood's *East Lynne* (1861) or Mary Elizabeth Braddon's *Lady Audley's Secret* (1862). In her novels of the 1860s, Yonge had used certain plot elements from the contemporary sensation school: *Hopes and Fears* (1860) involves two elopements and robbery with violence, *The Trial* (1864) is a murder story, and *The Clever Woman of the Family* (1866) includes fraud and forgery; all three novels have important courtroom scenes.[8] With *The Pillars of the House*, however, Yonge provides narrative drive – and presumably improves marketability – in a different mode, by shaping the novel as an economic survival narrative, a domestic *Robinson Crusoe*. The orphaned Underwoods, a middle-class family of thirteen brothers and sisters, struggle against poverty, dispersal and loss of class status. The novel's focus on economic and social survival inevitably entails engagement with women's traditional domestic work, as well as their work outside the home. The practical household necessities that are the basis of women's traditional occupations are foregrounded by means of constant reiteration of almost the entire range of domestic tasks: the young Underwoods are represented as washing and drying dishes, ironing and mending clothes, dusting, sweeping, cooking and shopping – essential activities, rarely recorded in nineteenth-century fiction. Wilmet, the eldest sister – one of the two 'pillars' of the title – engages in baby-care, nursing, sewing and other domestic tasks, while working full-time as a school-teacher. At the same time, she also exercises her naturally extraordinary capacity for budgeting and household management. Yonge represents Wilmet as the controller of the family finances. Her eldest brother Felix, the other 'pillar', refers to her as 'our financier' (vol. 1, p. 371), and it is in this role that she is regarded (rather resentfully) as 'our Pallas Athene' (vol. 1, p. 234). The main breadwinner of the family is Felix, but Wilmet's management is obviously just as necessary for the survival of the family as a unit. Felix comments gratefully near the end of the novel: 'If you had not been the girl you were, we [the Underwood family, that is] must have broken up; it could not have been done at all' (vol. 2, p. 478).[9]

Like the household tasks required by domestic economy, the necessary rigid control of the family's financial concerns is imagined in concrete form. At intervals in the novel Yonge provides information about the narrow means on which the two pillars must manage their large family. At the beginning their income is about one hundred and eighty pounds a year and we are given updates about their financial position after nine months and again after three years, as well as before they finally take possession of Vale Leston, the family estate, when they realise they must manage the needs of the family and a large property on an income of twelve hundred pounds (vol. 2, p. 316). As Jane Austen does in *Sense and Sensibility*, where we are aware of the precise financial position of virtually every character, Yonge in *The Pillars of the House* presents the concrete details of the economic circumstances on which her narrative depends. Wilmet's household management also involves the careful discipline of the younger children, especially the little girls. Through such scrupulous care, she enables the family to retain not only its unity but also its social status, maintaining its class position despite poverty, shabbiness and the demeaning nature of their housing ('over the shop') and employments ('in trade').[10] Her brother Edgar jeers that her prudence is aimed at keeping the 'family refinement' untarnished (vol. 1, p. 242); but then Edgar is the family scapegrace and is speaking a true word in his jest. Yonge makes both the precise observances of social code and domestic labour entertaining, by representing them as a necessary part of family survival in a narrative that assumes that family unity is sacrosanct. The necessity of Wilmet's endeavours in particular are highlighted through the threats to the family caused by her enforced absence for a month: during this period the family gets into debt for the first time, the invalid Cherry becomes ill, the seven-year-old Stella is lost, property is damaged, and Bernard and Angela (aged nine and ten) misbehave with a social inferior in a way that threatens the family's precarious social position.[11]

However, although retaining their social stature is important to the Underwoods, they are willing to sacrifice social position for financial stability. Of course Felix and later the younger brother, Lance, do this in dedicating themselves to trade (and both suffer for it). Wilmet too has no hesitation in moving to live 'over the shop', despite the fact that the pretentious Lady Price declares that such a step means that 'Miss Underwood did not expect to be visited' (vol. 1, p. 173). Moreover, Wilmet insists that the family should forego the rise in status that would result from Felix's appointment to a clerkship in the office of a 'South American merchant' because life would be more expensive in London. For Wilmet these particular status concerns are apparently nonessential. She maintains the Underwoods' class position by controlling acquaintance, education and manners, and she does this so effectively that Ethel and Gertrude May (reappearing from their own family chronicle, The Daisy Chain), though they fear the embarrassment of contact with a family which has gone through 'a life-struggle to preserve gentility over a stationer's shop' (vol. 2, p. 266), find themselves in the company of the Underwoods 'in that state of ease which comes of accordance of tone' (vol. 2, p. 268).

Despite her value to the family, her domestic talents and extraordinary beauty, Wilmet is never represented in terms of the Victorian Angel in the House. In fact, Felix is far more of a domestic angel than she is. She bears little resemblance to Dickens's Esther Summerson, Lucie Manette or Agnes Wickfield, those perfect dispensers of household order and tranquillity – 'angels of competence' as Elizabeth Langland calls them.[12] Yonge, unlike Dickens, chose to avoid the mystification of domesticity, in this novel at least, where the power of the narrative depends on the practical problems facing the Underwoods. The novel insists on the materiality of Wilmet's life. Clearly the persona of an angel of peace would be incompatible with Wilmet's achievement. The mature Wilmet acknowledged that in her heroic girlhood she was 'hard and narrow' (vol. 2, p. 479), but, as Felix points out, these characteristics were the inevitable product of living, as she had to, 'in a continued state of resistance' – resistance to the least unnecessary expenditure. Wilmet is represented as 'the spirit that had – since six years old – never known freedom from responsibility, and – since fifteen – had borne the burthen of household economies and of school teaching' (vol. 1, p. 310). The Pillars of the House celebrates the domestic, but it celebrates domestic reality rather than a domestic idyll.

The Pillars of the House also represents women's less traditional work in a positive light. All five Underwood sisters[13] engage in paid work, or plan to engage in it, and most value their work both for its intrinsic worth and for its earning power. The Underwoods' cousin Marilda successfully runs a large importing business after her father's death. Although Angela has fantasies about marrying a duke (vol. 2, p. 14), or being a 'lady-doctor' (vol. 2, p. 387) or both, 'nature designed her for a nursing sister', according to Felix (vol. 2, p. 464). Teaching is of course the traditional occupation for middle-class women in need and little Stella, who is in fact married before she is eighteen, originally intends to be a governess. Robina, the fourth sister, actually becomes a first-rate, well-paid, and much-respected governess and thinks of her work in terms of vocation (vol. 2, p. 271). At the same time she also considers it in financial terms, as a 'provision' for herself and as the basis of 'a nice little nest-egg' for her marriage with Will (vol. 2, p. 308). She is incensed by her old-fashioned godmothers who feel that 'no one worthy of the name of man will permit the ladies of his family to go out into the world for maintenance' (vol. 2, p. 276) – and the narrative implies that their beliefs are indeed outdated, and that women like Robina make a worthy choice.

However, the most interesting Underwood sister is surely Geraldine, or Cherry, the cleverest and most charming member of a charming and clever family. She has a less orthodox career than her sisters, making a 'real and brilliant' success as a professional painter (vol. 2, p. 113), receiving critical acclaim and eventually enabling herself to earn an estimated three hundred pounds a year (vol. 2, p. 126). Like Robina, she relishes her earning ability:

> Her first rise out of uselessness gave her more exultation in its novelty than did even the exercise of her art, or the evidence of its success. There was something exquisite in the sense of power. (vol. 2, p. 134)

Indeed, the sense of the power to earn and to act is represented as energising and stimulating to all the women in *The Pillars of the House*.

II

In *Magnum Bonum* again the economic vicissitudes of a large family – the Brownlows – play an important role in plot and structure, though to a lesser extent than *The Pillars of the House*, as the pursuit of the *Magnum Bonum* of the title also shapes the narrative. (This is one of Yonge's characteristic punning titles, referring to the 'great good' both of Dr Brownlow's medical discovery and of religious belief.) Like *The Pillars of the House*, *Magnum Bonum* has a comparatively loose structure and spans a long period in the life of a large middle-class family. And again like *The Pillars of the House*, it offers a fairly open account of possibilities for women. Indeed in *Magnum Bonum* women are often placed in a position of authority, either as property-owner or as sole responsible parent. Caroline Brownlow – the Mother Carey of the sub-title, *Mother Carey's Brood* – is both, for she is left a widow with six young children, and for seven years is the apparent heiress of a large estate.[14] Before and after her years of wealth she helps support the family financially, both as an artist and as a teacher, preferring to employ her skills in order to earn money rather than to devote herself to domestic tasks in order to save it. Her decision and the grounds for it are made quite explicit. She tells her conventional and super-domestic sister-in-law Ellen: "'On true principles of economy, surely it is better that Emma [the maid], who knows how, should mend the clothes, than that I should botch them up in any way, when I can earn more than she costs me!'" (pp. 121-22).

As she continues to insist on her position ("'I had rather do what I can – than what I can't'") she exasperates her sister-in-law further: 'Ellen heaved a sigh at this obtuseness towards what she viewed as the dignified and ladylike mission of the well-born woman, not to be the bread-winner, but the preserver and steward, of the household' (p. 123). Although Caroline has to learn the skills of household management and Ellen's beliefs are never explicitly controverted, the narrative as a whole suggests a justification of Caroline's position. At the end not only have all the children finally 'wakened' (p. 661) – that is, come to the sense of a spiritual life – but Ellen's children, too, as well as Elvira, the young cousin Caroline has adopted, all have a wider and deeper sense of social and spiritual existence through Caroline.

Although Caroline Brownlow (as a mother) is represented as less dedicated to her art than Cherry Underwood (as a single woman) – being of course devoted to her children, instead – her work has a degree of success. In fact, her work as an artist is represented in less traditionally feminine terms that that of her fictional predecessor. Cherry uses watercolours and works mainly on religious and domestic scenes, thus confining herself in both medium and subject matter to the conventionally feminine. Caroline, on the other hand, is a sculptor and chooses classical scenes (Astyanax, Hector and Andromache), more often associated with the privileged masculine genres. Indeed, her work is mistaken for that of Grinstead (the distinguished fictional sculptor of *The Pillars of the House*). Her youngest child Barbara shares her abilities and is represented as able to earn her keep through writing and more than willing to do so: 'In fact, she would rather prefer to have the whole family on her hands' (p. 413) – dependent on her earnings, that is. However, her mother insists that she and her brother should not become 'literary hacks' until they are twenty-one (p. 574).

In 1877, in *Womankind*, Yonge had written that 'there is much less every year of the fear of losing caste by absolute labour' (p. 238). Certainly in *The Pillars of the House* and *Magnum Bonum* Yonge excludes some forms of employment as unsuitable for women. The aspiring woman doctor was a fictional novelty at the period, introduced by Charles Reade in *The Woman-Hater* (1876); and indeed the first actual British woman doctor, Elizabeth Garrett (later Garrett Anderson) had only become fully qualified in 1870, after endless struggles.[15] In *Magnum Bonum*, Janet Brownlow, Caroline's eldest child, actually qualifies and practises as a doctor. Yet in representing Janet as the least attractive and amiable of the family and marrying her to a quack-doctor interested only in her money, Yonge surely implies a low opinion of this choice of profession. In *Womankind* she had already expressed grave doubts about medicine as a profession for women:

> No, except for certain kinds of practice, and for superior nursing, it does not seem as if enough would be gained to make it desirable to outrage feminine instincts, ay, and those of men, by the full course of scientific training.
>
> A person engaged in hospital nursing has told us that the hardening effect of witnessing constant suffering can hardly be counteracted without special religious discipline and training; and how much greater must be the danger of mischief to mind and soul alike in the technical display of the wonderful secrets of the temple of the human body without any special safeguard. We know that medical students often do not come out unscathed from the ordeal, and can it be well to let women be exposed to it? (p. 237)

That is, she disapproves of women in medicine as a threat both to gender identity and to religious faith. Janet Brownlow's wish to qualify as a doctor is represented as arising from emulation, from her wish to surpass her brothers, which in turn arises from her natural resentment that they rather than she will inherit the right to explore further their father's medical discovery, which the family refers to as 'Magnum Bonum' and which she eventually says has been only a

'Magnum Malum' to her (p. 629). Janet finally realises the importance of her faith and her mother's love and atones for previous doubts and hostility by dying while nursing in the 1878 Yellow Fever epidemic in New Orleans (in which 4,056 people died, according to the *Encyclopaedia Britannica*). Her name on the memorial for those who laid down their lives in the epidemic reads 'Janet Hermann, daughter of Joseph Brownlow', for Caroline feels that 'she died worthy of her father' (p. 659). As with the fallen women of other Victorian narratives, Janet's rather different sin can only be expiated in death.

III

In regard to women's work, as in most other respects, *The Three Brides* provides a striking contrast to the other two novels discussed here. It is rigidly and thematically structured to focus on women's role, and at its centre, literally, is a protracted debate on women's nature and rights. Yonge is especially concerned in this novel with women's role in marriage, as her title suggests, and her triple plot reiterates the wife's obligation to adapt to her husband's family. In accordance with its exceptionally hierarchical presentation of women's roles, this novel totally avoids the threats to hierarchy involved in presenting middle-class women as professionally active. The only serious alternative to marriage offered is a Sisterhood. The narrative implies an adverse judgement on the two women who are active outside their homes, Clio Tallboys and Bessie Duncombe. Moreover, *The Three Brides* is as silent on economic issues as it is on women's work.[16] Altogether it may seem perverse to force a comparison between this novel and the other two discussed here. However, the silences I have noted warrant close examination, while the comparison between the two family chronicles and the thematically structured novel helps elucidate the peculiar quality of Yonge's novels *as* novels.

As I have suggested, in contrast to *The Pillars of the House* and *Magnum Bonum*, in *The Three Brides* the main characters are in no financial need. The brides of the title are the daughters-in-law of 'a great English household' (p. 57), and the other central characters, though their financial positions may be rather more precarious, nevertheless assume that they are entitled to high status and to a high standard of living. As for work, while all the central male characters are employed in various socially acceptable professions – as Member of Parliament, sailor, clergyman, civil servant and soldier – none of the novel's women has a profession. This is hardly surprising, in view of their wealthy circumstances; what is more telling is that only one female character – Lady Rosamund, the clergyman's wife – seems reasonably active. Both the other two brides are wretchedly inactive and without function. Cecil, as wife to Raymond, the heir to the estate, and as the supposed support of her paralysed mother-in-law, who owns the family estate in her own right, lives in the parental house where she has little control and no sympathy. Her extreme unhappiness in this position eventually leads her husband to feel, as he is dying of typhoid fever after only a year of marriage, that his death will be a happy release for her. The third bride, Anne, who has suffered a miscarriage, who is exiled from her South African home and waiting for her sailor husband's return, cannot recover from her natural severe depression, simply because she has no role, no function:

> What could be a more unpropitious fate than for a Colonial girl, used to an active life of exertion and usefulness, and trained to all domestic arts, to be set down in a great English household where there was really nothing for her to do, and usefulness or superintendence would have been interfering. (p. 57)

Whereas *The Pillars of the House* and *Magnum Bonum* show women as happily and usefully active, *The Three Brides* shows them as suffering because they are deprived of useful activity. The novel is permeated with suggestions of impotence and disability. Besides Cecil and Anne, Mrs Charnock Poynsett, the brides' mother-in-law, is physically paralysed, while Eleonora Vivian, who will become the family's fourth bride, is psychologically 'petrified' (p. 103) by the manipulations of her elder sister.

As this description may suggest, *The Three Brides* is patently a serious novel, a novel that treats adult themes in a sophisticated manner. In many ways it is the most ambitious of Yonge's novels, possibly because she wrote it under the influence of her reading of *Middlemarch*, published four years earlier.[17] Despite her ambivalent feelings about Eliot,[18] she will have been aware of the general acclaim given a work that Virginia Woolf would later call 'the magnificent book which for all its imperfections is one of the few English novels written for grown-up people';[19] and to which Henry James had already applied superlatives: 'There is nothing more powerfully real [...] in all English fiction and nothing certainly more intelligent.'[20] *Middlemarch* set the standard for the intellectual novel in the 1870s. Whether or not it is a response to *Middlemarch*, *The Three Brides* certainly bears some of the hallmarks of 'serious' fiction. Not only does it deal with serious themes, it also directly addresses important public events and social issues. As Alethea Hayter has shown,[21] its treatment of drainage and drinking water addresses an important issue of the times. Its focus on marriage places it in the context of an urgent debate about marriage laws. And, as I have said elsewhere, in the chapter called 'The Monstrous Regiment of Women', where the nature and position of women is discussed, the organised discussion expressing divergent opinions on an important political issue is far beyond the normal scope of her writing.[22]

Moreover, this novel exploits myth and legend more than any of Yonge's other novels apart from the almost contemporary *My Young Alcides*. Its central myth is the Arthurian story of Vivien, the beautiful and seductive enchantress who lures the aged Merlin into giving her the spell which will enable her to immobilise him, to imprison him in an oak tree or under a stone, according to which version of the myth is used. It is the subject of many nineteenth-century paintings and poems,[23] including one of Tennyson's *Idylls of the King*. In *The Three Brides*, the beautiful, clever, and wicked Lady Tyrrell, whom Cecil's husband once loved, is represented as a social and sexual threat, an unusual figure for a Yonge novel. Significantly she is a member of the Vivian family, and lives at *Siren*wood. Like Tennyson's Vivien she controls almost everybody through her beauty, her manipulative intelligence, and through the appearance of affection and sympathy. Her younger sister, like many of the other characters, speaks of her as an enchantress: "'I thought her like mother and sister both in one [. . .] How could I have thought so for a moment? But she *enchanted* everybody. Clergy, ladies, and all *came under the spell*.'" (p. 100 – my italics.)

Like the Vivien both of Tennyson's *Idyll* and of Burne-Jones's painting, 'The Beguiling of Merlin' (1873-77), like Medusa (and like Eve), Lady Tyrrell is associated with snakes. Even dying, she is represented as 'beautiful still, but more than ever like the weird tragic head [of a medallion of Medusa] with snake-wreathed brows' (p. 257). Medusa turns men to stone; Vivien imprisons them under stone or in trees. They both immobilise other people, and Lady Tyrrell is represented as controlling others so skilfully that she robs them of their power, petrifies them, turns them to stone, as, according to Yonge's metaphor, she does her sister. In this novel, in which women are largely inactive or immobilised, they also are represented as immobilising each other.

Yonge's incorporation of myth into her text is significant in relation not only to theme but also to the literary claims she makes thereby. Yonge uses the Arthurian story of Vivien in *The Three Brides* much as Eliot uses the classical story of Ariadne in the Dorothea sections of *Middlemarch*. The mythological treatment, like the thematic structure, the serious political implications, and the staged debate, is one more indicator of Yonge's ambitions in this novel. She saw all of her novels as having a serious purpose, in that they were all part of her work for the Church. However, *The Three Brides* is among the very few that show the marks of the quest for the literary prestige of 'serious' fiction. In the following section I want to build further on this point.

IV

No reader of this collection is likely to question Dorothy Mermin's assertion that Yonge's novels are 'still eminently readable today'. They may have rather less sympathy with Laurie Langbauer's amazement at this readability – 'I especially can't believe how enjoyable they remain in spite of everything' – or her reluctance to enjoy novels she describes as 'almost unpleasantly attractive'.[24] All the same, Langbauer overcomes her reluctance enough to provide a stimulating general account of Yonge as novelist of the everyday. Langbauer's comments have helped me articulate my view on the contrast between *The Three Brides* and the other two novels discussed here, shaping them into an argument about Yonge's novelistic practice. Langbauer connects Yonge's insistence on the everyday, the commonplace, with the readability of her novels. However, in relation to *The Three Brides*, Ethel Romanes wrote long ago, in her appreciation of Yonge's life and works, that 'we do not think many people would greatly care for it' (p. 135), and I agree that, despite or because of its literary pretension and its very real interest, this novel lacks much of the charm, the attraction, the sheer readability of the 'chronicle' novels, and especially *The Pillars of the House* (my personal favourite). Because of these pretensions, *The Three Brides* works on a more generalised level than most of Yonge's fiction. It aspires to qualities traditionally associated with 'major' fiction rather than to the domestic detail which has always been associated with 'minor' fiction. Its comparative lack of success is surely explained by this sparseness of detail.

For Yonge's details, her careful evocations of the everyday, are surely her great strength. For instance, she convinces us effortlessly that the lame thirteen-year-old Cherry Underwood enjoyed a sense of usefulness in washing dishes, that she suffered from a guilty conscience if she drew pictures instead of mending clothes, that three-year-old Bernard quickly learnt to carry away her crutch before he did something especially naughty, that all these details are an essential part of the moral consciousness of a scrupulous adolescent, and that Cherry's sensitive moral consciousness is of interest. Yonge engages directly with the everyday and makes it significant.

As her reception among her contemporaries would suggest, in doing so Yonge places her work firmly in the feminine tradition.[25] For thousands of years the feminine has been associated culturally with details rather than with generalisation and detail has accordingly been subordinated to generalisation. In the mid-nineteenth century, Elizabeth Barrett Browning indicates the intellectual immaturity of Aurora Leigh's cousin Romney by putting this conventional speech in his mouth:

> 'None of all these things
> Can women understand. You generalise
> Oh, nothing! – not even grief! Your quick-breathed hearts,
> So sympathetic to the personal pang,
> Close on each separate knife-stroke, yielding up
> A whole life at each wound, incapable
> Of deepening, widening a large lap of life
> To hold the world-full woe.' (*Aurora Leigh* 2.182-89)

Barrett Browning's poem works towards unsettling gender assumptions, and Romney will eventually recognise how misguided are his attitudes both to the feminine and to the particular. But his attitudes were widely accepted enough, even in the intellectual circles of the period. Such assumptions were an important factor in the reception of Yonge's novel. As Langbauer notes, 'one argument contemporary reviewers made about Oliphant's and Yonge's novels (as well as Trollope's [. . .]) is that, although enormously popular, they must be by definition minor because they took as their subjects the

banalities of everyday life' (p. 49). Domestic novelists such as Yonge were categorised as belonging to a lower order of writers. George Eliot, for instance, dismissed another contemporary domestic writer, Dinah Mulock Craik, as 'a writer who is only read by novel-readers, pure and simple, never by people of high culture. A very excellent woman she is, I believe – but we belong to an entirely different order of writers'.[26] And there is no question, of course, as to which is the higher order of writer.

Yonge is not concerned to question the conventions of gender and literary genre: she rarely attempts to transcend her position as feminine domestic novelist, as she does in *The Three Brides*. For her, a focus on the everyday was not merely a matter of practice, but also of principle, a principle that pervaded her personal and professional life. As a Tractarian, as a dear friend of John Keble, she early accepted its importance. Probably these lines from 'Morning' are still the best-known lines from Keble's *The Christian Year*:

> The trivial round, the common task
> Will furnish all we ought to ask.
> Room to deny ourselves, a road
> To bring us daily nearer God.

Perhaps this principled concern with 'the trivial round, the common task' is the great strength of Yonge's work. 'For Yonge the register of true heroism lies in the everyday', according to Langbauer (p. 82), and Mermin makes a similar point: 'For Yonge, religion justifies the novelists' vocation by affirming the importance of uneventful, restricted lives' (p. 10). In writing about women's work, Yonge is especially interesting because she represents the way domestic and professional concerns constantly interact, and because she recognises, without trying to elevate, the seriousness of both. Cherry's painting is interrupted by the needs of the house, of the children, of the weekly paper that Felix edits and so on. (Many women will recognise this pattern very well.) All these concerns are made concrete and treated as worthy of respect. The domestic details of life are carefully written into the novels – the financial concerns, the household chores. Women's lives are recorded with a wealth of details of everyday existence that forbids any idealisation.[27] Felix Underwood may be the nearest thing to a domestic angel and Jock Brownlow might be well on the way to that position, but Wilmet and Caroline are fully imagined, as good women – and full of faults.

When characters are represented in such everyday terms, their narratives tend to resist closure; family chronicles similarly tend to resist closure. There is always another task, always another child or grandchild. Indeed *The Pillars of the House* is the beginning – one beginning – of a long chain of interconnected novels.[28] This refusal of closure, an aspect of the concern with the everyday, is again a refusal to ignore practical reality:

> One reason the series may be so closely connected with the everyday for these writers of domestic realism that the everyday seems to refuse ideal solutions. It insists that there is no utopia outside ideology's confines. An emphasis on the everyday may provide instead a way of inhabiting those confines, working within them, without simply overlooking them or accepting them as natural. (Langbauer, p. 58)

Yonge is free to work in this way because she believes that incompletion is inevitable in this world, and because she believes in completion in the next world. The quality which draws readers to these novels is surely their insistence on the everyday, an insistence which arises both from imagination and from principle.

I want to end by commenting on a quotation from a discussion of fiction by a very different novelist, Iris Murdoch:

> Reality is not a given whole. Understanding of this, a respect for the contingent is essential to imagination as opposed to fantasy [. . .] Real people are destructive of myth, contingency is destructive of fantasy and opens the way for imagination [. . .] Too much contingency of course may turn art into journalism. But since reality is incomplete, art must not be afraid of incompleteness.[29]

Murdoch is certainly talking about literature which would be considered 'major'; in her next sentence she writes about *Hamlet* and *King Lear*. Nevertheless, her literary criteria suggest one of the strengths of a kind of literature that is inevitably considered as minor. As a novelist, Charlotte Yonge works with the contingent and accepts the incomplete.

1   *My Young Alcides* was published in 1875. I have not included it in this discussion because it is so different in structure, being framed round the twelve labours of Hercules.

2   After 1876 she helped support her brother's family after he lost money speculating in a mine.

3   *The Monthly Packet*, new [second] series, 7 (1869) p. 414. The correspondent questions the 'obstacles which keeps these two yearning cries of "help help" and "work work" from mingling in one gladsome song of thanksgiving'.

4   This topic is discussed in more detail in J. Sturrock, 'Women, Work and *The Monthly Packet*, 1851-73', *Nineteenth Century Feminisms* 1 (1999) pp. 51-73.

5   Although these concerns are by no means ignored, the few relevant discussions focus on individual cases of financial hardship rather than the general social problem.

6   In *The Object in Life* the heroine must learn not to pine after charitable work but rather to submit to being a helpful sister and daughter – for her 'the only true and sufficient Object in life' is God and her proper field of activities her duties at home (*Monthly Packet*, first series, 15 [1858] p. 615). In *A Vantage Ground for Doing Good* the seventeen-year-old heroine must accept the primary duty of looking after her rather neglectful and frivolous parents before she can marry the vicar, thus freeing herself to concentrate on poor cottagers (*Monthly Packet*, new [second] series, 6 [1868] p. 102). Again, the hero of 'One Story by Two Authors' – the authors being Yonge herself and Jean Ingelow – complains that: 'half the girls one meets in society and all the girls one reads of in books want to be furnished with a mission and never look for it under their feet but always up aloft' (*Monthly Packet*, first series, 21 [1861] p. 465).

7   These words are taken from an article, 'Waiting', deploring the fact that the need for women's work is discussed in front of young girls making them think they, too, should work (*Monthly Packet*, first series, 23 [1862] p. 464).

8   For Yonge and sensation fiction, see J. Sturrock, 'Sequels, Series, and Sensation Novels: Charlotte Yonge and the Popular Fiction Market of the 1850s and 1860s', in *Part Two: Reflections on the Sequel*, ed. Paul Budra and Betty A. Schellenberg (Toronto: University of Toronto Press, 1998) pp. 102-17.

9   In *Nobody's Angels: Middle-Class Women and Domestic Ideology in Victorian Culture* (Ithaca: Cornell University Press, 1995) Elizabeth Langland writes (p. 8) of women's role as economic managers: 'a Victorian wife, the presiding hearth angel of Victorian social myth, actually performed a more significant and extensive economic and political function than is usually perceived. Prevailing ideology held the house as haven, a private sphere opposed to the public commercial sphere. In fact, the house and its mistress served as a significant adjunct to a man's commercial endeavours. Whereas men earned the money,

women had the important task of managing those funds towards the acquisition of social and political status.'

10 Langland, p. 17, discusses the way in which middle-class women's 'signifying practices [. . .] police the borders of polite society'.

11 Felix is also away, recovering from an illness. The relevant chapter is called 'The House without Pillars' (C. M. Yonge, *The Pillars of the House*, 1873 [London: Macmillan, 1893], vol. 1, ch. 19).

12 Langland, p. 80.

13 I exclude Alda who is brought up by wealthy cousins.

14 After seven years another will is found leaving the property to Caroline's second cousin, Elvira, who eventually marries Caroline's eldest son, Allen. He thereby comes to live on his wife's property, just as he had lived on his mother's property. In this he is like his uncle who also lives on property inherited by his wife, Ellen ' an heiress in a small way' (p. 2). Caroline's friend, Mrs Evelyn, is also a widow and the sole responsible parent for her children. (C. M. Yonge, *Magnum Bonum*, 1879 [London: Macmillan 1886]).

15 See Barbara Brook's excellent little book *Elizabeth Garrett Anderson, "A Thoroughly Ordinary Woman"* for a brief account of this remarkable woman's life (Aldeburgh: Aldeburgh Bookshop, 1997).

16 The Vivians are a wealthy family who have been 'ruined' but are living well on Lady Tyrrell's jointure (C. M. Yonge, *The Three Brides*, 1876 [London: Macmillan, 1892] pp. 13-14).

17 Mrs Poynsett reads *Middlemarch* during the course of the novel. Lady Rosamund, like Rosamund Vincy, bears a name that stresses her worldliness though it is of a very different kind and far more appealing.

18 Yonge wrote of Eliot, 'the farther she drifted away from the training of her youth, the more [her novels] failed even as works of art' (in a letter to Miss Ireland Blackburne, quoted by Ethel Romanes, *Charlotte Mary Yonge: An Appreciation* [Oxford: Mowbray, 1908] p. 179).

19 Virginia Woolf, 'George Eliot' in *The Common Reader* (London: Hogarth Press, 1984) pp. 162-72; passage cited is on p. 168.

20 In *Galaxy*, March 1873, quoted in Rosemary Ashton, *George Eliot: A Life* (London: Penguin, 1997) p. 32.

21 A. Hayter, 'The Sanitary Idea and a Victorian Novelist', *History Today* 19 (1969) pp. 840-47.

22 J. Sturrock, *"Heaven and Home": Charlotte M. Yonge's Domestic Fiction and the Victorian Debate over Women* (Victoria: University of Victoria English Studies 66, 1995).

23 Stephanie L. Barczewski, *Myth and National Identity in Nineteenth Century Britain* (Oxford: Oxford University Press, 2000) pp. 177-81.

24 Dorothy Mermin, *Godiva's Ride: Women of Letters in England, 1830-1880* (Bloomington: Indiana University Press, 1993) and Laurie Langbauer, *Novels of Everyday Life: The Series in English Fiction 1850-1930* (Ithaca: Cornell University Press, 1999) p. 84.

25 Nicola Diane Thompson, *Reviewing Sex: Gender and the Reception of Victorian Novels* (Basingstoke: Macmillan, 1996) pp. 190-214.

26 Sally Mitchell, *Dinah Mulock Craik* (Boston: Twayne, 1983) p. 104.

27 Violet in *Heartsease* and Amy in *The Heir of Redclyffe* may be idealised but the women characters in later novels are far less likely to be treated in this way.

28 Characters from earlier novels appear in *The Pillars of the House* (the Mays from *The Daisy Chain* and *The Trial*, Constance from *The Castle Builders*). This is the first novel in which they are woven together (although *The Trial* is an earlier example of the sequel).

29 Iris Murdoch, in *Existentialists and Mystics: Writings on Philosophy and Literature*, ed. P. Conradi, (London: Chatto and Windus, 1997), pp. 287-95.

CHARLOTTE YONGE: EMBODYING
THE DOMESTIC FICTION

Barbara J. Dunlap

Charlotte Yonge's domestic novels present characters whose lives become as vivid to us as our own. Readers come to know her characters through authorial description, and the skilful use of dialogue, but also through their bodies. As Lettice Cooper observed in her incisive essay, 'Charlotte Mary Yonge, Dramatic Novelist': 'How much it enhances the dramatic intensity of Charlotte's novels that she is so very good at bringing to life the physical presence of her characters.'[1] Analysis of ways in which the body is presented in literature has emerged as a challenging way in which to read nineteenth-century fiction.

She enhances her presentations of physicality through the use of dramatic description and codes which advance the narrative as they assist in her representations of the healthy body, the sick and invalid body, and what might be called the consoling body. In her presentation of the sexual body, coded though it is, she is sometimes capable of more directness than a self-conscious writer such as Thackeray would allow himself.[2] I will look at her use of these techniques in *The Daisy Chain*, *The Heir of Redclyffe*, and *The Pillars of the House* with glances at some instances in other domestic novels.

While Charlotte Yonge does employ static description, much of her description is dramatic: bodies are presented in motion which advances the narrative. It is difficult to demonstrate her skill here without extended quotation but parts of a few scenes must suffice. In *The Pillars of the House* (1873), Felix and Wilmet find that Lance's susceptibility to headaches after his sunstroke requires that he move from his hot attic bedroom to a cooler one on the first floor. They go to the warehouse he has sought as a refuge from the hot sun:

> Felix went up a step-ladder, Wilmet following; and there, sure enough, was Lance, lying in a nest of paper shavings, with head on his air-pillow. 'Oh, you've unearthed me, have you? I wish you'd let me stay here all night!' he said with some weary fretfulness; but the next moment burst into a peal of laughter as Wilmet's head appeared above the floor. 'Pallas Athene ascends! Oh! what a place it would be to act a play – only then all the fry would find it out [. . .]!'
>
> 'My poor dear Lance, is this the only quiet place you could find? and you let us all neglect you, and never complained!' exclaimed Wilmet, kissing his hot forehead.
>
> 'Why, it's only my stupidity,' said Lance, wearily but gratefully; 'and you can't make places quiet or cool! If you would just let me sleep here!'
>
> 'No; but you shall have Mr. Froggatt's room. He will not want it now. Come along, Lance, we'll bring your things down. The barrack is a great deal too hot for you to go into!'
>
> He did not make any resistance; but as they landed from the ladder, threw his arm round Wilmet, and leant against her with a sort of lazy mischievous tenderness, as he said, 'Isn't the Froggery wanted for – somebody else?' and tried to look up into her face [. . .]
>
> [T]hey paused while entering the house and going upstairs, but no sooner were they in the barrack [. . .] than Lance returned to the charge.
>
> 'But when is *he* coming? Not Fernan – he's an old story.'
>
> 'Yes,' said Felix, walking up to Wilmet to fold together the corners of the sheets they were stripping from Lance's bed [. . .] 'I want particularly to improve my acquaintance, if you don't.'[3]

In this short passage, Lance's delightful temper, the physical affection which flows between the Underwoods, and Felix's willingness to perform domestic work reinforce the permanent harm the sunstroke has done Lance; the loving teasing which goes on as they attend to the bed leads, in the rest of the chapter, to Wilmet's full avowal to Felix of her feelings for John Harewood and acceptance of him as a suitor.

Equally skilful is the body language Charlotte Yonge gives to Arthur Martindale of *Heartsease*, the younger son of a peer, as he tells his brother John about his sudden marriage to a sixteen-year-old girl from modest circumstances:

> 'She is very lovely!' said John, in a tone full of cordial admiration.
>
> 'Isn't she?' continued Arthur, triumphantly. 'Such an out-of-the-way style; – the dark eyes and hair, with that exquisite complexion [. . .]'.

After listening to Arthur describe Violet's 'points' as if she were a race horse, John asks, 'How did your acquaintance begin?'

> 'This way,' said Arthur, leaning back, and twirling a chair on one of its legs for a pivot. 'Fitzhugh would have me come down for a fortnight's fishing to Wrangerton. There's but one inn there fit to put a dog to sleep in, and when we got there we found the house turned of window for a ball. [. . .] I thought I might as well give in to it, for the floor shook so that there was no taking a cigar in peace. So you see the stars ordained it, and it is of no use making a row about one's destiny,' concluded Arthur, in a sleepy voice, ceasing to spin the chair.[4]

The Arthur of the next 300 pages is before us in all essentials: his ability to see only the surface (he has no notion of the depths of Violet's character or her capacity for development), his desire not be 'bothered', and the physical restlessness which leads him to the unreflecting pursuit of pleasure as a remedy for ennui.

Both static description and this type of narrative description are easily 'read'. The last two decades have produced critical works that present more complex ways of 'reading' the body in fiction, and particularly in Victorian fiction.[5] In looking anew at Charlotte's Yonge's presentation of the body, I have found especially helpful a recent book by Elizabeth Langland, *Nobody's Angels: Middle-Class Women and Domestic Ideology in Victorian Culture*. The author does not mention Charlotte Yonge but does look at 'classed bodies' or 'class as bodily inscription' in novels by Elizabeth Gaskell and Margaret Oliphant, and their dramatization of those 'signifying practices [. . .] which belong to the genteel bourgeoisie' and which 'functioned not only to manage working-class dissent but to police the borders of polite society from the incursions of the vulgar middle-class or the petite bourgeoisie'.[6] She maintains that 'Class *is* a representation, inscribed on the body through characteristic postures, and modes of speech.'[7] This observation is certainly relevant to the work of Charlotte Yonge.

In developing her large families, all having the basic signs of 'gentle' or 'county' breeding, Charlotte Yonge differentiates family members through bodily signs which go beyond mere descriptions of appearance. Among the eleven May siblings of *The Daisy Chain* (1856) the dexterity and general 'handiness' of the eldest son, Ritchie, partially compensate for his academic mediocrity and are physical adjuncts to his 'calm good sense'. Flora, the most conventionally attractive, has a smoothness which allows her manipulate the social environment of Stoneborough to her advantage; but this surface conceals the passion for praise which drives her. Ethel, ardent, impetuous, clumsy, has looks which caricature her father's sharp, sallow features and at fifteen finds her great desire for usefulness 'thwarted by the awkward ungainly hands and heedless eyes that Nature had given her'.[8] Unable to manage her long skirts, she treads on the hem of her own trailing mourning dress, pulling out the gathers, dragging her skirts in the mud of the unpaved streets, and earning a sharp reprimand from Dr May. Assisted by the patient Richard she subdues her body to more of the graceful calmness which should belong to a lady. In a few years, 'she held herself better, had learnt to keep her hair in order, and the more womanly dress [. . .] improved her figure' (Vol. II, ch. 1, p. 335 = p. 300M). She learns to make and pour the tea without spilling or scalding and to keep her belongings in order. Her achievements in learning to perform the role of a well-bred young lady confound Flora's prediction that 'Richard would never succeed in making a notable or elegant woman of Ethel [. . .]' (Vol. I, ch. 8, p. 75 = p. 69M). Along with her impetuosity, Ethel has largely given up her Greek studies for the French which 'dear Mamma' preferred as one of those accomplishments befitting a lady. But Ethel retains her intellectual and religious ardour, and they are more respected by the men around her – father, brothers, clergy – as she learns to perform her role as a lady. Indeed, this role is vital to her desire to improve the neighbouring rural slum of Cocksmoor and establish a church there. She becomes her father's confidant and in a subsequent novel, *The Trial* (1864), almost a substitute wife.

What Dr May calls his brilliant son Norman's 'morbid sensitiveness' (Vol. II, ch. 12, p. 474 = p. 425M), is a temperament which unfits him to take up his father's profession. 'Every patient he lost, he would bring himself in guilty of murder,' the doctor exclaims. (Vol. II, ch. 16, p. 517 = p. 463M). This temperament has been exacerbated by witnessing the accident which killed his mother. His intellectual precocity wins him high honours at Oxford, but Norman experiences religious doubts which almost disable him and tell on his body through restlessness, sleeplessness and general debility. Unable to resolve the tension between a desire to gain worldly success and a doubt of its ultimate value, he finds relief for his psychosomatic debility by going as a missionary to New Zealand accompanied by a wife whose happy temperament is reflected in her buoyant health. As a family, the Mays are not particularly handsome, with real beauty given only to Flora and little Blanche and Harry, their sailor brother. When Harry is thought to have perished in shipwreck, Dr May valorises him as 'my yellow-haired laddie, with his lion look! He was the flower of them all! Not one of these other boys come near him in manliness [. . .]' (Vol. II, ch. 14, p. 497 = p. 445M). In *The Trial* the development of the two youngest May sons bear out this partiality. 'Professor Tom' with his spectacles and quixotic marriage and Aubrey with his weak chest have admirable qualities, but Harry retains a special hold on his father's heart.

Miriam Bailin's observation in *The Sickroom in Victorian Fiction* that illness in the Victorian novel serves as a focus for social interaction and calls on service is exemplified in the presentation of Alan Ernescliffe, a young naval lieutenant whom Dr May was called in to attend when he fell ill at the local hotel.[9] The doctor brings Alan home to the house on the High Street to convalesce and the initial doctor–patient relationship progresses to a strong friendship with the entire May family. Indeed, it is 'dear Mamma's' desire to constrain the growing attraction between Alan Ernescliffe and her oldest daughter which leads to Margaret's accompanying her parents on a carriage ride while the others walk to Cocksmoor with Alan. The overturning of the carriage, due as much to Dr May's 'headlong driving' as to a startled horse, kills her mother and leaves Margaret paralysed. Presented at the outset as 'a fine, tall, blooming girl of eighteen', she finally becomes a bedridden invalid with a 'complexion [which] had assumed the dead white of habitual ill-health' (Vol. II, ch. 1, p. 335 = p. 300M).[10]

Placed in her mother's room, she is initially the focus of her family's attention, but Charlotte Yonge did not valorise or privilege invalidism for its own sake. She did understand how bodily discomfort could prey on the temper and in *Womankind* (1876) pointed out:

> The invalid of books, who lies on the sofa ready to do everything for everybody, and to hear every care and trouble, is an excellent ideal for the invalid herself [...] But all invalids have not the free head and nerves, lively spirits, and unfailing temper, required for such a post to be easily fulfilled.[11]

She noted that while families and friends would rally round in the early days of disability, as the condition becomes fixed,

> You feel it very hard and neglectful if you are left alone, yet you do not know how to bear with the others when they come, and you are glad when you can manage to be only dull, not snappish. People petted you, and thought nothing too much for you, when you were very ill; now that ailment is permanent, they are getting tired of you, when you really want them.[12]

As a member of a large family, Margaret is not neglected but her lingering invalidism wears on her family, and she herself begins to yearn to join Alan Ernescliffe and her mother. While belief in the afterlife partially accounts for Ethel being able to awake the day after Margaret's death with a sense 'more fraught with relief than with misery', the feeling is also due to the fact that the 'long watching is over' (Vol. II, ch. 25, p. 641 = p. 575M.). And seven years of attendance to bodily functions which are never discussed but always present.

For Charlotte Yonge and her contemporaries, the reality was that illnesses and physical disabilities forced a limited life on many whose only resource was their family. *The Heir of Redclyffe* (1853), her first novel to have a wide success, opens with the contrast between the body of the crippled Charles Edmonstone and his active cousin, Philip Morville. Philip enters their comfortable drawing room and is first seen as a 'tall, fine looking young man', whose vigour contrasts with Charles's peakiness as he lies on the sofa with his crutches, the badges of his dependence, near him.[13] Their cousin, Guy Morville, has just lost the grandfather who raised him and is coming to live with his guardian's family. From the beginning of their acquaintance Guy longs to look up to his older cousin Philip, hoping to find in him the friend his sheltered boyhood never afforded and thereby heal the generations-old enmity between the two branches of the Morville family. Over a period of four years Philip thwarts and belittles Guy with a supercilious criticism masked as concern for his younger cousin's moral welfare. By convincing Mr Edmonstone that Guy is a habitual gambler he causes the engagement with Charles' sister Amy to be broken off for a time until the truth is revealed.

Guy is seventeen when he first comes to the Edmonstones and to Charles he has 'the unformed look of a growing boy, and was so slender as to appear taller than he really was' (ch. 3, p. 18). But Guy has grown up in a free outdoor life and throughout the novel he is vividly physical – riding, bathing, romping with his dog, gardening or hay-making. He reveals his strength by leading the rescue party to the wrecked ship in Redclyffe Bay and on his wedding trip in Switzerland where he saves Amy from falling down a precipice: 'Joy unspeakable to feel his fingers close over her wrist, like iron' (ch. 30, p. 305).

Charles' rage against his physical limitations reaches a crescendo during the period when Philip is 'investigating' Guy's conduct. To avoid the painful tedium of crutching himself upstairs, he resentfully accepts Philip's arm but the cousins continue to argue:

> 'Take care what you say!' exclaimed Charles, flushing with anger, as he threw himself forward, with an impatient movement, trusting to his crutch rather than retain his cousin's arm; but the crutch slipped, he missed his grasp at the balusters, and would have fallen to the bottom of the flight if Philip had not been close behind. Stretching out his foot, he made a barrier, receiving Charles' weight against his breast, and then, taking him in his arms, carried him up the rest of the way as easily as if he had been a child. (ch. 17, pp. 185-86)

Charles is soon exclaiming to Amy:

> 'I say there is no greater misery in this world than to have the spirit of a man and the limbs of a cripple. I know if I was good for anything, things would not long be in this state. I should be

> at St. Mildred's by this time, at the bottom of the whole story, and Philip would be taught to eat his words [. . .] But what is the use of talking? This sofa' — and he struck his fist against it — 'is my prison, and I am a miserable cripple, and it is mere madness in me to think of being attended to.' (ch. 17, p. 210)

Of course, Charles is very much 'attended to' in one sense, absorbing a great deal of his mother's and sisters' time; but in his view he is very much *not* attended to in the way that counts for him now — as a normal young man whose vigorous body could impose its will on others. His reaction to Philip's persecution of Guy, the jar on the stairs, and his rebellion against his body occasion a severe recurrence of his hip pain. Before succumbing to the opium which will give him some hours of oblivion, he bids Philip good-bye with a bravado taunt which reverses their advantages: 'I had rather have my hip than your mind' (ch. 20, p. 212.

Philip's persecution of Guy clearly springs from concern that the younger man will supplant him as the centre of Edmonstone veneration, for Guy is the possessor not only of a title and a fine estate but of true natural humility and a sunny disposition which make him generally popular. But Philip's conduct as presented betrays a sexual anxiety which Charlotte Yonge may not have intended to convey. In a foreshadowing of the fever which will consume him in Italy, he several times arrives at the Edmonstone estate from the town of Broadstone where his regiment is quartered in what might be described today as 'in a sweat'. After one hot walk, 'heated and dusty' he arrives to discover Guy and Laura singing together and determines he must protect her from the instability of Guy's character. Thus after another such hot walk a few days later he finds her sketching in a field; taking advantage of her lifelong adoration of him and his physical command, he gets her to agree to a secret understanding — the kind of proceeding which is at variance with the high moral position he has taken toward Guy but which he justifies to himself through rationalization which displays an egotistical selfishness: 'He believed sincerely that a long, lingering attachment to himself would be more for her good than a marriage with one who would have been a high prize for worldly aims [. . .]' (ch. 8, p. 93). A few years later when, despite his best efforts to prevent it, Guy and Amy are married, Philip meets them at Bellagio while he is on a walking tour. Once again he is 'hot and dusty', almost terminally so, and watching his youthful cousins he reflects: 'They both looked so young, that [. . .] he was ready to charge them with youthfulness, if not as a fault, at least as a folly; indeed the state of his own affairs made him inclined to think it a foible, almost a want of patience, in any one to marry before thirty' (ch. 30, p. 310). Philip is annoyed at the deference Guy's title and his generous spending command and at the 'playfulness' and laughter which characterise his relations with Amy – a suggestion of the physical concord which crowns their mental and spiritual sympathies.

Philip becomes ill because of his overweening pride in his body. When the itinerary the three have agreed on for the next stage of their journey proves to lie in way of a fever district and Guy wishes to change it, Philip snorts: 'I say that I cannot see any occasion for our being frightened out of our original determination. If a fever prevails among the half-starved peasantry, it need not affect well-fed healthy persons, merely passing through the country.' In the argument which ensues, Philip 'perhaps, in his full health and strength, almost [regarded] illness itself as a foible, far more the dread of it' (ch. 30, p. 316). He continues with the original itinerary and, naturally, becomes ill. His attack of fever includes delirium, delusions and 'violent ravings'. Guy, finding him abandoned and alone at an inn, stays to nurse him. He too becomes ill, but his fever, though ultimately fatal, 'never ran as high as in Philip's case, and there was no delirium' (ch. 33, p. 340). Previously censorious of Charles for giving in to his pain and absorbing the attention of his sisters, Philip's pride is reduced as he submits to the ministrations of his cousins. While fevers from unspecified infections are a staple of Victorian fiction, this one which reduces Philip is here the ideal correlative of the fever of social and sexual jealousy which has been devouring him all along.

Amy bears Guy's child several months after his death, and Charlotte Yonge, usually so reticent about pregnancy and childbirth that infants sometimes make startling appearances in the novels, is quite direct about her pregnancy. As the Redclyffe estate is entailed, the question of whether the baby will be of 'the right sort' is important to both her and to Philip. Her mother fears that Amy's unnatural calm following Guy's death must eventually tell on her body. This reaction is occasioned when her younger sister tries to comfort her by bringing in some Noisette roses, the same kind Guy was holding when he proposed. The roses bring Guy's living body vividly before her:

It was too much. It recalled his perfect health and vigour, his light activity, and enjoyment of life, and something came on her of the sensation we feel for an insect, one moment full of joyous vitality, the next, crushed and still. She had hitherto thought of his feverish thirst and fainting weariness being at rest, and felt the relief, or else followed his spirit to its repose, and rejoiced; but now the whole scene brought back what he once was; his youthful, agile frame, his eyes dancing in light, his bounding step, his gay whistle, the strong hand that had upheld her on the precipice; the sure foot that had carried aid to the drowning sailors, [. . .] all came on her in contrast with − death! The thought swept over her, carrying away every other, and she burst into tears [. . .] The bodily frame had been overwrought to obey the mental firmness and composure, and now nature asserted her rights [. . .]. (ch. 37, pp. 384-85)

Once back in England, Philip, though essentially recovered, is still troubled by recurrent headaches, that complaint so often associated with women; his proud, lofty manner is subdued into gentleness toward the family to whom he used to condescend. He stays with his married sister, who has become a caricature of his former self and his diminished body shrinks from her 'stately presence' and uncomprehending sympathy which equally overwhelm him. When, a year later, Philip marries Laura, Charles drives to the station to meet her and reports to Amy that she is: 'As large as life, and that is saying a good deal. She would make two of Philip. As tall and twice as broad. I thought Juno herself was advancing on me from the station' (ch. 44, p. 456). If Charles finds Margaret Henley's bulk off-putting, for her part she rejoices that Philip has chosen a wife with suitable physical attributes. She views Laura as 'a fine-looking person, like her own family, and fit to be an excellent lady of the house; [. . .] she perceived that her brother's choice had been far better than if he had married that poor pale little Amabel, so silent and quiet that she could never make a figure anywhere, and had nothing like the substantive character her brother must have in a wife' (ch. 44, p. 458). But Amy is now the moral centre of the Edmonstone–Morville connection, not only through her status as Guy's widow, mother of his child, but because she always gave her parents her full confidence while Laura, like Mrs Henley herself, has lost status in the family. Laura, characterised by her drooping head, 'had too much failed in a daughter's part to go forth from her home with the clear, loving, hopeful heart her sister had carried from it!' (ch. 44, p. 461). Philip goes to his marriage ceremony with a 'throbbing, burning brow', and throughout his distinguished career as a member of Parliament and exemplary landowner, Laura's main duty will be 'watching him and tending his health' (ch. 44, p. 463). His own moral failings have branded his body while Amy and Charles have regained health. Indeed, Charles looks forward to a useful career as assistant to Philip's secretary, and tutor to Guy's daughter. The moral events of the novel have marked the bodies of Philip, Laura, Charles and Amy but the facades they show to outsiders do not accurately represent their values within the family.

Nearly twenty years and several long domestic novels separate *The Heir of Redclyffe* and *The Daisy Chain* from *The Pillars of the House*, which was serialised in *The Monthly Packet* for two years before its book publication in 1873. Here Charlotte Yonge develops her largest family on a canvas which has England firmly in the foreground but includes scenes in California, Egypt and France, and narrates travels to New Zealand and Australia. The narrative of *Pillars* says that hard work, a disciplined religious life and the cultivation of one's talents are the signs of true worth at least as valid as are inherited wealth and title. Thus the Underwoods do not regain Vale Leston until, in the material sense, they no longer need it, and their disciplined way of life allows Felix to serve its community and restore some monies to the church. Yet although the Underwoods may have fallen into trade from their inherited position as country gentry, their bodies retain irremediable signs of their class.

For the thirteen siblings, Charlotte Yonge creates a set of 'family features' which reflect their 'high', 'county' heritage. Among the children sitting or tumbling on the stairs at the beginning of Chapter One are the twins, Wilmet and Alda who have 'the family features in their prettiest development – the chiseled straight profile, the clear white roseately tinted skin, the large, well-opened azure eyes [. . .] the long, slender, graceful limbs' (Vol. I, ch. 1, p. 7). Sixteen years later, among the party which greet Felix as the new Squire of Vale Leston is Robina Underwood's friend, Lord Ernest de la Poer, who has 'rather aquiline features, but with that peculiar whiteness of complexion which is one of the characteristics of old nobility, and though not exactly handsome, with a very pleasing countenance, and an air of birth and breeding' (Vol. II, ch. 36, p. 243). Such marks of class serve Alda well when she is launched in London society by the Thomas Underwoods, but are almost a disadvantage for Wilmet left behind in Bexley to assist her oldest brother in keeping the family afloat. Indeed, her once lovely but worn-out mother has suffered from the stings of the rector's pretentious wife to whom 'the soft movement, the low voice, the quiet sweep of the worn garments were a constant source of vexation' (Vol. I, ch. 1, p. 5). Though impoverished, the young Underwoods maintain their upper-class bodies as a silent reproach to those in Bexley who would condescend to them. Fulbert, a younger brother, who is 'stout, square, fat-cheeked, and permanently rough and dusty, [and] looked as if he hardly belonged to the rest' (Vol. I, ch. 1, p. 7) has a physical energy which cannot be contained within the confines of life at Bexley or the Clergy Orphan school and happily emigrates to Australia. Marilda, daughter of Edward Underwood's cousin Tom, has her Underwood features marred by inheritance from her coarse mother. To Edward Underwood, she is an 'Underwood all over [. . .] although entirely devoid of that delicacy and refinement of form and complexion that was so remarkable in himself and in most of his children [. . .] There was a sort of clumsiness in the shape of every outline, and a coarseness in the colouring, that made her like a bad drawing of one of his own girls' (Vol. I, ch. 2, p. 27). Marilda also lacks the social delicacy of the Underwoods and is full of inconvenient questions and remarks.

Though Marilda's mother tries to ape the gentry through expensive dress and furnishings, her thin veneer of gentility cracks when she becomes excited. In the clamour caused by Alda's engagement to Fernando Travis, 'Tom, who after all was an Underwood, and whose better breeding had come to the perception how [his wife's] ravings compromised his daughter's dignity' takes her brother Felix off for a private conference (vol. I, ch. 15, p. 260). Her body betrays her real status. As an index of her status Mrs Thomas Underwood's pretensions are dramatically contrasted with the affectionate portrait of her own mother, that thorough Cockney Mrs Kedge, whose wealth does not prevent her from nursing Fernando when he is ill, wearing pattens and doing some of her own housework and cooking.

Though generous and loving to her cousins, and especially to Edgar and Alda who are almost adopted by her father, Marilda never really gains their acceptance. After Alda reveals how she schemed to blight the early attachment of Marilda and Fernando, Felix reflects: 'Even though the essential vulgarity of Alda's nature had been so painfully evident, the delicate contour of her face, her refined intonation and pronunciation, and elegance of appearance and manner, returned on him in contrast with poor Marilda's heavy uncouthness' (Vol. II, ch. 28, p. 80). He recognises that her bluff manner and appearance put her at a disadvantage compared to Alda who 'performs' the outward role of the lady. Fernando Travis, who is not related at all to the Underwoods, is 'adopted' by them and his own striking appearance, while different from theirs, is a feature that is not unimportant here. Fernando is literally precipitated into their lives by the fire at the Fortinbras Arms during which his black servant wraps his own body around Fernando and jumps from an upper window, saving the young man at the cost of his own life – a dramatic example of body loyalty which much impresses the eldest brother, Felix. Fernando, the son of a Mexican mother and a raffish English father, is so dark-skinned as to be the objects of slurs from the nouveau riche Sir Adrian Vanderkist but has the look of a Hildago or Spanish nobleman. Association with the Underwoods triggers the development of a deep, disciplined religious life and this endears him to the family. At the novel's end, Fernando, now a wealthy merchant, has acquired 'the matured nobleness of countenance stamped on naturally fine outlines by a life of brave, unselfish activity and dutifulness. It was a calm, serious, dignified face [. . .]' (Vol. II, ch. 47, p. 477). After Fernando rescues Edgar's young son and brings him from America to Vale Leston Felix confers the ultimate Underwood accolade: 'You are more than ever one of ourselves,' a tribute never paid to their cousin Marilda. (Vol. II, ch. 45, p. 432). However, by the novel's end she has for several years been directing the hide-importing business inherited from her father and has 'somewhat fined down, and actual work in business and charity had given meaning to her countenance' (Vol. II, ch. 47, p. 475). This improvement makes her now a suitable wife for Fernando. Marilda's inability ever to be 'one of ourselves' is emphasised by Geraldine's fierce reaction to her wish to adopt young Gerald, Edgar's son. A few months later, during the preparations for Stella's marriage to the wealthy Charlie Audley who has an appointment at the British Embassy in Munich, Felix wishes her to purchase a trousseau suitable for the life she will be leading there. Though Marilda has offered to buy it, Wilmet accompanies Stella to

London for this purpose because: 'It was due to the Ambassadress that [Stella's] outfit should neither be countrified nor left to Marilda's taste' (Vol. II, ch. 47, p. 467).

The opening chapter of *The Pillars of the House* seem to be preparing the thirteen-year-old Geraldine for either an early death or the social role of family invalid, but Charlotte Yonge belies the reader's expectations. On her first appearance, Geraldine's face is marked by an 'expression of wasted suffering' due to a tubercular ankle joint and she looks almost older than her parents. But Geraldine is never allowed to become the pathetic, attention-absorbing invalid her jealous sister Alda accuses her of being. Several years later she shows great determination in deciding to have her troublesome foot amputated, and the operation improves her overall health and allows her to move fairly easily on her 'cork foot' with the aid of a walking stick. The artistic talent she has been quietly developing during her confined years blossoms with some good instruction in London and she begins to earn critical praise as well as handsome commissions.

In *The Flesh Made Word*, Helena Michie examines the presentation of the heroine's body in Victorian fiction and notes that the novels

> are frequently about women's hands: hands that stand for hearts, and hands that are won and offered by themselves. The hands that are offered with hearts, that represent in themselves something higher, constitute one of the centre of value in the nineteenth-century novel. They form a synecdochal chain where the heart represented by the hand is in itself a synecdoche for the more obviously sexual part of the body that enter into a heroine's decision about whom to marry [. . .] [The] touch of a hand [is] frequently the first touch between lovers.[14]

Michie does not note that in Victorian novels the primary uses of a *gentleman's* hands as shown in that same fiction are only to guide horses, hold a gun, and deal cards. By contrast, the hands of the most admirable Underwood siblings are useful hands: Felix's hand which writes newspaper articles and soothes Theodore; Geraldine's hand which skilfully manipulates pencil and brush; Lance's hands which play the violin and organ. And of course, Wilmet's hands, which demonstrate Michie's thesis but are also essential to the welfare of the Underwood siblings.

Wilmet Underwood is known by the usefulness of her hands as much as by her beauty. It is by her hands that she lives her role as one of the two pillars of the house. Useful in mending, knitting, cooking and teaching, her hands also stand for the physical affection and comfort she provides her brothers and sisters. In the desolate weeks following her father's death, she herself receives and expresses comfort through the body which she is yet unable to feel in her heart: 'She had felt as if she could hardly have lived over these weeks save for fondling the younger twins and waiting on her mother' (Vol. I, ch. 5, p. 78). When Alda leaves, 'Wilmet went up and quietly lay down by her mother on her bed, feeling as if there was nothing she cared for in all life, and as if youth, hope, and happiness were gone away from her for ever [. . .] But then her mother's hand came out and stroked her; and presently one of the babies cried, and Wilmet was walking up and down the room with it, and all activity with her outward senses, though her heart felt dead' (Vol. I, ch. 5, p. 79).

Some years later when she returns home after nursing Lance through his sunstroke, having left Alda in charge, the Underwoods' old servant exclaims, 'sure 'tis you that has got all the heart, and the head, and the hands' (Vol. I, ch. 19, p. 328). Her first act upon seeing Lance lying almost unconscious from the sunstroke is to lay 'her hand on the helpless fingers, and ben[d] to kiss the brow'. He responds to her touch sufficiently to speak for the first time: 'Wilmet, Wilmet, bring me back!' (Vol. I, ch. 17, p. 296). When yielding to John Harewood's proposal, she draws off her glove, revealing 'the shapely, notable fingers' (Vol. I, ch. 22, p. 393). In allowing him to take her hand, Wilmet is giving the essence of her being. The 'bracing severity' towards her variable sister Geraldine is all gone after this encounter and she is so caressing that 'Cherry felt a thrill of delicious surprise' (Vol. I, ch. 22, p. 394). Throughout the novel her hands and arms stand in for the physical comfort her body affords her brothers and sisters at times of stress.

When Wilmet first learns that it was Edgar, on the run from having killed a man in a duel, who took time to care for John immediately after his accident, her first reaction recognises the power of the hand: '"And he had done this when he touched you', said Wilmet, shuddering' (Vol. II, ch. 33, p. 179). Her hand is the last trace she leaves in the novel, as her 'white resolute fingers' attempt to take the photograph which Geraldine is using as a model for the series of miniatures she is painting of the recently deceased Felix (Vol. II, ch. 49, p. 517).

After the death of a loved one, characters frequently face a conflict of feeling between their religious faith which tells them that the dead are better off – spared the toils and corruption of this world and enjoying perfect happiness in a better one – and the 'selfish' wish to have them back. While religious consolation is ultimately triumphant, in the immediate loss, the consolations of the body can be as vital as those of the spirit. In *The Pillars of the House*, the death of Edward Underwood is immediately followed by this scene:

> Presently after, Felix was sitting in the large arm-chair in the dining-room, with his sister Geraldine on his lap, his arms round her, her arms tightly clasped round his neck, her hair hanging loosely down over his shoulder, her head against him, his face over her, as he rocked himself backwards and forward with her, each straining the other closer, as though the mechanical action and motion could allay the pain.' (Vol. I, ch. 4, p. 61)

Felix is sixteen and Geraldine thirteen. This form of comfort remains one of the marks of the special, almost marital relationship they develop and several years later, at a difficult moment in her life, their brother, Edgar, will urge Geraldine to remain with him in London, although 'Felix might be tempted to take his baby home to rock' (Vol. II, ch. 26, p. 56).

Another kind of physical consolation concerns the youngest of the Underwood sisters, Stella, who is seventeen when the retarded twin brother for whom she has been an inseparable companion is drowned. The youthful Charlie Audley finds her solitary in the garden making crosses of flowers and in her lonely state his reverent affection receives a swift return in which consolation and desire seem to mingle, 'bringing such an approach to caressing as would have startled her at any moment when her heart was not so yearning for tenderness and sympathy' (Vol. II, ch. 43, p. 390). Together they complete making the crosses and bring them to Theodore's open coffin where Stella in a sense accepts Charlie's love. She kisses Theodore 'and seemed to expect Charles to do the same, as a great favour to him, after which she let him help her to lay her cross with the wreath round it on the breast, and change the now closed Star of Bethlehem that lay

under the waxen fingers [. . .] They went away hand in hand [. . .]'
(Vol. II, ch. 43, p. 391). The death of the retarded Theodore, Stella's
engagement and marriage to Charlie and acceptance by the wealthy
Audley family are the signal for Felix to lay down the burden
bequeathed to him eighteen years ago by the sexually reckless Edward
Underwood. The father's heedless career of parenthood (which
Charlotte Yonge criticises only obliquely through its effect on his
wife), unchecked by poverty, or his own tuberculosis, has ensured
that his responsible oldest son will see celibacy as his only option.
Immediately after the wedding ceremony the already weakened Felix
has a final fatal attack and dies after a few days of terrible suffering.
For Stella

> the loss to her was as of a parent, and no father could have been
> more beloved than her 'Brother,' but the change in her life had
> made it just not the utter desolation it was to the home sisters,
> and the strength of the new bond, and the soothing bliss of her
> husband's caresses, lifted her up enough to make her sympathy
> a support. (Vol. II, ch. 48, p. 495)

Observations such as this strengthen the view that Charlotte Yonge
was not an unsophisticated writer, but rather a most unself-conscious
one.

In *The Sickroom in Victorian Fiction* Miriam Bailin notes how, '[t]he
rigid inhibition of physical and emotional exposure in the Victorian era
is also suspended in the sickroom, which thus becomes a privileged
site of untroubled intimacy while staying within the moderating
decorum of social propriety and realist convention.'[15] This is much the
case in *The Pillars of the House*. In her few days of attendance on the
dying Edward Underwood, Sister Constance enters deeply into
spiritual communion with him; Fernando becomes intimate with the
Underwoods during an enforced stay in their home while recovering
from his injuries in the fire.

The experiences Charlotte Yonge gives Wilmet in *Pillars* further
bear out Bailin's contention. Necessarily concerned with domestic
detail and maintaining propriety among the large family, her nursing
roles both release her from routine and render her body susceptible to
deep feeling.[16] After seeing Lance through the worst of the effects of
the sunstroke she can begin to enjoy the beautiful surroundings of the
cathedral where Lance has been a chorister. Freed from planning

meals and other practicalities, she allows herself to explore her own feelings while sitting in the Deanery garden at Minsterham 'full of still sweet sounds, midsummer hum above, the soft ripple of the water close by, the cawing of the rooks in the Close'. Lance's favourite sister, Robina, has just paid him a welcome visit and Wilmet realises that 'Lance had been everything to her, and she to Lance, for full four weeks; but she should never awaken the look on his face she had seen for Robin' (Vol. I, ch. 18, p. 310-11). During Lance's illness she has been assisted by his friend's brother, John Harewood, and the four weeks they spend together in the intimacy of the sickroom propel their relationship much further forward than could have occurred at home in Bexley, with its claims and restraints upon her.

They become engaged and two years later, when Major Harewood is injured on his way home from India in the explosion of a train engine, Wilmet overturns her life to accompany his father to Egypt. In tending John's terrible scalds whose great extent included intimate parts of his body: 'The pleasure and comfort she gave him were really serving to bear him through. Not only was her touch unusually light, firm, dexterous, and soft, but pain from her hand was not like that given by any one else, when each dressing was tortured [sic]' (Vol. II, ch. 31, p. 144). Wilmet is so bonded to John through her physical care of him that, when his father's duties at the Cathedral require his return to England and he fears she cannot remain unless another family member come out to act as chaperone, Wilmet's reaction is that 'her little proprieties most entirely vanished into oblivion.' Her body echoes the passion of her words: 'The colour flew into her cheeks, 'I could do very well alone if you were only to marry us.' (Vol. II. ch. 31, p. 145). At their wedding, 'on African soil, between two Europeans, and one spectator came from Asia, another from America, to say nothing of the lesser distinctions of France, Germany, Greece, Egypt, and Arabia' (Vol. II, ch. 31, p. 150), John lies motionless on the bed, 'covered by a bright striped silk quilt'. Over a nearby chair his servant has placed the emblem of his masculinity: 'his master's uniform coat and medals, of which he would not be denied the display' (Vol. II, ch. 31, p. 151). Wilmet kneels by the bedside, so her hand will be in reach of John's 'poor weak one over which her long soft fingers seemed to exercise cherishing guidance, with that sense of power and protection she had been used to wield through life' (Vol. II, ch. 31, p. 151). But just as Charlotte Yonge does not conclude *The Heir of Redclyffe* with Guy's exemplary death but shows how Amy and her family 'come to terms' with his loss, she does not say farewell to John and Wilmet with this exalted moment. Wilmet has to learn that she has not married her patient, and her lesson is taught through the hand. Stopping at Pau during the later stage of John's recovery, they have their first, polite, disagreement. Wilmet is in the wrong and John, feeling the necessity to pay a visit she refuses to make herself, overtaxes himself. The edge of Wilmet's apology is blunted by John's falling 'asleep in her very face', in their hotel sitting-room and in such a position that she is unable to rise to get her knitting and 'the deprivation of mechanical employment for her fingers was trying enough to take away serenity or connection from her thoughts. [. . .] Perhaps in truth, nothing in her whole life was so difficult to Wilmet Harewood, or of so much service to her, than using such abstinence' (Vol. II, ch. 33, pp. 181-82).

At the time of his father's death Felix is sixteen, a healthy, well-made schoolboy verging on manhood. Over the next eighteen years, as he grows into his role as head of the family, Edgar will grow away from and eventually abandon it. Their bodies are marked by the choices they make. Edgar is initially the most handsome and talented of the Underwoods, 'the King Oberon of the nursery' in his father's phrase. At seventeen, after three years on the continent,

> Edgar had grown very tall, and had inherited his father's advantages of grace and elegance of figure, to which was added a certain distinguished ease of carriage, and ready graciousness, too simple to be called either conceit or presumption, but which looked as if he were used to be admired and to confer favours. Athletics had been the fashion with him and his English companions, and his complexion was embrowned by sun and wind, his form upright and vigorous [. . .] Edgar's appearance was a perfect feast of enjoyment, not only to little loving Geraldine, but to sage Felix. They recreated themselves with gazing at him, and when left alone together would discuss his charms in low confidential murmurs, quite aware that Wilmet would think them very silly; but Edgar was the great romance of both. (Vol. I, ch. 9, p. 146)

In contrast, Felix, at nineteen, 'seemed almost to have ceased growing for the last three years [. . .] his indoor occupations had given his broad square shoulders a kind of slouch' (Vol. I, ch. 9, p. 146). Edgar's physical advantages, which become even more splendid a few years later when he adopts a moustache, Tyrolean knickerbockers, and guitar, fail to make him a strong pillar of the house of Underwood. Rejecting Christianity and scorning bourgeois life, he yet is undisciplined in his art work and is ultimately eclipsed by Geraldine who works patiently. Edgar casually attracts the young woman to whom Felix is attracted, although he knows he must not think of marriage. It is Felix who plays out one kind of masculine role as he supports his sisters and becomes a partner in the bookselling and local newspaper business while Edgar becomes a forger, murderer and fugitive from his family. Yet Felix also has characteristics Victorians would have identified as feminine; indeed, he is a Victorian forerunner of today's nurturing father. He acts as mother to the retarded Theodore, even to the extent of having him sleep in his room; he blushes even as an adult; he is the recipient of the kinds of confidences from his brothers and sisters which a mother would traditionally receive. Yet Felix's role as the masculine pillar of the house of Underwood to Wilmet's female one is never in doubt. In *Pillars* Clement is the brother presented ambiguously. Indeed, at a point in this brother's late adolescence, Felix reflects that 'Clement always seemed to him like a girl' (Vol. I, ch. 12, p. 207), and there is an almost palpable physical antagonism between the attenuated Clement and the physically charismatic Edgar, the brother nearest him in age.[17]

When Felix finally does inherit (or in a sense re-inherits) the wonderful Vale Leston estate his practical and moral qualifications to be a good 'Squire' are never in doubt. Rather, his sister Geraldine is anxious to determine if his body has maintained the marks of class which will make him accepted among the 'county' families. They are invited to stay at the home of 'Sir Vesey Hammond, the patriarch of the county [. . .] the very picture of a country gentleman, white-haired, clear-eyed, ruddy-cheeked, tall and robust, all vigorous health [. . .]' (Vol. II, ch. 37, p. 279).[18] At the dinner party Sir Vesey gives for Felix, Geraldine 'first saw Felix there as a country gentleman, and could judge of his appearance among others. [. . .] And how did her own Squire hold his place compared with others? Looking at him critically, as she tried to do, she saw that his complexion was devoid of the embrowning of sun and wind, his hands were over-white and delicate, and too many cares had pressed on his young shoulders not to have rounded them; so that he did not look like the active, athletic men who had led an out-of-door life; but in look, movement, and tone, he was as thorough a gentleman as any one. Evening dress was perhaps most favourable to him [. . .].' The others find him intelligent and 'if he did not shoot or hunt, that was his own affair [. . .]. If he did sell books elsewhere, that was nothing to them; they felt he was a gentleman, and that was all they wanted' (Vol. II, ch.37, pp. 280-81).

If years in a shop and newspaper office have marked Felix but not diminished his aura of class, Edgar's fugitive life cannot obliterate his. After following the fortune of a travelling group of minstrels around Europe and the Antipodes, he comes to the United States and eventually works his way to California in a wagon train. When Fernando Travis, travelling in California, finds a man near death from an Indian attack, he finds on the wall of his shack a photograph of Edward Underwood. 'He turned hastily to the bed. Yes, the face, weather-stained yet ghastly, overgrown with neglected beard, stained with blood and dust, still showed the delicate chiselling of eyebrow and nose, the Underwood characteristic!' (Vol. II, ch. 44, p. 418).

The Pillars of the House seems to want to say unambiguously that effort, uprightness and faith are of more value than inherited wealth, and that those with innate nobility cannot lose it by stepping behind a shop counter. Yet this message is periodically undercut by the text's indications that class has bodily signs which trump life experiences. Charlotte Yonge is deeply concerned with her characters' moral and religious lives (indeed, the two are inseparable); her ability to embody these characters so vividly (and to make telling observations about their dress) is a vital factor in the readers' belief in the world she creates.

---

1   Lettice Cooper, 'Charlotte Yonge, Dramatic Novelist', in A *Chaplet for Charlotte Yonge*, ed. Georgina Battiscombe and Marghanita Laski (London: Cresset Press, 1965), pp. 31-40 (p. 36).

2   Camilla Vivian of *The Three Brides* (1876) is several times said to resemble the Medusa: 'not the Gorgon, but the beautiful winged head, with only two serpents on the brow and one coiled around the neck' (London: Macmillan, 1889) ch. 5, p. 36. In *Body Work: Objects of Desire in Modern Narrative*, Peter Brooks discusses Freud's view that the 'snaky locks' of the Medusa represent both female genitals and an 'attempted reassurance against the threat of castration' (Cambridge, MA: Harvard University Press, 1993), p. 12. Camilla has a petrifying effect on Raymond Charnock Poynsett's marriage. His

thwarted passion for her has exaggerated his devotion to his mother to the degree that he views his bride primarily as a daughter for her. Even Mrs Charnock Poynsett finds something exaggerated in his attitude. Her own paralysis is greatly mitigated when both Raymond and Camilla die of the fever. Charlotte Yonge does not explore all the implications of this charged material.

3   C. M. Yonge, *The Pillars of the House; or, Under Wode, Under Rode*, 1873 (London & New York: Macmillan, 1893) Vol. 1, ch. 21, pp. 380-81.

4   C. M. Yonge, *Heartsease; or, The Brother's Wife*, 1854 (London: Macmillan, 1897) ch. 1, p. 7.

5   Among a number of many interesting studies of the past two decades which have come to my attention are: Peter Brooks, *Body Work* (Cambridge, MA: Harvard University Press, 1993); Laura Fasick, *Vessels of Meaning: Women's Bodies, Gender Norms and Class Bias from Richardson to Lawrence* (DeKalb, IL: Northern Illinois University Press, 1997); Janet Gezari, *Charlotte Bronte and Defensive Conduct: The Author and the Body at Risk* (Philadelphia: University of Pennsylvania Press, 1992); Pamela K. Gilbert, *Disease, Desire and the Body in Victorian Women's Popular Novels* (New York: Cambridge University Press, 1997); Toril Moi, *Sexual/Textual Politics: Feminist Literary Theory* (London and New York: Routledge, 1985); and Athena Vrettos, *Somatic Fiction: Imaging Illness in Victorian Culture* (Stanford: Stanford University Press, 1995).

6   Elizabeth Langland, *Nobody's Angels: Middle-Class Women and Domestic Ideology in Victorian Culture* (Ithaca: Cornell University Press, 1995) p. 17.

7   Langland, p. 60.

8   C. M. Yonge, *The Daisy Chain; or, Aspirations* (London: John W. Parker & Sons, 1856) Vol. 1, ch. 8, p. 69 = p. 64M. [The second reference in this format indicates the 1888 Macmillan reprint.]

9   Miriam Bailin, *The Sickroom in Victorian Fiction: The Art of Being Ill* (New York: Cambridge University Press, 1994) p. 8.

10   Bailin uses the case of Margaret May in *The Sickroom*, but her comment that Margaret is a 'delicate, sickly and sensitive' invalid who 'presides over the novel with a moral authority and saintliness of manner for which pain is both the origin and the sign' (p.11) misrepresents her presentation in the novel. The seven years remaining to Margaret after the accident are a struggle for patience and resignation, especially after Alan Ernescliffe's death. While she is able to direct the household for some years, she is several times shown to be deficient in judgement.

11   C. M. Yonge, *Womankind* (London: Mozley and Smith, 1876) p. 261.

12   *Womankind*, p. 263.

13   C. M. Yonge, *The Heir of Redclyffe*, (London: John W. Parker, 1853). References are from the 1897 Macmillan reprint: ch. 1, p. 1.

14   Helena Michie, *The Flesh Made Word: Female Figures and Women's Bodies* (New York: Oxford University Press, 1986) p. 98.

15   Bailin, p. 22.

16   The skein of concerns which enfold her are dramatised not only by the condition of the household after her return from Minsterham, but by this dialogue several months later. Ten-year-old Bernard stages a rebellion at having to wear hand-me-down clothes. Felix sees the humour in Wilmet's explanation when she says 'there *could* be no objection to those trousers. They were almost new when Fulbert left them, and Lance has only had them for best one winter' (vol. 1, ch. 23, p. 418).

17   Claudia Nelson has pointed out that '[s]o firm was the cultural connection between the ideal of domesticity and that of womanhood that a man seeking to be the centre of the family (in a literary work if not in real life) had to take on at least some feminine characteristics.' See her *Invisible Men: Fatherhood in Victorian Periodicals, 1850-1910* (Athens, GA: University of Georgia Press, 1995) p. 201.

18   In that almost unpleasant novel, *Dynevor Terrace; or, The Clue of Life* (1857), where duty to parents is pushed to lengths which might have seemed excessive even in its year of publication, the exemplary Mary Ponsonby the elder is made to suffer from an imprudent marriage. Robert Ponsonby's infidelities over the years and his verbal (and possibly physical) abuse have attenuated her until she dies from an unspecified wasting illness. When his daughter, Mary, straining dutifulness to the utmost, returns to her father in Peru to 'sponsor' his teenage bride in society (a sponsorship which proves most unnecessary), the man who has blighted her mother's life and apparently doomed her own hopes, 'held out his arms, Mary fell into them, and it was the same kind rough kiss which had greeted her six years back. It seemed to be forgiveness, consolation, strength, all at once' (London: Macmillan, 1888, ch. 27, p. 286). Almost a caricature of an English sportsman, Robert Ponsonby has a physicality lacking in the men whom Mary has left behind in England: the boyish Louis, his melancholy father, and even her scholarly cousin James Frost: 'Mr. Ponsonby was a large man, with the jovial manner of one never accustomed to self-restraint; good birth and breeding making him still a gentleman, in spite of his loud voice and the traces of self-indulgence. He was ruddy and bronzed [. . .]' (*Ibid.*) When they discuss Louis and Lord Ormersfield, Ponsonby 'poured one of those torrents of fierce passion which had been slowly but surely the death of his wife [. . .].' Mary withstands this but agrees to break off all contact with Louis: 'when her father would have kissed her, she laid her head on his shoulder and wept silently but bitterly'. She draws back to say: 'I give him up because you command me, father, but I will not hear him spoken of unjustly.' (ch. 27, pp. 289-90). Her reward for this is to be allowed to prepare his tea in the morning, a reward that even Charlotte Yonge regards ironically.

Photo by

W. T. Green.

C. M. YONGE'S WRITING-TABLE AT ELDERFIELD.

THE GENEALOGIES OF THE INTERLINKED FAMILIES APPEARING IN CHARLOTTE YONGE'S NOVELS SET IN HER OWN TIMES

John Alves and Hilary Clare

Characters in Charlotte Yonge's contemporary novels frequently appear in more than one of her stories. She thereby creates her own microcosm of Victorian society, or at least that portion which reflected her interests and preoccupations. It is a world in which the Church exerts a stronger influence than do politics, art or literature, and the personalities that Charlotte Yonge has created play their parts within her chosen framework.

The family is the most important unit in the world that she created, and the family members' relationships with one another and with other families provide the main themes. Charlotte Yonge's skill in establishing each character and the differences between characters might be held to make these family trees superfluous since we can quickly recognise each individual in the novels from ways of speech and behaviour. But memories are fallible, and Reader's Companions and Reader's Encyclopaedias will always have their uses. We can at least be helped to avoid traps such as that which caught out Vera Prescott in *Modern Broods*, where she read despairingly onward through *Rudder Grange* not aware that the character 'Lord Edward' was a big dog. More importantly, some of the connexions between families are complicated and guidance is then most welcome.

When it comes to *writing* about the novels, we can assure you that these genealogical tables are indispensable. Are you unable to remember if Maurice Devereux Mohun was born before or after his brother Redgie? Here is the answer immediately to hand. Did Felix Underwood really have twelve younger brothers and sisters? Or was it fourteen? You do not have to go very far to find the answer!

Just to glance through these tables, or to enjoy browsing among the names of all these well-loved characters, the eight tables of family relationships are a treasure to possess. We are delighted that we can now make them more widely available to the members of our Fellowship through the kindness of the Charlotte Yonge Society.

The Charlotte Yonge Society (established with limited membership thirty-five years earlier than our Fellowship) published these tables in their collection of Charlotte Yonge studies entitled *A Chaplet for Charlotte Yonge* (1965). Many Fellowship members own this book, many do not. The genealogical tables were compiled by Violet Powell, who acknowledges her great debt to the extensive researches carried out by Marghanita Laski. The latter discussed in detail many of the problems and inconsistencies which manifest themselves as earlier and later books are compared ('Some Chronological Cruces', *Chaplet*, pp. 79-89). Georgina Battiscombe also contributed to the compilation of the tables. At a recent meeting of the Society, the members kindly agreed to allow our Fellowship to reproduce the Society's tables in one of our publications, making them available for the convenience and edification of our own membership.

Over the years, certain members of the Society, and others in the Fellowship, have taken note of minor slips, misprints and discrepancies in the eight tables. Rather than attempting a revision we have reproduced the tables as originally printed and have then added an Appendix listing all such corrections. If you notice any that should be added to that list, please notify one of the Editors of the present volume.

TABLE I

SCENES AND CHARACTERS *begins 1845*
TWO SIDES OF THE SHIELD *begins 1878-80*
BEECHCROFT AT ROCKSTONE *begins 1879-81*
LONG VACATION *begins 1888*
MODERN BROODS *begins 1889*

Sir William de Moune *[Roll of Battle Abbey]*

Sir John de Mohun *[Early Garter Knight]*

Sir Maurice de Mohun *(Cavalier)* m. Phyllis de Crossthwayte

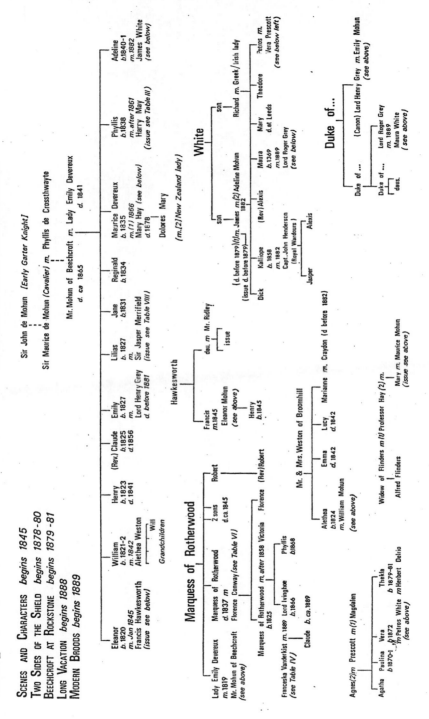

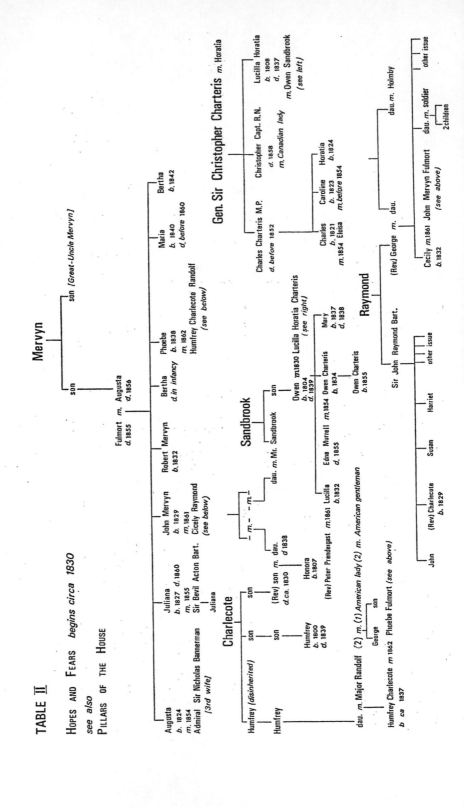

TABLE III

The Daisy Chain *begins 1847*
The Trial *begins 1859*

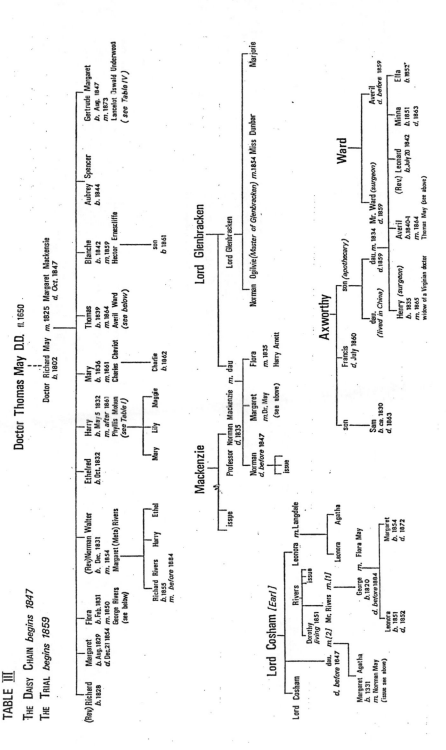

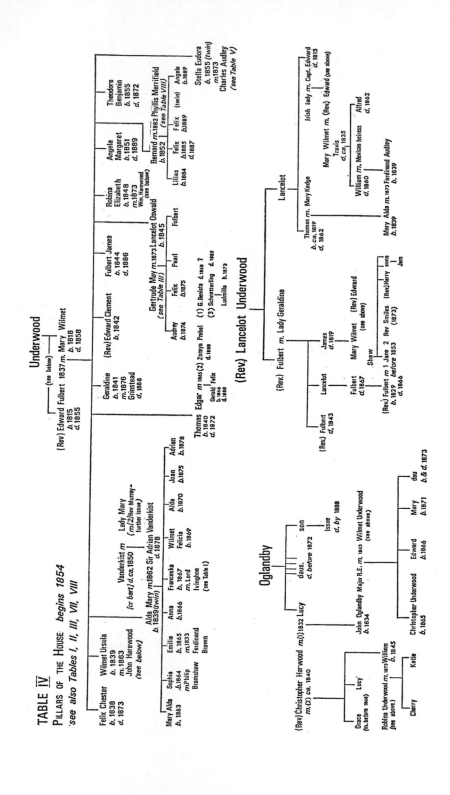

TABLE IV

PILLARS OF THE HOUSE: *begins* 1854

see also Tables I, II, III, VII, VIII

Underwood

Oglandby

(Rev.) Lancelot Underwood

TABLE V

THE CASTLE BUILDERS *begins 1849*

see also:

A LINK BETWEEN THE CASTLE BUILDERS
& PILLARS OF THE HOUSE

PILLARS OF THE HOUSE
BEECHCROFT AT ROCKSTONE
MODERN BROODS

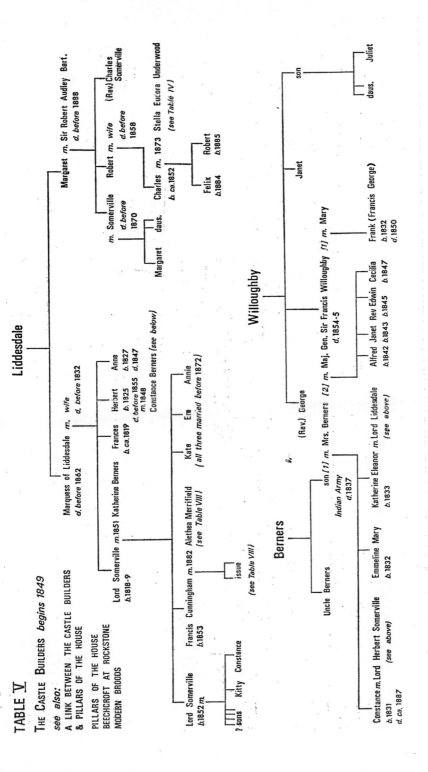

Liddesdale

Berners

Willoughby

TABLE VI

DYNEVOR TERRACE *begins 1847*

see also:

TWO SIDES OF THE SHIELD
BEECHCROFT AT ROCKSTONE

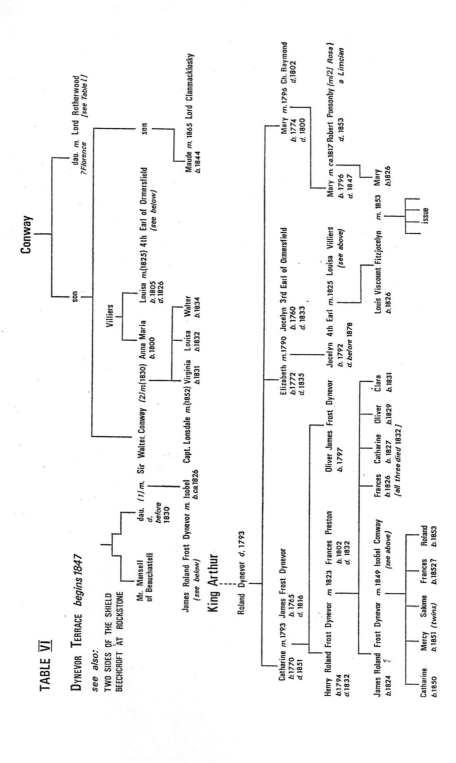

Conway

son

dau. *m.* Lord Rotherwood [*see Table I*]
?Florence

Villiers

son

Louisa *m.*(1825) 4th Earl of Ormersfield
*b.*1805
*d.*1826
(*see below*)

Maude *m.* 1865 Lord Clanmacklosky
*b.*1844

dau. (1) *m.* Sir Walter. Conway (2)/*m.*(1830) Anna Maria
d.
before
1830
*b.*1800

Mr. Mansell
of Beauchastell

Virginia
*b.*1831

Louisa
*b.*1832

Walter
*b.*1834

James Roland Frost Dynevor *m.* Isobel
(*see below*)   *b.ca.*1826

Capt. Lonsdale *m.*(1852)

King Arthur

Roland Dynevor *d.*1793

Elizabeth *m.*1790 Jocelyn 3rd Earl of Ormersfield
*b.*1772   *b.*1760
*d.*1835   *d.*1833

Mary *m.*1796 Ch. Raymond
*b.*1774   *b.*1802
*d.*1800

Mary *m.ca.*1817 Robert Ponsonby (*m.*/2) Rosa)
*b.*1796   *d.*1853   a Limcian
*d.*1847

Jocelyn 4th Earl *m.*1825 Louisa Villiers
*b.*1792   (*see above*)
d. before 1878

Louis Viscount Fitzjocelyn   Mary
*b.*1826   *b.*1826

                    m. 1853

                    issue

Catharine *m.*1793 James Frost Dynevor
*b.*1770   *b.*1765
*d.*1851   *d.*1816

Oliver James Frost Dynevor
*b.*1797

Frances   Catharine   Oliver   Ciara
*b.*1826   *b.*1827   *b.*1829   *b.*1831
                [*all three died 1832*]

Henry Roland Frost Dynevor *m.*1823 Frances Preston
*b.*1794   *b.*1802
*d.*1832   *d.*1832

James Roland Frost Dynevor *m.*1849 Isobel Conway
*b.*1824   (*see above*)

Catharine   Mercy   Salome   Frances   Roland
*b.*1850   *b.*1851 (*twins*)   *b.*1852?   *b.*1853

TABLE VII

COUNTESS KATE *begins 1858*

see also:

PILLARS OF THE HOUSE

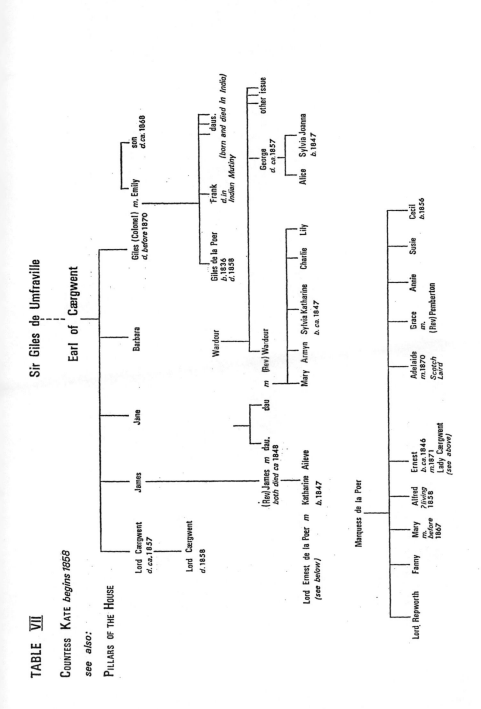

Sir Giles de Umfraville

Earl of Cargwent

Lord Cargwent
d. ca.1857

Lord Cargwent
d.1858

James

Jane

Barbara

Giles (Colonel) *m.* Emily
d. before 1870

son
d.ca. 1868

(Rev) James *m* dau.
both died ca 1848

dau

Wardour

Giles de la Poer
b.1836
d.1858

'Frank
d.in
Indian Mutiny

daus.
(born and died in India)

other issue

Katharine Alieve
b.1847

m (Rev) Wardour

George
d. ca.1857

Alice

Sylvia Joanna
b.1847

Lord Ernest de la Poer *m*
(see below)

Mary Armyn Sylvia Katharine
b. ca.1847

Charlie

Lily

Marquess de la Poer

Lord Repworth

Fanny

Mary
m.
before
1867

Alfred
?living
1858

Ernest
b.ca.1846
m.1871
Lady Cargwent
(see above)

Adelaide
m.1870
Scotch
Laird

Grace
m.
(Rev) Pemberton

Annie

Susie

Cecil
b.1856

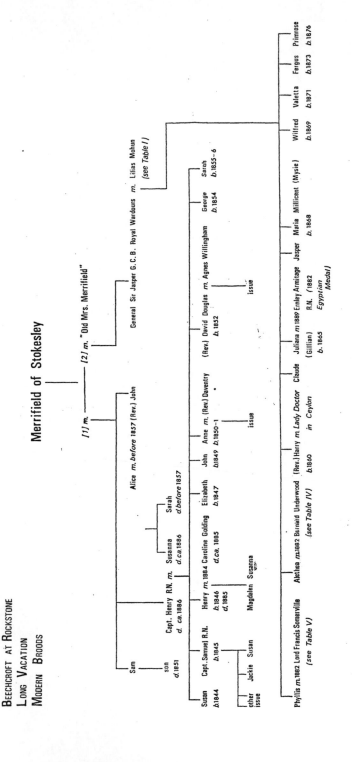

TABLE VIII

STOKESLEY SECRET *begins 1857*
TWO SIDES OF THE SHIELD
BEECHCROFT AT ROCKSTONE
LONG VACATION
MODERN BROODS

Merrifield of Stokesley

CORRECTIONS TO GENEALOGICAL TABLES I - VIII

Table I – Mohun

Eleanor Mohun married Francis Hawkesworth on 13 January 1845 and they had a son Henry (Harry) born later the same year.

William Mohun married Alethea Weston in September 1846, not 1845.

Lilias Mohun was born in 1829, not 1827. (But as Emily, Lilias and Jane are said to be eighteen, sixteen and fourteen in January 1845 they may in fact have been born respectively in 1826, 1828 and 1830 rather than in 1827, 1829 and 1831.)

Reginald and Maurice Devereux Mohun are shown the wrong way round; Maurice's age is not given in *Scenes and Characters*, but he seems to be the older of the two. In *The Two Sides of the Shield* Lilias says she is four years older than Maurice, which would make him born in 1833 (according to the table), whereas Reginald was born in 1834; in the same book, Maurice is specifically said to be the elder.

Dolores Mary Mohun, Maurice's daughter, was born in 1865.

TABLE I White

Maura was born in 1869, not 1369.

The children correctly shown as born in the 1850s and 1860s to Richard White and his 'Greek/Irish' wife are also attributed (incorrectly) to his brother James White and wife Adeline (née Mohun), to whom no children were born.

TABLE I – Prescott

Mr Prescott's first marriage to a Magdalen is included, but their daughter, also Magdalen, is omitted despite her playing an important role in the story of *Modern Broods*.

TABLE II – Mervyn

Great-uncle Mervyn's Christian name was Robert.

Juliana Fulmort (1827-1860) married Sir Bevil Acton in 1855. Their only child is shown as Juliana but was actually Elizabeth.

TABLE II – Charlecote

Humfrey Charlecote (disinherited) married late in life and had an only daughter, who married Major Randolf as his first wife. Major Randolf's second wife, an American lady, married as her second husband a merchant from Buffalo.

Humfrey Charlecote Randolf married Phoebe Fulmort in 1860, not 1862. His half-brother George was born in 1853.

Humfrey Charlecote, born 1800, died in 1840, not 1839. His sister Sarah (omitted from the table) married the Rev. — Savile, and died before 1838.

TABLE II – Sandbrook

Owen Charteris Sandbrook the elder married Edna Murrell on 14 July 1854. His younger sister was Mary Caroline.

Lucilla Sandbrook's husband, the Rev. Peter Prendergast, was born in 1815.

TABLE II – Charteris

Charles Charteris, M.P. had as wife Caroline — , who died in 1852.

Captain Christopher Charteris, R.N., died in 1859, not 1858.

TABLE III – May

Dr Richard May's third daughter (born in 1832) is shown as Ethelred. She was in fact called Etheldred (more often Ethel). Her mother's name, Margaret Mackenzie, should be spelled in that way, not as Mackensie.

Harry May was born on 5 May 1835, not 1832.

TABLE III – Lord Cosham

Margaret Agatha ('Meta') Rivers, who married Norman May in 1854, was born in 1831, not 1331.

TABLE IV – Underwood

Emilia Vanderkist (born in 1865) married Ferdinand Brown in 1883, not 1833.

Thomas Edgar Underwood (1840-1872) is shown as marrying Zoraya Prebel in 1865, after Giovanni Benista, her first husband, died. Marghanita Laski noted that it is *The Pillars of the House* that should establish Gerald: by its chronology, he was born between 1864 and 1866. According to *The Long Vacation* Benista died on 12 February 1868 and the marriage was in April 1868 – but Gerald was born in January 1868. There is thus an irresolvable discrepancy between the two books, which is not materially helped by emending Benista's death from 1868 to 1865. Gerald's legitimacy remains in doubt.

The daughters of Lance Underwood and Gertrude May, although referred to as Audrey (or Awdrey) and Pearl, were actually Etheldred and Margaret, and in both *The Long Vacation* and *Modern Broods* Pearl is the elder. Their younger brother is, in *Modern Broods*, called Richard (Dickie), not Fulbert.

There is no warrant for the name Felix for the second son (Angela's twin) born to Bernard and Phyllis Underwood.

TABLE IV – Oglandby

Harewood should be spelled in that way, with an 'e', not Harwood as in the entry for (Rev) Christopher.

TABLE IV – (Rev.) Lancelot Underwood

Ferdinand Audley Travis married Mary Alda ('Marilda') Underwood in 1873. He was later known as Ferdinand Travis Underwood and was knighted.

TABLE V – Liddesdale

Charles Audley married Stella Eudora Underwood in 1873, and their sons are, in *The Long Vacation*, named Robert (Robbie) and Theodore, not Felix and Robert.

TABLES VI & VII

No errors detected.

TABLE VIII – Merrifield of Stokesley

The two eldest daughters of General Sir Jasper Merrifield and his wife Lilias (née Mohun) have 'exchanged husbands' in this Table, although they are correctly shown in Table IV and Table V, respectively. The correct entries are as follows:

Phyllis Merrifield m. Bernard Underwood in 1882.
Alethea Merrifield m. Lord Francis Somerville in 1882.

THE DEPUTATION.

THE CASE FOR ANGLICANISM
IN CHARLOTTE YONGE'S
HISTORICAL FICTION

Maria Poggi Johnson

In the preface to *The Chaplet of Pearls*, a novel set during the Huguenot wars, Charlotte Yonge remarks,

> It is the fashion to call every story controversial that deals with times when controversy or a war of religion was raging; but it should be remembered that there are some which only attempt to portray human feelings.[1]

It would be foolish to foist on Charlotte Yonge a controversial agenda which she is at pains to disclaim. It would be equally foolish, however, in reading any of the novels, to forget that Charlotte Yonge, in her literary life no less than in other aspects, saw herself as a woman with a mission: 'an instrument for the popularisation of Church views.'[2] In the domestic novels the 'Church views' which she is concerned to popularise by rendering them lively and attractive to her readers are primarily those notions of virtue, propriety and duty which she learned from her father and from John Keble. To a considerable degree her works of historical fiction, of which there are more than twenty, share with the better-known (and, in fact, better in most senses) domestic novels, a focus on the moral development of her young protagonists who are often most persuasive when they seem most like young Victorians.[3] The same is true, for that matter, of her volumes of 'straight' history, which are largely written for the schoolroom. After briefly describing, for instance, the death of Charles I, hero-saint of the Tractarians, she focuses at considerably greater length on the fates of his children, exploring the circumstances in which they found themselves and how those circumstances combined with their characters to shape the moral development of each; a theme very similar to that which she explores in *The Daisy Chain* or *Hopes and Fears*, among others.[4]

There are other elements at play, however, in the historical novels. First of all there is Charlotte Yonge's passion for history: she wrote a considerable number of historical works, directed primarily towards a young audience, and her novels were often conceived around ideas or episodes she encountered in her reading and research, to the breadth of which the prefaces to the novels often give testimony. To give but two from many possible examples: *Unknown to History*, set during the captivity of Mary Stuart, was suggested by a hint about a lost daughter of Mary and Bothwell that captured Charlotte Yonge's imagination. *The Dove in the Eagle's Nest*, set in Germany in the years immediately before the Lutheran Reformation, stems from her personal attraction to the much maligned figure of Maximilian whose undeniable faults she found to be emphasised by historians at the expense of his virtues.

Although her sources and concerns are diverse, although her interest is primarily in her characters' emotional and moral development, and although she is right in disclaiming the term 'controversial,' it is still fair to say that there is a consistently didactic element running through, although not dominating, the historical novels. In these works the 'Church view' which Charlotte Yonge is particularly concerned to popularise is the Tractarian ecclesiology of the *via media*: the notion that the Church of England, in its doctrine and practice, represents a pure and authentic Catholic Christianity, a middle way between the excesses and corruptions of Romanism and the modernizing irreverence of Protestantism.

To this end the historical novels, for all their differences in initial inspiration, have two things in common. First of all her protagonists, as I said above, are young people coming to maturity. Secondly these protagonists are coming of age in turbulent times, marked by religious and other conflict. This conflict can be violent – the St Bartholomew's Day massacre, for instance, is the historical centrepiece of *The Chaplet of Pearls* – or primarily cultural and intellectual, but in all cases Charlotte Yonge guides her protagonists through competing religious options that are central to their moral formation. She seeks to delineate, and to steer her characters along, a *via media* between the extremes of Catholicism and Protestantism in periods where the two see each other as enemies. In the delineation of this middle road Charlotte Yonge is always concerned to introduce certain themes, either by narrative illustration or by editorial comment as best suits the context. Firstly she affirms the status of the historical Catholic Church as the true Church. Secondly she is critical of the corruptions, perversions and superstitions into which the Roman Church has lapsed. Thirdly she is convinced that the interiority and sincerity of Reformed theology is a rediscovery of the heart of the true faith of the Church. Lastly this reformation, although at bottom a re-discovery, is in its turn often perverted by disrespect and irreverence.

All of the novels are furnished with situations or comments which at least hint at these four ideas, and with a character or location which, to greater or lesser depth and with greater or lesser expertise, represents the middle path and upholds the virtues of each option while resisting the corresponding dangers. In *The Chaplet of Pearls*, for instance, the *via media* finds a home with the Walwyn family, friends to the family of the late Thomas More. Hurst Walwyn provides a home to Cicely St. John, a nun until the dispersion of her convent, who continues to keep the Benedictine rule, and who fancies herself 'firm to old Romsey doctrine'. At the same time Cicely delights 'in the use of the vernacular prayers and Scripture', and when summoned by Mary as a consultant on the reestablishment of her order, her views are found to have sufficiently altered as to render her safer at home than at court. Hurst Walwyn offers a home also to the stern but admirable Baron de Ribaumont, a French convert to the faith of the Huguenots, who is delighted to raise his son Berenger in England, although 'not indeed among such strict Puritans as he preferred, but at least where the pure faith could be openly avowed without danger.'[5] Raised as a bluff frank Englishman in an atmosphere which embraces the reverence of the ancient faith and the fervour of the new while rejecting the excesses of both, Berenger is able to rescue his child-bride, the convent-raised Eustacie, from the degeneracy and violence of France. While he is being held captive by the forces of Guise, an old priest is summoned to attempt his conversion. Berenger, 'bred up [. . .] in doctrines that, as he had received them, savoured as little of Calvinism as of Romanism'[6] finds the *via media* sure proof against the pressure. The priest 'at first thought the day his own,' we hear, 'when he found that almost all his arguments against Calvinism were equally impressed upon Berenger's mind,' but he finds himself increasingly ill-equipped for the task: 'He knew nothing of controversy save that ad-apted to the doctrines of Calvin; so that in dealing with an Anglican of the school of Ridley and Hooker, it was like bow and arrow against sword.'[7]

Curiously, one of Charlotte Yonge's most explicit descriptions of the *via media* occurs in *The Dove in the Eagle's Nest*, although the novel is set largely in the years before Luther challenged the Roman *status quo*. The plot concerns the coming together of the old, proud, violent world of feudal Germany and the new, sedate world of the German burghers who will form the basis of the Protestant revolution. When these worlds are united in the marriage of the burgher maid Christina Sorel and the robber baron Eberhard von Adlerstein, they bring forth the twins Ebbo and Friedmund, nobility for a new age, who are ready to embrace the best of the new teaching, while maintaining their ancestral virtues. When the storm of the reformation does break Ebbo's mixed lineage and moral education enables him to resist the polarising forces that tear apart the religious world of Germany. 'Into schism I will *not* be drawn,' he assures his mother. 'I have held truth all my life in the Church, nor will I part from her now!' At the same time he and his mother have this to say to those who accuse him of bearing the taint of the new doctrine:

> 'New? Nay, it is the oldest of all doctrine.'

> '[. . .] As I ever said, Dr Luther hath been setting forth in greater clearness and fulness what our blessed Friedel and I learnt at your knee, and my young ones have learnt from babyhood of the true Catholic doctrine.'[8]

If *The Dove in the Eagle's Nest* is notable for its explicit treatment of the parameters of the *via media*, equally notable for its subtlety and complexity is a lesser-known work which focuses in some depth on religious issues, and which concerns itself specifically with the origins and authenticity of the Church of England. Charlotte Yonge described *The Armourer's Prentices* modestly as an attempt 'to sketch civilian life in the early Tudor days'.[9] At first glance indeed it is little more than that: a well-informed and colourful, but second-rate, historical romance. If we read it with Charlotte Yonge's apologetic purposes in mind, however, we will find at the heart of the novel an ambitious, elaborate, and imaginative apology for the *via media*.

This apology is three-pronged. To survive the turmoil of the Reformation, the Church in England needed first to define itself as an historical body: Charlotte Yonge ascribes to Henry VIII, in the early years of his reign, the skills and virtues necessary to create a safe middle path through the delicate terrain of national and international statesmanship. The Church needs also to define itself as a religious body: she adopts the figure of John Colet to act as a mouthpiece for her theological and ecclesiological views. Finally, and most interestingly, the political and religious conflicts of the Reformation had their roots in deep and complex tensions about meaning and value which shaped all of society, and which could not be resolved by any historical individual. To represent the stabilising power and primitive authenticity of the via media, therefore, Charlotte Yonge creates the *morisco* swordsmith Miguel Abenali, whose personal history transcends destructive class, guild and national interests and whose race links him to the earliest roots of Christianity.

Charlotte Yonge was well aware that to situate an apology for the Church of England in the reign of Henry VIII, as she does in *The Armourer's Prentices*, was an exceedingly bold move. The circumstances of the Church's birth were the greatest liability to the Tractarian claims for her legitimacy; the Oxford Movement, indeed, was born in part out of concern for the effects of the Erastian settlement on the Church in an increasingly secular society,[10] and the Tractarian apology for Anglicanism typically concentrated on the great seventeenth-century divines of her 'Golden Age'. Charlotte Yonge, for the most part, prudently avoids the struggles of the 1530s and sets the bulk of her narrative between 1515 and 1517. Thus she can portray the religious and cultural forces from which the Anglican *via media* would eventually emerge without having to confront the painful and compromised process of that emergence. Her choice of the century's second decade allows her to paint a more appealing portrait of the Church of England's first Supreme Head than a later date would have allowed. By concentrating on the attractive figure of the gallant young king in the early years of his reign, before Katharine's failure to provide a son had become a problem, and by largely ignoring the events of the thirties and forties, she avoids having to choose between the image of Henry VIII as the 'plaything of factions' in the religious struggles of the Reformation and that of the older Henry as a corpulent tyrant executing a phalanx of wives and advisors with gay abandon.

Henry VIII is introduced in the aftermath of the protectionist riots of Evil May Day 1517, in which English tradesmen and apprentices attacked foreign tradesmen working in London. The king's response to the violence demonstrates those virtues of government proper to a political *via media*. He acknowledges the need to maintain the integrity of the English court in European politics. 'The King,' he declares publicly, 'being in amity with all Christian princes, it was high treason to break the truce and league by attacking their subjects resident in England. The terrible punishment of the traitor would thus be the doom of all concerned.'[11] In the interests of international relations King Henry administers the sternest justice; over one hundred apprentices are sentenced to hang. But in the interests of domestic harmony, he also represents and administers mercy. He orchestrates a huge public spectacle in which the mothers, sisters, and sweethearts of the condemned apprentices plead tearfully for clemency, and the king relents and pardons the boys.[12] Henry's response to the riot is a skilful middle road through a delicate crisis: he satisfies the demands of both justice and mercy, and the exigencies of both foreign and domestic politics. Although the Anglican communion is undeniably the offspring of political strategy, Charlotte Yonge seems to be suggesting, it is nonetheless the child of a wise and honourable strategist, capable of forging a path for his people through the multifarious demands of a complex situation.

Charlotte Yonge also provides a trustworthy spiritual and moral guide for the infant Church in the person of John Colet, Dean of St Paul's. The gentle, learned and saintly Dean Colet, like all good clergymen in Charlotte Yonge's novels, is essentially a mouthpiece for the Tractarian position, and a portrait of her mentor, the gentle, learned and saintly John Keble. Colet first appears ascending the pulpit of St Paul's. Ambrose, the more reflective, pious, and sensitive of the novel's two young protagonists, hears his sermon and is captivated by Colet's psychological insight and by the challenging demands which he makes of his congregation. 'Sinfulness stood before him,' Charlotte Yonge tells us, 'not as the liability to penalty for transgressing an arbitrary rule, but as a taint to the entire being, mastering the will, perverting the senses, forging fetters out of habit'.[13] The sermon is a turning point for Ambrose, who seeks more such soul-stirring teaching in the Lollard subculture of London. He soon finds himself painfully torn between his attraction to the new teaching and his deep loyalty to the Catholic system in which he had been educated but which his new friends were bent on undermining. 'He was wretched under the continual tossings of his mind', Charlotte Yonge writes:

> Was the entire existing system a vast delusion, blinding the eyes and destroying the souls of those who trusted to it; and was the only safety in the one point of faith that Luther pressed on all, and ought all that he had hitherto revered to crumble down to let that alone be upheld? Whatever he had once loved and honoured at times seemed to him a lie, while at others real affection and veneration, and dread of sacrilege, made him shudder at himself and his own doubts![14]

Ambrose takes his perplexity to Colet as many young Victorians, including Charlotte Yonge herself, would come to Keble with their anxieties about the validity of their faith and communion.[15] Colet directs him to the safe middle path, warning him both against the corruptions of the Roman system and against the destructive passions of the dissenters. He welcomes the work of the reformers as 'an outpouring of cleansing and renewing power' to return the Church to its true vocation. Yet Colet's faith in the care of Providence for the Church is tempered by a sorrowful realism about the complexities of human life and religion. 'Whatever is entrusted to man will become stained, soiled and twisted,' he warns Ambrose, and predicts 'some great and terrible rending and upheaving that may even split the Church as it were asunder.'[16] He counsels the boy to seek salvation through faith in Christ, but to seek it within the confines of the Church, which, although tainted by human error, is nonetheless the place appointed by God for the union of human souls with Christ.

Colet's advice echoes that which Keble offered to troubled souls. Keble insisted that the path of duty was to be found by 'only the simple principle, "*quieta non movere*: where a man is, let him abide with God."'[17] The Church of England, for all its faults, was where God had placed him and therefore the Church of England was where God intended him to remain. Colet acts and advises on the same principle of personal dutifulness: his final words to Ambrose are that 'our Mother-Church is God's own Church and I will abide with her to the end, as the means of oneness with my Lord and Head, and do thou the same, my son'.[18]

The third prong of Charlotte Yonge's apology for Anglicanism is by far the most interesting and sophisticated, involving as it does the startlingly contemporary insight that a new religious way cannot be forged merely by political or theological compromise, but must navigate also cultural allegiances and economic interests and must ultimately take into account the ways in which religious meaning is grasped and communicated: as we shall see this last is the issue at the heart of the conflict between Catholic and Protestant to which Anglicanism proposes a middle way. Charlotte Yonge takes as the setting for this third element neither court nor cathedral, but two places of trade, each 'a little world in itself',[19] twin microcosms that echo the concerns of the great worlds of Reformation Europe. Dragon Court, workshop of the armourer Giles Headley, represents the old order of Catholicism, while the new world of Protestantism finds a home in Warwick Court, where the Dutch printer Lucas lives and works. The transactions between the two locations demonstrate that matters more momentous than political order, and more delicate even than doctrine, are at stake in the English Reformation and the birth of the new church.

The armourer's work of production and ornamentation largely serves the extravagant world of pageantry, the 'ostentatiously ritual-ized displays' for which Henry's court was famed.[20] The artifacts produced at Dragon Court function primarily as tokens in the grammar of object and ornament by which means the English nobility and the royal courts of Europe negotiate and stabilise relations of power and precedence. To the denizens of Dragon Court objects also provide an iconic language by which they interpret the invisible world. Their relationship to the sacred is mediated through images, relics, holy water, *ex voto* offerings and the like. When Headley is rescued from attack by a dog, his immediate reaction, to 'vow to St. Julian a hound of solid bronze a foot in length, with a collar of silver, to his shrine in St. Faith's, in token of my deliverance in body and goods',[21] shows how intimately the sacred and the material are linked in his mind.

Even as the Church physically encloses the symbols that order the spiritual worlds of her subjects, so also does she reduce words to tokens in spiritual transactions that operate on the model of commercial transactions. Charlotte Yonge presents it as part of the pastoral practice of the Church to alienate the laity from language by reducing speech to performance, words to tokens, and significance to value. The typical sermon of the day, she tells us, is a vigorous practical affair, offering its hearers,

> the consolation of hearing that a daily 'Hail Mary,' persevered in through the foulest life, would obtain that beams should be arrested in their fall, ships fail to sink, cords to hang, till such confession had been made as should insure ultimate salvation, after such a proportion of the flames of purgatory as masses and prayers might not mitigate.[22]

In sharp contrast to this robustly material religion, Warwick Court, where Ambrose finds a place after Colet's sermon awakens him to the interiority of religious experience, represents a Protestant world of text and word. The young industry of printing exists outside of the guild system, and Ambrose encounters a constant traffic of European scholars and printers who occupy a socially marginal space with regard to the structures of economic power which shape life in the city. This social fluidity is mirrored by an intellectual and hermeneutic fluidity. The reformers react against the Catholic alienation of words from their meanings and against the conversion of religious language into a currency of act and object impervious to the activity of the individual mind. Through their work as translators and editors of the sacred text, they reappropriate the spoken and written word as the bearer of religious meaning, and make it available to the comprehension, interpretation and manipulation of the individual subject, removing even the barriers which language itself throws up to the understanding.

By her analysis of the different forms of inner life and religious awareness in Dragon Court and Warwick Court, Charlotte Yonge portrays the Reformation as a struggle between systems of meaning. The Church in England is faced not merely with an historical conflict of belief which has the potential to be mediated, resolved, or finally won by one party or another. At stake also is the confrontation between two symbolic worlds which are not so much incompatible as incommensurable; no effective communication between them is possible. This incommensurability is thrown into sharp relief when Ambrose, under the guidance of the dour Protestant Tibble, joins a crowd gathering at St Paul's.

'Is there a procession today? or a relic to be displayed?' asked Ambrose, trying to recollect whose feast-day it might be.

Tibble screwed up his mouth in an extraordinary smile as he said 'Relic, quotha? yea, the soothest relic there be of the Lord and Master of us all.'

'Methought the true Cross was always displayed on the High Altar,' said Ambrose, as all turned to a side aisle [. . .]

'Rather say hidden,' muttered Tibble. 'Thou shalt have it displayed, young sir, but neither in wood nor gilded shrine. See, here he comes who setteth it forth.'[23]

'The soothest relic [. . .] of the Lord and Master of us all' is not a fragment of the physical cross but the Bible, with its message of atonement, and 'he who setteth it forth' the preacher, Colet. The incongruity between Catholic and Protestant worlds which Tibble's dry punning exploits is again revealed when Ambrose's cheerful and unreflective brother Stephen, happily apprenticed at Dragon Court, visits him in his new home. But when he finds Ambrose reading a scroll 'covered with characters such as belonged to no alphabet that he had ever dreamt of',[24] Stephen drags his brother into a nearby Church and drenches him with holy water, terrified that he is bewitched and instinctively seeking material protection from the threatening power of the written word.

The political crises of the Reformation can be solved by a skilful and noble statesman. Doctrinal and ecclesiological conflicts eventually can be resolved by wise and faithful divines in the model of Colet. But this problem of incommensurability between Protestant and Catholic worlds, which provides Charlotte Yonge with the greatest challenge to her apology for the Anglican way, is beyond the reach of any individual. She wisely does not try to provide an historical figure capable of bringing resolution at this level of the novel. Instead she offers an emblem of hope in the person of the *morisco* swordsmith Miguel Abenali, the third prong of her case for the *via media* and, as its representative, a figure considerably more intriguing, subtle and pro-found than either Henry or Colet.

Abenali is important to Charlotte Yonge's apologetic purpose not because of his personal virtues or activities, but because of his history, which Charlotte Yonge recounts in considerable detail.[25] Born to a family of wealthy Saracen Muslims in southern Spain he was baptised as a young man during the conquest of Granada, so that his family would be allowed to retain their property. By the time he reached maturity Abenali's Christianity, initially the insincere product of economic self-interest, had taken root in his heart through his reading of a vernacular translation of the Scriptures. Although he comes wholeheartedly to share the faith of the conquerors Abenali remains in some ways culturally distinct from the Catholic society around him. 'The inbred abhorrence of idolatry had influenced his manner of worship' Charlotte Yonge tells us,

> and when [. . .] the Inquisition had begun to take cognisance of new Christians from among the Moors as well as the Jews, there were not lacking spies to report the absence of all sacred images or symbols from the house of the wealthy merchant, and that neither he nor any of his family had been seen kneeling before the shrine of Nuestra Señora.[26]

As the Spanish distrust of the 'Nuevos Christianos' deepens into severe persecution, Abenali's only recourse is to flee the country. 'Having known the true Christ in the Gospel, he could not turn back to Mohammed,' we learn, 'even though Christians persecuted in the Name they so little understood.'[27] Thus, rather than returning to Muslim territory, Abenali settles in London. He is an armourer of extraordinary, mystifying skill, whom the local armourers are forced sometimes to consult 'though unwillingly, for he was looked on with distrust and dislike as an interloper of foreign birth, belonging to no guild'.[28] He lives and practises his craft in Warwick Court, where the atmosphere is tolerant of foreigners and their strange ways, and where his continued 'abstinence from all cult of saints or images',[29] his devotion to the Bible, and the persecution he had suffered at the hands of the Catholic establishment earns him the respect of Lucas' circle. Abenali, however, does not 'join in their general opinions', and holds aloof from those secret conferences at the workshop, so disturbing to Ambrose, where reformation texts and ideas are disseminated by visitors from Holland or Germany.

Abenali thus occupies a unique social space amid the conventional physical, economic and religious boundaries that separate the worlds of the novel; he has dealings in both Dragon Court and Warwick Court, but is fully at home neither among the hearty English Catholics nor among the fervid international Protestants. He deals with both object and word, but his religious life is determined by neither. His notable skill as an armourer, his love and knowledge of scripture, and his detachment from the local interests and obsessions of both worlds make Abenali uniquely able to mediate and cement relationships between Dragon Court and Warwick Court, and to offer a way through the conflicts threatening society and faith in England. The depth and complexity of his personal history affords him the moral and spiritual weight to be an anchor in an unstable world, tossed in the currents of history. Abenali's faith, poised between the excesses of Catholic brutality and superstition and Reformation irreverence and iconoclasm, is at once the most mature and stable of the novel, and a earnest of the coming *via media*.

In appointing a converted Muslim to stand as a representative of the Anglican way, Charlotte Yonge is also making a characteristically Tractarian claim about Anglicanism. A central part of the Tractarian apology for their Church was 'the note of antiquity' – the continuity of Anglican beliefs and practices with the purity of the apostolic faith from which, they claimed, both the Protestant Reformation and the Roman Church had diverged. Abenali's Middle Eastern ancestry reflects the importance that the Tractarians attached to antiquity. His spiritual home is not in the revolutionary turmoil of Reformation Europe, and his mistrust of religious images has more ancient roots than the iconoclastic spirit of Protestantism. Charlotte Yonge indulges herself in her portrait of the swordsmith: his flowing robes and beard and his elaborately courteous sentences are redolent of the exotic mysteries of the East as the spinster from Hampshire imagined them. But there is a deeper purpose than glamour to Abenali's origins. The 'inbred abhorrence of idolatry' which marks him as a Muslim has its roots in the Semitic culture that Islam shares with Judaism, and which Charlotte Yonge is at pains to draw out in her treatment of Abenali. She describes him repeatedly as 'patriarchal', and compares his figure as he sits in a doorway of Warwick Court to that of Abraham in his tent.

Thus, just as Abenali's ancestral connection to the ancient Semitic roots of Christianity secures the purity of his faith, so by implication are the roots of Anglicanism in apostolic and patristic theology and worship a guarantee of its stability and purity. These are roots deep enough to establish and steady the Church amidst the storms of violence and folly that rage through human history. The initial conversion of the young Abenali, like the birth of the Church of England, is motivated by a cynical expedience, and a self-serving compromise with political power. His life, like that of the Church, is darkened by the bigotry and cruelty of ignorant fanatics. Yet amid all the turbulence of a world in transition he, like the Church, is nourished and sustained by the most ancient springs of divine revelation.

Neither Charlotte Yonge, of course, nor the High Church party, was alone in seeing history as providing resources for their personal agendas. In an era which tended all too easily to see itself as having reached the apex of history it was only natural for writers to turn to the past for material to support their own interpretations of the present: Victorians of all shades of opinion did so, and in part as a result of the influence of Scott, did so often in the form of novels, many of which are far more deserving of the label 'controversial' than are Charlotte Yonge's romantic moral tales. Charles Reade's *The Cloister and the Hearth* is perhaps the best known example. Thinkers as prominent as Newman and Kingsley found the genre of historical fiction a useful place to engage in combative exchange about the mission of the contemporary Church.[30] All of these authors and others were confident that they could read and correctly interpret both the lessons of history and the signs of the present times.

Charlotte Yonge is wisely more cautious. She is certain only of the reliability of the dutiful conscience as a guide through the uncertainties of history. The truly dutiful conscience, wherever and whenever it finds itself, will respond to the complex conflicts of its world by finding a middle path. In the final scene of *The Dove in the Eagle's Nest* Ebbo, son of the Freiherr and the burgher maid, laments that obedience to his sense of right and wrong has landed him between the contrasting moods of the moment, and thus out of favour with all parties. The Emperor, he tells his mother,

> 'never forgave me for shaking hands with Luther at the Diet of Worms. I know it was all over with my court favour after I had joined in escorting the Doctor out of the city. And the next thing was that Georg of Freundsburg and his friends proclaimed me a bigoted Papist because I did my utmost to keep my troop out of the devil's holiday with the sack of Rome! It has ever been my lot to be in disgrace with one side or the other!'[31]

Christina reassures him:

> 'I doubt me whether it be ever easy to see the veritably right course while still struggling in the midst. That is for after ages, which behold things afar off; but each man must needs follow his own principle in an honest and good heart, and assuredly God will guide him to work out some good end, or hinder some evil one.'[32]

The final word on the Reformation goes, as do most great issues in Charlotte Yonge's fiction, to a virtuous parent. Equally characteristically, that final word is an exhortation to resignation and perseverance in virtue despite all manner of hardship and sacrifice. Resignation and perseverance, virtues central to the moral system which Charlotte Yonge learned from Keble, stem from a profound trust in the divine providence that orders both individual human paths and the broad movements of history. These virtues are the root and the flower of the *via media*, its historical and divine sanctions.

The author and the editors of the present volume thank the Editorial Board of *Clio: A Journal of Literature, History and the Philosophy of History* for permission to reprint this article, which first appeared as 'The King, the Priest and the Armorer: A Victorian Historical Fantasy of the *Via Media*', in *Clio* 28.4 (1999) pp. 399-413.

---

1   C. M. Yonge, *The Chaplet of Pearls*, 1868 (London: Macmillan, 1894) p. vii.

2   Quoted in Georgina Battiscombe, *Charlotte Mary Yonge: The Story of an Uneventful Life* (London: Constable, 1943) p. 14.

3   For a survey of Charlotte Yonge's historical fiction, see Alice Fairfax-Lucy, 'The Other Miss Yonge', in *A Chaplet for Charlotte Yonge*, ed. Georgina Battiscombe and Marghanita Laski (London: Cresset Press, 1965) pp. 90-97.

4   C. M. Yonge, *Young Folks' History of England*, 1873 (Boston: Estes and Lauriat, 1879) pp. 282-87.

5   *Chaplet of Pearls*, p. 12.

6   *Chaplet of Pearls*, p. 360.

7   *Chaplet of Pearls*, p. 241.

8   C. M. Yonge, *The Dove in the Eagle's Nest*, 1866 (London: Macmillan, 1912) pp. 285-86.

9   C. M. Yonge, *The Armourer's Prentices*, 1884 (London: Macmillan, 1889) p. vii.

10   The traditional date for the beginning of the Movement is John Keble's 1833 Assize Sermon on 'National Apostasy,' in which he decries the recent parliamentary decision to suppress ten Irish Bishoprics as an 'unquestionable symptom of enmity' to Christ and the Church. See John Keble, *Sermons Academical and Occasional* (Oxford: John Henry Parker, 1847) p. 136.

11   *Armourer's Prentices*, p. 216.

12   Charlotte Yonge takes her account of Evil May Day and its aftermath largely from Hall's *Chronicle*, although she adapts the latter episode to give the Queen and the women of London an importance which they do not have in Hall's account. Her motivation may have been that, in this manner, she could at least hint at what Hall discusses thoroughly elsewhere, namely, Henry's genuine devotion to his first wife. For a recent account, see Susan Brigden, *London and the Reformation* (Oxford: Clarendon Press, 1989), pp. 129-132.

13   *Armourer's Prentices*, pp. 71-72.

14   *Armourer's Prentices*, pp. 190-91.

15   See Georgina Battiscombe, *John Keble: A Study in Limitations* (New York: Knopf, 1963) p. 246.

16   *Armourer's Prentices*, pp. 241-42.

17   Keble, *Sermons Academical*, p. xvii.

18   *Armourer's Prentices*, p. 242.

19   *Armourer's Prentices*, p. 59.

20   Simon Schama, 'Heavy Metal,' *New Yorker*, 21 December 1998, p. 92.

21   *Armourer's Prentices*, p. 42.

22   *Armourer's Prentices*, p. 71.

23   *Armourer's Prentices*, p. 70.

24   *Armourer's Prentices*, p. 135.

25   Charlotte Yonge acknowledged that since the time of Scott, who claimed freedom of the 'Muse of the historical romance [. . .] to bend time and place to her purpose', the historical novel has become 'the meek handmaid of Clio, creeping obediently in the track of the greater Muse, and never venturing on more than colouring and working up the grand outlines that her mistress has left undefined'. (C. M. Yonge, *Stray Pearls*, 1883 [London, Macmillan, 1909], p. v.) In view of this, albeit grudging, sense of duty to the facts of history, the importance which she attached to Abenali's religious history is demonstrated, ironically, by the fact that she is willing to manipulate the chronology of the period to align the events of his life with the early years of Henry's reign: while the dating of Abenali's conversion is plausible, the serious persecution of the *moriscos* in Granada did not occur until after the time of the novel, and

the 'gallant and desperate warfare' between Muslims and Christians in the Alpuxarra mountains to which she alludes took place in the 1560s.

26　*Armourer's Prentices*, p. 138. Charlotte Yonge, an enthusiastic supporter of Victorian missionary work, has this to say elsewhere about the missionary tactics of the Church after the reconquest of Spain: 'Christianity, as popularly understood in the Spain of the fifteenth century was in the form most repellent to a Muslim, especially to a philosophical and scientific one. The essential points of Christianity are startling enough to a mind trained to the brief Moslem creed, and when to these were added a passionate adoration of the Blessed Virgin and the Saints, the teaching seemed to the Moors degrading in itself as well as hateful because coming from the conquerors. In old times the Mozarabic liturgy and the free use of the Scriptures had made conversion far less difficult than since the strictest uniformity with Rome had been enforced, and with more ardour in consequence of the distant echoes of the Reformation in Germany.' C. M. Yonge, *The Story of the Christians and Moors of Spain*, (London: Macmillan, 1879), p. 295.

27　*Armourer's Prentices*, p. 139.

28　*Armourer's Prentices*, p. 140. On the superiority of Spanish to English arms at this period, and the dependence of English armourers on the expertise of foreign craftsmen, see Charles ffoulkes, *The Armourer and his Craft* (London: Benjamin Blom, 1912), pp. 121-23.

29　*Armourer's Prentices*, p. 191.

30　John Henry Newman's *Callista* (1855) and Charles Kingsley's *Hypatia* (1853) anticipate some of the issues that resurface in the two authors' much more famous public clash in 1864.

31　*Dove in the Eagle's Nest*, p. 407 (= Macmillan ed., pp. 289-90).

32　*Dove in the Eagle's Nest*, p. 408 (= Macmillan ed., p. 290).

CHARLOTTE YONGE AND THE CLASSICS

Clemence Schultze

One hundred and fifty years ago, Charlotte Yonge was in her prime; and classical learning was taken for granted as the basis of education and the touchstone of culture. Its dominance in the formation of the elite had a spin-off effect upon non-elite groups within society: classics was both foundational and aspirational. By the time of Yonge's death in 1901, this classical predominance had come to feel the shock of sustained challenge as other disciplines asserted themselves and different values began to prevail.[1] While Yonge was not entirely unaware of this development, her works throughout largely reflect traditional assumptions about the curriculum. Both her own non-fiction writings and also the abundant material drawn from the magazine for girls which she edited, *The Monthly Packet*, tend to bear out the view that classics was assumed as a foundation and constituted (especially for marginal groups) an aspiration. In her contemporary fiction, by contrast, it is striking to see how that which is taken for granted can also be problematised; and how the assumed and shared background of classical culture can foreground conflict and ambiguity.

In order to demonstrate the all-pervasiveness of classical culture in Yonge's own milieu, I begin by examining her own education, and the advice and assumptions expressed in *The Monthly Packet*. These amply illustrate the extent to which the language of classics (if not necessarily always the actual Greek and Latin tongues themselves) formed the stuff of learning for girls as well as for boys. A brief look at her non-fiction confirms that she envisaged classical material at an appropriate level as being available to all age groups and classes. Then with reference to that small subsection of her fiction which has a classical theme, I discuss how Yonge exploits myth and history to address at one remove religious issues which might otherwise be too sensitive to handle. Finally, the allusions to classical learning in the novels with a contemporary setting reveal that while the classics sometimes represent a source of enjoyment and pleasure, they are much more often employed as the setting for potentially perilous competition and emulation, and as such, stand as an aspect of experience which must be regulated or even forsworn. In this sense, they constitute a touchstone of right behaviour in a way which goes far beyond a mere acceptance of classical culture as a badge of belonging, a marker of class or gender.

CLASSICAL EDUCATION FOR GIRLS: REALITIES AND RECOMMENDATIONS[2]

Charlotte Yonge imbibed classical history and mythology from an early age. At almost seven years old she suggested the names 'Alexander Xenophon' for her new-born brother;[3] about four years later she was evidently well acquainted with the main myths:

> I remember the first evening [Warden Barter of Winchester College] dined with us his talking to me about Flaxman's designs to Potter's *Aeschylus*, and telling me that Clytemnestra was a wicked woman who killed her husband, while I felt preternaturally virtuous for not saying I knew it already. (Was this a more elaborate form of conceit?)[4]

Both the cleverness and the scruples seem entirely characteristic. Yonge's education took place at home and was conducted almost entirely by her parents: her father undertook mathematics, Latin and Greek. Yonge began Latin when she was eleven, and consolidated it by helping her five-year-old brother;[5] Greek followed in due course. William Yonge's competence to teach was founded on the conventional classical education he had enjoyed at Eton before leaving school early to enter the army. Thus, as she puts it, she had acquired by the age of twenty 'such Greek [. . .] as had furnished forth the Etonian and soldier of sixteen'.[6] Her father, who demanded absolute rigour in the foundations of mathematics, no doubt applied the same standards to languages. Yonge will have been thoroughly grounded in grammar and syntax, and was doubtless able to cope with a fair range of ancient texts, as well as to read the New Testament and Septuagint in Greek.

Yonge's *Womankind* gives a good notion of girls' classical education at home a generation later.[7] After a brief outline of 'the *lowest* standard for a lady' – which includes French and 'history enough not to confound Romans with Greeks' (p. 39) – Yonge proceeds to develop a somewhat more demanding programme, which presumably cannot have been too untypical. A girl's first foreign language will be French, but the second should be Latin rather than German, because it is the key to so much beyond itself; at least the minimum of Greek which allows the looking up of words in the dictionary is desirable too (p. 41); both languages 'may be studied more effectually after eighteen' (p. 84). Classical mythology begins with simple retellings for young children, then proceeds to Homer and Greek tragedies, read in translation; Virgil's *Aeneid* should be read in Latin (p. 48; cf. p. 71). Classical history (which is regarded as almost as essential as English) is to be covered systematically from the age of seven or eight (pp. 46-48). Yonge also envisages that it may well be mothers who start small boys upon their Latin (p. 30).

The chapters collected into the book *Womankind* had already appeared as papers in *The Monthly Packet* between 1874 and 1877. Other articles in the magazine, and such items as the Editor's 'Hints on Reading' and 'Conversations on Books', as well as the competitions, fill out *Womankind's* general principles of education with detailed particulars of actual implementation. Self-education for older girls is regarded as very desirable,[8] and it is plain that it was not extraordinary for such education to encompass the Greek and Latin languages, and certainly ancient history, classical authors (possibly studied in translation rather than in the original), and classical mythology. From the 1870s, there is also an increasing awareness that a number of the readers of *The Monthly Packet* are addressing themselves to organised study under the Local Examinations system.

To take the languages first: the most remarkable instance comes in an anonymous series entitled 'Polyglott [*sic*] Parsing'.[9]. This is a sustained course of instruction in comparative philology, couched as holiday conversations in the schoolroom among the boys and girls of a family. They are represented as having between them a command of Greek, Latin, Italian, Spanish, French and German, and a shared interest in language structure and the interrelationship of the Indo-

European family, termed 'the Aryan Languages'. The aspects covered include articles, cases, the verb 'to be', and declensions; every topic is based upon a sentence from one of the New Testament Epistles – with the proviso that the treatment will involve no irreverence.[10] The text is given in Greek but is also transliterated in a footnote; translations into the other languages follow. The participants discuss such matters as phonetic changes, morphology, and the syntactical differences between the various tongues. The didactic aim is obvious enough, but the questioning and explanation is done in a lively manner, and nothing in the handling suggests that acquaintance with such a range of languages is inherently improbable for schoolroom girls in their teens.

An important benefit of learning Greek was the access it permitted to the New Testament in the original. A. M. W. devoted three articles to 'The Greek Testament for Ladies', and offered very sensible advice about choice of texts and grammars.[11] The assumption is that some teaching will probably be available, but also that a good deal may be done by those working on their own. There will be a considerable amount of rote learning until the inflections are thoroughly familiar, and grammatical rigour is enjoined as the basis of a really sound understanding. Other classical topics relate to Christianity and its cultural background in the Graeco-Roman world without demanding linguistic knowledge. The Revd Peter Lilly contributed several articles on 'Greek Forerunners of Christ', which covered Socrates, Alexander and the Successors, the Septuagint, and Philo of Alexandria.[12] An article on 'My First Greek Book', by P., discusses the so-called *Tabula* (i.e. *Picture*) of Cebes.[13] While the title appears to imply that it was read in Greek, this is not explicitly discussed in the text; the chief interest is in applying to Cebes the recommendation of Lactantius (*Divine Institutions* 8.7) that classical philosophers be read in such a way as to extract Christian truths.

In one notable instance we glimpse the interaction, on a classical topic, of author with adviser: Yonge and Keble. Keble sends some comments on one of the 'Conversations on the Catechism', advising a small revision to sharpen up a contrast Yonge wished to draw between natural religion and religion as a principle of action. She has included a passage from Aeschylus (given in translation) to illustrate how the Greeks had attained to a belief in a moral God. By way of afterthought, Keble adds:

It occurred to me whether, when the ladies quote Greek, they had better not say they have heard their fathers and brothers say things.[14]

As published, the Aeschylean quotation is obediently introduced thus (the speaker is one of the girls participating in the conversation):

'I see now what papa meant when he made me learn some lines from a translation of Aeschylus, and said, I might see how the true philosophy was clearing itself from the mists of the evil superstitions of the Greeks.'[15]

Greek subject matter is not, however, invariably oriented towards Christianity. Various major classical authors are treated in translation, as if to assure access to a wider readership, but with literary-critical discussion at a level which could well have been helpful to those reading them in the original. Homer's *Iliad* and Plutarch's *Lives*, considered as exemplary heroes, are among these.[16] There is also a series of translations from the Greek tragedians.[17] Two explanations (not necessarily mutually exclusive) can be suggested for the fact that Latin authors are not accorded this sort of treatment: they may have been more familiar in the schoolroom whereas the learning of Greek merited encouragement from the wider learning community provided by the readers of *The Monthly Packet*; alternatively, Greek may be privileged precisely because it is regarded as more sacred.[18]

Expectations with regard to ancient history can be gleaned from the numerous articles which advise on reading, and in the answers to correspondents. The editor is aware of differing target audiences: for example, in praising *Ancient History for Village Schools*[19] there is also the *caveat* that, when dealing with village children, the topic 'is too utterly remote from all their interests' actually to be remembered or applied intelligently.[20] Expectations for the girl in the schoolroom or the young woman pursuing self-education are much higher. Abridgements and *rechauffés* are spurned in contrast to tackling a full work by a serious author: for example, 'the first volume of Professor Rawlinson's *Five Empires*.[21] If you are a sensible reader, or wish to become one, you could not do better than begin with his *Herodotus*[22] which would give you double interest in this book, relating the conclusions formed from the remains at Nineveh.'[23] Thus the most up-to-date and comprehensive scholarly work is here being recommended to the teenage readers of *The Monthly Packet*.

Several essay-type societies (which required a small additional subscription, and whose members contributed under a pseudonym) flourished at various times under the aegis of *The Monthly Packet*. Some were specialist (mathematical, botanical), others general: 'Spider Subjects' was set by Arachne (Yonge), while under Christabel Coleridge's ('Chelsea China's') editorship there was 'The China Cupboard'. The usual form was essays on a set topic, but sometimes notes or translations were required. The subjects are broadly historical and cultural, and demand wide-ranging knowledge; it is evident that those whose contributions are praised and printed had access to a fair range of books and had made intelligent use of them. Classical topics (historical and mythological) are well represented here: for example, 'The Battle of Cannae', 'The History of the Parthenon and its Sculptures', and 'The Myth of Perseus'.[24]

Mythology makes a frequent appearance in the magazine, and not at the level of mere simple retellings: it is plainly assumed that the basics are already known. It can be treated typologically, so as to derive a Christian meaning from an ancient tale. This is explicitly the aim of a series by Yarach, entitled 'Mythological Legends'.[25] The intention is pointed by an epigraph from Isaac Williams' poetic cycle 'The Cathedral' (1839): 'They spoke of things more glorious than they knew' ('The Psalms', stanza 22). Thus Atlas is explained as 'the type of an inhospitable man' and is hence turned to stone (hardening of heart).[26] The treatment of Eros and Psyche as 'a type of the soul thirsting after perfection, yet subject to the weaknesses attendant upon being united to a mortal nature'[27] could have been the germ of Yonge's handling of the theme in *Love and Life* (see below). But typology is not the only mode of mythological interpretation: there is an effort at comparative mythology in a discussion of the Adoneia.[28] This compares the cult of Adonis with those of Tammuz and Osiris, and offers a lively adaptation of Theocritus' sixteenth poem describing the Adonis festival in third-century B.C. Alexandria. Finally, the general assumption of a shared classical background is illustrated by various original poems on subjects from the Greco-Roman world as well as translations of actual ancient poems; there is also the occasional piece of fiction – for example, a story about Spartacus.[29]

This brief selection from *The Monthly Packet* demonstrates how the classics were perceived as an essential element of a shared and valued culture. The aim of the magazine was certainly in part educational and improving, and not the least important aspect of this was the role it played in creating a notional community for learning amongst a readership whose education was often limited by social convention and lack of access to appropriate schooling. Even if readers never aspired to learn Greek or to enter the essay competitions, they were made aware that such topics were not only of potential interest but were also accessible to themselves. And as external opportunities for the education of girls widened, the journal continued to supplement formal teaching by its sustained emphasis on self-directed study at a serious level.

CLASSICAL CULTURE IN YONGE'S NON-FICTION

While the pages of *The Monthly Packet* represent a means of transmitting and extending classical learning to a readership of middle- and upper middle-class girls, they cannot be said to constitute an original work of scholarship. But one work of Yonge's could, in its day, justly claim that description: the *History of Christian Names*. The discussion of the origins of names demanded an acquaintance with most of the European languages, classical and modern, an understanding of philology, and wide reading in folklore and history. Interestingly, sources are differentially cited: the underlying assumption is that readers will possess a sound knowledge of 'matters of universally known history or mythology'; for these, Yonge states that she has 'not always given an authority, thinking it superfluous. Indeed, the scriptural and classical portion is briefer and less detailed than the Teutonic and Keltic, as being already better known.'[30] Thus the classical is here treated on a par with the biblical as the shared cultural heritage of an educated readership.

Classical culture is, however, by no means solely the privilege of an elite minority. The near-universal recognition, among all classes, of its significance is illustrated by *What Books to Lend and what to Give*. This work offers guidance to those responsible for choosing fiction and non-fiction books (arranged by topics) for parish or school libraries, reading groups and working parties. Brief notes explain the suitability of the books for different readerships, ranging from young children to mothers' meetings and working lads. The introduction to the section on 'Mythology' takes for granted the value of an intelligent understanding of the subject.[31] Yonge's own experience of teaching is apparent: Nathaniel Hawthorne's retellings can 'delight clever village children and utterly perplex dull ones'; C. H. Hanson's volumes *Old Greek Stories* and *Wanderings of Aeneas* constitute '[e]xcellent prizes for boys aiming at cultivation of mind' (though the illustrations, drawn from the antique and depicting some nude figures 'must be shown with caution'). The aspirational element is noteworthy, but clearly *rechauffés* largely suffice for readers such as these.

Yonge herself provided a number of reworkings of classical themes, aimed at children from the age of ten or so. *A Book of Golden Deeds*,[32] *A Book of Worthies*,[33] and the Greek and Roman volumes of *Aunt Charlotte's Stories*[34] include both mythological and historical topics. The retellings are very readable and they manifest considerable awareness of the limits of historical reliability; some reference is also made to the ancient sources from which the tales derive. A notable feature is Yonge's careful discrimination of act and motivation: it is never forgotten that the springs of action are different from and inferior to those which impel a Christian to a similar undertaking. This insistence is natural, given the age of the readership; it is, however, worth pointing out that the readers of *The Monthly Packet* are treated as considerably more sophisticated in their understanding of myth and history by the authors of the various articles mentioned above: it can be inferred that Yonge, as Editor, approved.

What stands out when the classical elements within Yonge's non-fiction are examined is the range of readerships to whom she directs herself. While she indeed retains an awareness of appropriate levels of treatment for different age groups, classes and levels of learning, she is far from sharing any Gradgrindian notion of limiting the training for the lower class to the merely useful and factual. On the contrary, the classics are valuable on two counts: as forming part of a liberal education, and in providing raw material for what might be called 'comparative ethics'. Thus the classical world is regarded as one where high culture prevails and where excellent instances of moral behaviour on occasion manifest themselves: Yonge implicitly or explicitly reminds her readers to pose to themselves the question of the satisfactoriness – or otherwise – of such a basis for morality.

FICTION WITH A CLASSICAL THEME

The treatment of classical material in Yonge's fiction comprises two aspects: the employment of historical or mythological matter for entire novels; and the dispersed allusions to the classics and the learning of Greek and Latin within the contemporary novels.

In three full-length novels (*The Slaves of Sabinus*, *My Young Alcides* and *Love and Life*), Yonge undertook classical themes, always adapting them to convey a Christian message. Only one of the novels can be termed 'historical': *The Slaves of Sabinus: Jew and Gentile* (1890).[35] It is set in the reigns of Vespasian and Domitian, and deals with the story of Sabinus and Eponina (derived from Plutarch, *Erotikos* 25.770D-771C). Their story is combined with that of Flavius Clemens, whose death under Domitian is treated as martyrdom.[36] This is one of the dozen or so National Society books which Yonge wrote more or less annually in the last years of her life, and is not among the best of these. It drew praise from the *Guardian* as 'a story on a theme to draw all hearts – Christian faith and martyrdom'.[37]

The other two novels, both retellings of Greek myths, are considerably more successful.[38] *My Young Alcides: A Faded Photograph* is the legend of Hercules, transposed into a mid-nineteenth-century English setting.[39] All twelve Labours and numerous other incidents are recounted, and the detail extends down to ingenious parallels of character and place names. But the work is more than a clever exercise: it is a typological reading of the ancient myth, as is indicated in the Preface (pp. v-vi). This is brought out fully towards the end, where the hero is memorialised in chapel windows which refer to Samson as Type and to Christ as Antitype (pp. 350-51). Entailing as it does violence, madness and murder, the plot enables Yonge to deal more overtly with the theme of wickedness and sin, repentance and redemption, than she normally does in her novels of contemporary life. This certainly does not mean that she abandons regard for the typically Tractarian virtue of Reserve, which enjoined both sparing reference to holy names and subjects, and also the avoidance of any intrusive examination of the spiritual state of another. But by comparison with the extreme Reserve applied to the characters in the linked family stories, the religious awakening of Harold (the Hercules figure), first to a sense of sin and then gradually to confidence in salvation, is brought out very clearly. Yonge achieves this largely by

167

means of allusions to the Bible and the Book of Common Prayer: the General Confession and Psalm 51 denote the stage of penitence (pp. 198-200), mentions of 'the power of the dog' represent the hero's recurrent struggle with madness (pp. 181-82, 305), and finally the recognition that 'Christ has conquered' upholds him at the approach of death (pp. 341-3). Biblical and classical references thus intertwine to express the hero's typological significance. Moreover, inasmuch as Harold is Hercules and hence a figure of male physical prowess and, ultimately, of manly moral strength, he allows Yonge to reflect upon the nature of masculinity as her less overtly masculine heroes do not. The classical theme is thus of great advantage in enabling Yonge to address issues and emotions which normally lie outside her self-appointed limits.[40]

The same applies, in a lesser degree, to *Love and Life*.[41] Here Yonge takes the story of Eros and Psyche, first told in Apuleius' *Metamorphoses* (also known as *The Golden Ass*), adds overtones of 'Beauty and the Beast', and puts the whole into an eighteenth-century context. This allows for such plot devices as a secret marriage and an abduction, which Yonge would scarcely have allowed within a contemporary setting. *Love and Life* could, just conceivably, be read as a straight historical novel by someone who had no acquaintance whatsoever with classical mythology in general, or Apuleius in particular. Second-level reading would involve appreciation of the classical parallels; full understanding requires that the story be interpreted, in allegorical fashion, as tracing the course of a Christian soul reaching, despite obstacles and setbacks, towards ultimate union with Divine Love. The Soul comes to feel love for the Bridegroom, Christ: it knows him, but only partially. Trust and faith are not fully present but must be learnt through an ordeal of separation, and by the sustained practice of virtue when under threat; failure in faith must be confessed and repented. Only after death will there be full union of the Soul with Christ.

That this is the intended mode of reading is clear from Yonge's 'Preface' (pp. viii-ix). Important in her method is her choice of names for the characters, and the constant equation of light with truth, both factual truth and religious, revelatory truth. Aurelia Delavie (Psyche) falls in love with Sir Amyas Belamour (Eros), and undergoes a secret and unconsummated marriage in a darkened room; despite a warning, she attempts to see his real face, and this action appears to kill him. His mother Lady Urania Belamour (Venus) imprisons Aurelia, subjects her to various ordeals, and finally arranges for her abduction and sale abroad into an enforced marriage (tantamount to rape), through the agency of druggist and procuress Mrs Cora Darke (Proserpina/Kore). Mrs Darke represents the goddess of the underworld and death, the death of unrepented sin: she is utterly without remorse or pity. By means of a drug she produces a death-like sleep in Aurelia, but husband and father bring rescue at the last moment. Aurelia gradually comes back to life in the glow of sunset and twilight (pp. 399-404). At the time of dusk she is restored to her family, but it is only after confessing at dawn 'in the early summer morning' (p. 405) how wrong were the mistrust and disobedience which led her to try and see her lover's face that she finally (for the first time ever) beholds her Love properly: he is 'dazzling' in the full light of day (p. 407). An important sub-plot concerns the winning back to hope from the sin of despair of a 'prisoner of darkness' (p. 110): spiritual light finally breaks into his dark night of the soul.

On another level, the novel is also an interesting combination of the realistic and Gothic modes: the former at the start, in the detailed depiction of Georgian *mores* when Aurelia lives at home in the country, merging into the latter as she encounters change, isolation and imprisonment. A serious weakness in the work lies in the excessive propriety with which Yonge treats the abduction motif and the threat of rape: the reader lacks any sense that the heroine is ever in the real physical danger which represents the moral peril endangering her soul. The use of the classical fable does, however, enable Yonge to handle the theme of Christian spiritual growth as a timeless and universal one, and show the development of a female hero who preserves her spiritual innocence as a fit Bride.

In these two novels, the myths provide Yonge with strong basic plots for narratives which can be read as allegories of the spiritual development of Everyman or Everywoman. Here then, the classical is ancillary to Christianity, in that the message of the stories can be taken home by the reader as a warning against sin and a weapon against temptation without overt preaching or intrusiveness into areas of religious experience which should properly be kept private.

CLASSICS WITHIN THE CONTEMPORARY NOVELS

When we have a friend's account of a lively discussion with Yonge on the relative self-consciousness of Aeschylus, Euripides and Cicero, and on current mythological theories,[42] it comes as something of a surprise that such engagement with the classics is rarely reflected in the novels. Few authors are discussed, quoted or even named. Admittedly, boys construe Virgil, and Philip Morville is appalled by the way Guy turns a line of Horace in a joke and, in so doing, perpetrates a metrical false quantity,[43] but on the whole, the allusions are generalised rather than particular. Thus the notion of reading or studying the classics found in the novels seems to be almost content-free, a shared but undifferentiated *tabula rasa* upon the wax of which a number of experiences can be inscribed.

Classics will here be considered under four heads: a source of enjoyment; the stamp of the gentleman and clergyman; the learning process; and the locus of emulation and competition. Negative or ambiguous connotations attach to a number of these aspects.

Enjoyment

In the first place, it is only for the few that the experience represents enjoyment and stimulation. Ulick O'More and Mr Kendal are brought together in a lengthy discussion of Aeschylus' *Prometheus Vinctus*.[44] Lilias Merrifield's girlhood enthusiasm for Vercingetorix, which led her to make her own translation of Caesar, is recalled by her sister Jane Mohun (*Beechcroft at Rockstone*, ch. 10, p. 107).[45] For the clergyman Uncle Willoughby a Greek book is an intense pleasure, its purchase a temptation which he denies himself (*The Castle Builders*, ch. 4, p. 49).[46] The most appealing picture of real delight is that of Mr Potts, as described by his former pupil, Guy Morville:

> 'He is very clever, I assure you, and very patient of the hard, wearing life he must have of it there; and oh! so enjoying a new book, or an afternoon to himself [. . .] I am sure he has done the best he could for me; and he made the readings very pleasant by his own enjoyment. If Philip had known the difficulties that man has struggled through, and his beautiful temper, persevering in doing his best and being contented, I am sure he could never have spoken contemptuously of him.' (*The Heir of Redclyffe*, ch. 4, p. 42)

The Potts regime has imparted enjoyment but not accuracy to Guy:

> 'Oh!' cried Guy, eagerly, 'to be sure I delight in Homer and the Georgics, and plenty more. What splendid things there are in these old fellows! But, I never liked the drudgery part of the affair, and now if I am to be set to work to be accurate, and to get up all the grammar and the Greek roots, it will be horrid enough in all conscience.' (*The Heir of Redclyffe*, ch. 4, p. 42)

The rigorous programme of learning which Guy proceeds to impose attests to his self-discipline. It finally transpires that 'it was a great pity that he had not gone up for honours, as he would certainly have distinguished himself' (*The Heir of Redclyffe*, ch. 28, p. 285): he has thus renounced the competition for honours while in fact having worked hard enough to achieve them.

Philip Morville, on the other hand, has not only been trained to correctness by a public school education but is a lover of the classics and a scholar *manqué* – though his sacrifice of a university career has been in vain (*The Heir of Redclyffe*, ch. 2, p. 16; ch. 4, p. 44).

> 'Ah!' said Guy, laughing, 'how I wished Mr. Potts had been there to have enjoyed listening to Philip and Mr. Lascelles discussing some new Lexicon, digging down for roots of words, and quoting passages of obscure Greek poets at such a rate, that if my eyes had been shut I could have thought them two withered old students in spectacles and snuff-coloured coats.' (*The Heir of Redclyffe*, ch. 4, p. 42)

This points up not only different modes of acquisition of learning but also of enjoyment. Philip has learnt according to the public school norms but Guy's love is more spontaneous and just as sincere, for all that he has not been educated in the proper gentlemanly way. Other modes of learning classics (it is implied) may be no less valid than this 'proper' way; perhaps there is no need to fetishise the mode of acquisition. This message may have been encouraging to those disqualified, by class or by gender, from participating in the normative public school experience.

Gentlemen, clergymen and scholars

The classics could stand as a touchstone for judgement – judgement of gentlemanliness, of ability and achievement, even, perhaps, of moral worth: Yonge sometimes employs them to problematise these values. Thus, for many in the nineteenth century, classics denoted the gentleman. Yonge does not however agree that the study of classics is what turns a man into a gentleman.

> 'Has Latin and Greek made Harrison [the head gardener] a gentleman?' (*Heartsease*, part l, ch. 4, p. 38)

Clearly the expected answer is 'No'. And there can be no appeal from Theodora Martindale's final verdict on Harrison as 'an educated man though a coxcomb' (p. 148). So while the study of the classics may mark the gentleman, it does not make him. Harrison will forever lack the discrimination, the sense of fitness, the tactful consideration which reveal Yonge's true gentlemen.[47]

Still less do the classics make a man a good clergyman, although they are an indispensable precursor for Ordination. It is this which accounts for the health-destroying efforts made by Ulick O'More to keep up his Latin and Greek, and for Alexis White's gratitude for Gillian Merrifield's help with Greek lessons and books: both young men feel a clerical vocation, which circumstances force Ulick to resign but Alexis is able to pursue.[48]

But for many of Yonge's most admirable clergymen, the classics are an uncongenial study, an obstacle which only a sense of duty and the requirements of their calling stimulate them to overcome. For every Norman May, Bill Harewood or Lord Herbert Somerville, there is a Richard May, a Clement Underwood and a Frank Willoughby (a would-be clergyman). The one bright point the last-named finds in obeying his father's wish that he become a soldier is that he will be 'quit of an awful lot of Latin and Greek' (*The Castle Builders*, ch. 11, p. 127). Herbert Bowater is another such. He has required intensive coaching from his sister Jenny, he takes any excuse not to do the reading prescribed for his examination, and finally he is rejected for Ordination. Then comes the critical time of the fever at Willansborough, in which Herbert serves with the utmost devotion until he breaks down and nearly succumbs to it himself. The following year is one of probation and hard study for him:

> [. . .] the examining chaplain did not recognize the lean pale, anxious man, for the round-faced, rosy, overgrown boy of a year ago. His scholarship and critical knowledge were fairly

above the mark [. . .] and his written sermon [. . .] revealed, all unconsciously to himself, what treasures he had brought back from the deep waters which had so nearly closed over him. (*The Three Brides*, ch. 37, p. 326)[49]

It is the reality of the active service which makes men in this latter group conscientious and admirable clergymen, not the ordeal by classics which they have undergone.[50]

Another instance is the assumption that the life devoted to classical scholarship embodies a form of the good life: this too is challenged. University dons are in fact rare in the novels: a college Fellowship is generally a staging post for the abler men before they marry and move to a parish. Bill Harewood, who has been a active and inspiring tutor at Christ Church, Oxford, takes on the parish of Vale Leston: this is not large, and is so well-organised that he will be able to continue his valuable engagement in the world of theological scholarship (*The Pillars of the House*, vol. 2, ch. 49, p. 523).[51] But one imagined portrait of a college don appears, and this, significantly, is couched in a satirical tone rarely employed by the authorial voice. Albinia Kendal reflects upon her husband's character:

> Nature must have designed him for a fellow of a college, where, apart from all cares, he might have collected fragments of forgotten authors, and immortalized his name by some edition of a Greek Lyric poet, known by four poems and a half, and two-thirds of a line quoted somewhere else. In such a controversy, lightened by perpetually polished poems, by a fair amount of modern literature, select college friendships, and methodical habits, Edmund Kendal would have been in his congenial element, lived and died, and had his portrait hung up as one of the glories of his college. (*Young Stepmother*, ch. 4, p. 32)

Judged on the scale of values which endorsed the writing of Greek and Latin verse as the touchstone of scholarship and gentlemanliness, this is the pattern don (necessarily, at this period, a clergyman). He deals only with fragments – the more obscure the better – and passes his time in a collegiate milieu of amiable near-idleness and gentle self-indulgence rather than in any active exercise of his office. But Yonge's scale embodies different values. Just as this don's pointless existence is a shadow of that of an active scholar-clergyman such as Bill Harewood or Mr Clare (in *The Clever Woman of the Family*), so is Edmund Kendal's present life merely a sad caricature of the don's. Uncongenial work and an unstimulating first marriage have driven him within himself. He has indeed earned his living for a time in India, but has retreated as soon as opportunity offered to retirement in the claustrophobic world of Bayford. Now married and with children, he can never become the don intended by nature, but he can at least cut himself off from uncongenial society within his inviolable study. He renders himself an amateur scholar who is busy only with the inessential, a father who is distant from his children, and a layman who is indifferent to the life of the Church. To promote his emergence from this physical and spiritual self-seclusion is the prime achievement of Albinia's love. The classical don stands as here one who pursues a life of the utmost triviality and unreality.

Similarly, in the passage from *The Heir of Redclyffe* quoted above, it is noteworthy that 'obscure Greek poets' form the topic discussed by Philip in the imagined persona of aged scholar. There is a implication that scholarship – worthy and enjoyable though it may be – is, in the end, life-denying.

The learning process

The whole process of learning of classics measures not only ability and diligence but also character. Teaching often begins at home, as with the boys of the Winslow family:

> [. . .] my father heard them a short bit of Latin grammar at his breakfast (five was thought in those days [*c.* 1815] to be the fit age to begin it, and fathers the fit teachers thereof) [. . .] (*Chantry House*, ch. 2, p. 12)[52]

Women (mothers and sisters) can also be the teachers. Mr Ogilvie is delighted when the second set of Brownlow children do not share their cousins' sluggish indifference to learning.[53] Having been taught by his gifted mother, Armine (aged about seven) already knows a fair amount of Latin; the story of the Gallic Sack of Rome is vivid to him because he has acted Romans, Gauls and geese with his mother and siblings (*Magnum Bonum*, ch. 5, p. 55).

When boys proceed to school, the staple diet of Latin and Greek proves tough for some, as the scenes of literal construing that turns the text into nonsense illustrate.[54] The regime suits others admirably, and the standard of the best is extremely high – for example, Norman May and Bill Harewood, whose Latin verses leap the bounds of mere 'verse composition' into the realm of poetry.[55] For those who are able but whose natural bent is not towards the classics, there is little scope for other branches of learning.[56]

One significant passage criticises the classics, and offers a justificatory response. The dramatic date is early 1850s.

> 'Besides,' proceeded Bobus, warming to his subject, 'I see no good in nothing but classics. I don't care what ridiculous lies some old man who never existed, or else was a dozen people at once, told about a lot of ruffians who never lived, killing each other at some place that never was.[57] I like what you can lay your finger on, and say, it's here, it's true, and I can prove it, and explain it, and improve upon it [. . .] I know languages are necessary; but if one can read a Latin book, and understand a Greek technical term, that's all that is of use [. . .]'

He explains his aim of studying physical science, and Mr Ogilvie replies:

> 'Your chances will be much better if you go up from a public school, trained in accuracy by the thorough work of language, and made more powerful by the very fact of not having followed merely your own bent. Your contempt for the classics shows how one sided you are growing. Besides, I thought that you knew the days are over of unmitigated classics. You would have many more opportunities, and much better ones, of studying physical science than I can provide for you here.'
> (*Magnum Bonum*, ch. 13, pp. 177-8)

Plainly, there is little notion of such radical change in the curriculum as actually dropping classics: it is the training, the mental drill that shapes the intellect to engage with any higher branch of learning. This has both a practical effect and a moral one, as is shown when Clement Underwood buckles down to study after a well-founded rejection at Oxford, which, in a spirit of partisanship, he has attributed to prejudice against his spiritual home at St Matthew's, Whittingtonia.[58] Similarly, the stages by which the delicate and ever-priggish Armine Brownlow reconciles himself to an ordinary active life are marked by the degree of his commitment to his classical studies.[59]

It is precisely the tough reality of Greek that attracts the clever girls, and they are often helped by supportive fathers or brothers. Emmeline finds her Greek 'good hard satisfying work' (*The Castle Builders*, ch. 11, p. 119). For her, as for other girls educated at home, the classical languages are an exception, perhaps a privilege and certainly not a right, and hence a source of enjoyment rather than a dread imposed task. Emmeline is taught by her step-brother Frank, although he affects to think it 'nonsense' (p. 126). Geraldine Underwood's various studies, which include Greek and Latin, were begun with her father and continued with Mr Audley (*The Pillars of The House*, ch. 5, p. 81); Ethel May famously keeps up with her brother Norman. One of the attractions is undoubtedly the participation in the male world of learning.[60]

Competition

One consequence of elevating classics to the supreme position in the curriculum is that the subject becomes not only the object of effort and achievement but also the locus of cheating and deceit. For example, the timid youngster Tom May seems already to have got hold of a crib when learning Latin at home with his brother Richard. The latter is resigned to Tom's going to Stoneborough School, even though he rightly foresees that in the atmosphere there prevailing Tom is bound to shirk (*The Daisy Chain*, Part 1, ch. 16, p. 142).

> [Tom] was taught the most ingenious arts of saying a lesson without learning it, and of showing up other people's tasks; whispers and signs were directed to him to help him out of difficulties [. . .] (*The Daisy Chain*, Part 1, ch. 19, pp. 167-68)

Kenminster School too is riddled by various forms of cheating:

> 'Bobus would do anybody's exercises at a penny for Latin, two for French, and three for Greek,' said John, not aware of the shock he gave. (*Magnum Bonum*, ch. 14, pp. 185-6)

All this remains unsuspected by parents until the crisis of bullying (for not condoning cheating) in which Armine is nearly killed by his cousin.

Once girls' schools adopt the curriculum and the ethos of those for boys,[61] they likewise fall liable to the same dangers.[62] Valetta Merrifield's class at the High School at Rockstone is preparing for a language prize but this supposedly healthy stimulus occasions first strain, and then cheating. Valetta's need for help is unrecognised, so she resorts to using her mother's translation of Caesar. When other girls get to hear of it, she is bullied into providing more material until eventually the facts come to light. The blame is shared by Valetta and the other girls involved, but also by Gillian, too concerned with her own examinations to have time to attend to her little sister (p. 109), and by the teacher (pp. 108, 147, 152). The authorial voice seems to endorse Aunt Jane's opinion that the underlying fault is the system of 'general over-hurry' (p. 108). There is a strong sense that to learn in this way and for these motives is not only valueless but positively harmful. Aunt Jane Mohun reflects

> 'having opposed the acceptance of the system of prizes by competition at first, I thought it would look sullen if I refused to let Valetta try. Stimulus is all very well, but competition leads to emulation, wrath, strife, and a good deal besides.' (*Beechcroft at Rockstone*, ch. 10, p. 112)

Even where there is no question of cheating, Yonge still fears competition and emulation; again, these are often sited within the classics. Norman May is a prime example: his rivalry with Harvey Anderson focuses at first upon the position of Dux [Head Boy] of Stoneborough Grammar School, then upon the Randall closed scholarship; at Oxford it widens to include more momentous aspects. At school, Norman is undeniably brilliant at his classical work, but lacks the personal authority which would make him an effective Dux: for a short time, he is humbled, in a worldly view, by losing the position. This disqualifies him from trying for the Randall; however, he gains the more striking prize of a Balliol open scholarship – on the basis of a classical examination – and, when the truth emerges about the disorders in the school which had led to his demotion as Dux, he is triumphantly reinstated.[63] Thus far, then, the classics are linked to recognition and success. But the *leitmotif* of Norman's school and university career is the story of Publius Decius Mus, the Roman consul of 340 B.C., who deliberately sacrificed himself in battle in order that his country might win and not – as is several times made clear – for posthumous personal fame.[64] Norman's fame, within the world of the University, as the author of the Newdigate prize poem on the topic of Decius, comes at the same time as he is striving in theological controversy against Harvey Anderson ('imbued with [. . .] Rationalistic

177

ideas': *The Daisy Chain*, part 2, ch. 9, p. 377). The two are recognised as the foremost men of their undergraduate generation, and stand for opposing views on the nature of faith and the Church. Such encounters Norman is capable of winning, though at great personal cost in terms of intellectual and nervous strain – but should he endanger his health, and, more important, his faith by trying to win?

> 'They told me I ought to read this book, and that. Harvey Anderson used to come primed with arguments. I could always overthrow them, but when I came to glory in doing so, perhaps I prayed less. Any way, they left a sting. It might be, that I doubted my own sincerity, from knowing that I had got to argue, chiefly because I liked to be looked on as a champion.'(*The Daisy Chain*, part 2, ch. 16, p. 460)

Norman decides against the public controversy which the life of prominent champion of the Church would entail, and in favour of 'the simplest, hardest work' (p. 461). He therefore becomes a colonial clergyman; even in this capacity, he serves in a school and not in the more glamorous missionary field. He has been tempted (in the sense of 'tried', 'tested'): classics and the prizes it could lead to constituted the temptation, which was all the more dangerous for being bound up with duties, the right use of talents, and genuine intellectual pleasures. In Ethel's case, classics constitutes the sphere in which she can emulate her beloved brother.

> [...] meantime she spouted with great emphasis an ode of Horace, which Norman having learnt by heart, she had followed his example; it being her great desire to be even with him in all his studies, and though eleven months younger, she had never yet fallen behind him. On Saturday he showed her what his tasks were for the week [...]

> Ethel would not, for the world, that anyone should guess at her classical studies – she scarcely liked to believe that even her father knew of them, and to mention them before Mr. Ernescliffe would have been dreadful. (*The Daisy Chain*, part 1, ch. 1, pp. 6-7)

But a girl's emulation of a brother is only for the home.[65] No outsider is supposed to know that Ethel is learning Latin and Greek on a par with boys. Harry reports how

'Norman [. . .] had taken to school, by mistake, Richard's old Gradus that Ethel uses, and there were ever so many rough copies of hers sticking in it [. . .] Why, Anderson junior was gaping about in despair for sense for his verses – he comes on that, and slyly copies a whole set of her old ones, done when she – Norman, I mean – was in the fifth form. His subject was a river, and hers Babylon; but altering a line or two, it did just as well. He never guessed I saw him, and thought he had done it famously. He showed them up, and would have got some noted good mark, but that, by great good luck, Ethel had made two of her pentameters too short, which he hadn't the wit to find out, thinking all Norman did must be right. So he has shown up a girl's verses – isn't that rare?' [. . .]

'I hope no one knows they were hers?' [said Margaret.]

'Bless you, no!' said Harry, who regarded Ethel's attainments as something contraband. (*The Daisy Chain*, part 1, ch. 9, p. 82)

While the authorial voice endorses learning as praiseworthy in that it is right for talents to be developed, there is an early hint as to right priorities. At the family Bible reading the mother says:

'I am glad you have found in the Gospel a practical lesson, that should be useful to you both. I had rather you did so than that you read it in Greek, though that is very nice, too,' she added, smiling, as she put her hand on a little Greek Testament, in which Ethel had been reading it, within her English Bible. (*The Daisy Chain*, part 1, ch. 1, p. 6)

The significance of the Gospel in question for the characters is brought out by the ensuing discussion.[66] Ethel applies its lesson as referring to

'Caring to be clever, and get on, only for the sake of beating other people [. . .] caring to do a thing only because nobody else can do it – wanting to be first more than wanting to do one's best.' (p. 6)

Later, Ethel is advised greatly to reduce her classical reading: the time her Greek absorbs interferes too much with her other lessons, her household duties and the teaching she has undertaken in the school for the poor of Cocksmoor. Her governess complains that

> '[. . .] she is at every spare moment busy with Latin and Greek, and I cannot think that to keep pace with a boy of Norman's age and ability can be desirable for her.' (*The Daisy Chain*, part 1, ch.18, p. 159)

When Margaret discusses the issue with her, Ethel adopts a tone of voice which is 'a little sentimental':

> 'From *hic haec hoc up* to Alcaics and *beta* Thukididou[67] we have gone on together, and I can't bear to give it up. I'm sure I can –'

> 'Stop, Ethel, I really doubt whether you can. Do you know that Norman was telling Papa the other day, that it was very odd Dr. Hoxton gave them such easy lessons.'

> Ethel looked very much mortified. (p. 162)

The compromise is that she will limit the time spent on Greek to half an hour a day, giving up the verse-making. This is the culminating goal of the study, and thus, of course, its most gendered element.[68] Ethel, 'mortified' and 'melancholy', hopes that Norman will not be 'vexed'. Her brother, however, is far from taking the same view of the case as she does, for he answers with brisk realism that

> '[. . .] it is really time for you to stop, or you would get into a regular learned lady, and be good for nothing. I don't mean that knowing more than other people would make you so but minding nothing else would.'

> This argument from Norman himself did much to reconcile Ethel's mind to the sacrifice she had made; and when she went to bed, she tried to work out the question in her own mind, whether her eagerness for classical learning was a wrong sort of ambition, to know what other girls did not, and whether it was right to crave for more knowledge than was thought advisable for her. She only bewildered herself, and went to sleep before she had settled anything, but she knew she must make all give way to papa first, and, secondly, to Cocksmoor. (p. 164)

Ethel's viewpoint is presented with full and sympathetic clarity, but the authorial voice evades explicit decision as to the rights and wrongs of the issue, and instead asserts the supremacy of duty to others; this is tantamount to endorsing the view espoused by Norman and Margaret. Ethel has two prior duties: the natural one owed to her father and the self-imposed vow to work for Cocksmoor. That there might even be a duty not to neglect one's talents is perhaps implied by Margaret's compromise that Ethel should not entirely give up her Greek, but should limit the time spent on it. The danger to Ethel in classical study is that it is likely to become an attachment which will hinder the fulfilment of her right duties.[69]

In Yonge's moral scale, an excessive attachment is a perilous matter. From ideal to idol is an easy step, whether it is people or things that are at issue. A number of characters are shown as giving too high a regard to the affection, opinions, or judgement of another person. Examples include Honora Charlecote in relation to both the Owen Sandbrooks (*Hopes and Fears*); Emma Brandon to Theresa Marstone (*Heartsease*); and Laura Edmonstone and Margaret Henley, in their different ways, to Philip Morville (*The Heir of Redclyffe*).[70]

Where things – whether concrete or abstract – are concerned, there are similar dangers. The temptation of paying undue attention to matters such as personal beauty, possessions, status, respectable appearances or comfort is obvious enough, and only shallower personalities are represented as doing this. But the more insidious and dangerous idols manifest themselves in forms with a strong admixture of the good and the admirable. So with Philip Morville: his idolatrous tendency has been directed towards his own good judgement: he has come to believe himself always in the right, and as infallible in his handling of every person and situation. In this he deceives himself, and the damaging consequences include injustice towards Guy and the warping of Laura's character. Philip's own assessment of himself is, of course, not entirely without foundation: his abilities are excellent, he deserves much of the esteem he receives, his judgement is indeed often sound. But he is not perfect, and his self-image receives a devastating blow as he recognises his own misjudgement and its effects upon the innocent. It is when he sees his own opinions exaggerated into a caricature by his sister Margaret that he fully realises how gross has been his failure in understanding and charity (*The Heir of Redclyffe*, ch. 38, pp. 394-95).

> 'Every word you speak is the bitterest satire on me,' said Philip
> [...] 'Say no more, unless you would drive me
> distracted!'(p. 395)

Ethel May's case is different, and the verdict of the authorial voice, in the passage quoted above, is less harsh. An enthusiasm for leaning Greek is far from wrong in itself: the harm lies in what it stands for. Ethel has come near to idolising the distinctiveness which – in a woman's case – classical study represents. It has become a case of 'caring to do a thing only because nobody else can do it', the danger of which she herself has earlier recognised. The study of the classics also represents the uniqueness of Ethel's relationship with Norman: this too she later has to renounce, for Norman marries Meta Rivers, and goes to the other side of the world.[71]

Might Yonge then have endowed Norman with a passion for the natural sciences (such as drives Maurice Mohun in *Scenes and Characters*), or perhaps for mathematics, or architecture, and made Ethel follow him in that? In one respect the answer could be in the affirmative: any shared object of study would serve for the plot's renunciation theme. But in fact classics proves especially suited to this crucial role. It lacks any dangerous connotations of modernity or irreligiousness which might be perceived in the study of science: these would tend to obfuscate the issues of duty and attachment. It is a known quantity, and traditional within the curriculum, whether loved, endured or hated: hence Ethel's passionate enjoyment represents one extreme of a familiar scale. And pursuing its higher reaches is not likely to be of any great practical usefulness, which might be a distracting consideration with other topics of study. So the classics here provide a particularly appropriate test by which to assess the genuineness of Ethel's 'aspirations' (the novel's subtitle). Ethel's willingness to sacrifice something which is wrong, not for what it is, but for what it stands for in her case, prove that the 'practical lesson' of that early Gospel reading is indeed more to her than the Greek itself.

In the case of another Yonge heroine, deficiencies of attainment and of attitude are also pointed up by reference to the biblical languages of Latin, Greek and (unusually) Hebrew. Rachel Curtis evidently knows all three. For Hebrew she claims enough knowledge 'to appreciate the disputed passages', whereas her husband modestly states:

'I learnt enough [. . .] to look out my uncle's texts for him.'

She felt a little abashed by the tone. (*The Clever Woman of the Family*, ch. 24, p. 293)

This should be understood not as a mere contrast between Rachel's slight boastfulness and Alec's modesty, but also as a difference in motivation: she has read in order to achieve a superficial understanding, of current criticism, whereas Alec has subordinated himself to the needs of his uncle, the real biblical scholar. Her scanty command of the languages is immediately underlined, for when she insists on using a real Latin text of St Augustine to provide Mr Clare with a reference he requires, her pronunciation is so incorrect as to be virtually unintelligible to him (false quantities again!) and she realises that in this regard too 'her flight of clever womanhood had fallen short'.

CONCLUSION

That classical learning – like everything else – must and should be subordinate to the supreme end of religion is manifest in the way it is treated throughout Yonge's works, fiction and non-fiction. Two passages from the novels finally illustrate the wrong and the right use of the classics.

Firstly, ancient literature, however noble in sentiment, can never be compared to the inspired word of God:

> '[Mr Faulkner] talked of the Old Testament as if it was just like the Greek mythology, and then he compared it to Homer, and Aeschylus, and the Koran. To be sure he did say it was better poetry and morality; but the idea of comparing it! I don't mean comparing as if it must be better, but as if it stood on the same ground.' (*The Two Guardians*, ch. 14, p. 278)

And secondly, any form of learning is only valid if it is ancillary to the teaching of the Church. Geraldine explains the lesson of her two versions of Raphael's 'School of Athens':

> 'I mean that while woman works merely for the sake of self-cultivation, the clever grow conceited and emulous, the practical harsh and rigid, the light or dull vain, frivolous, deceitful, by way of escape, and it all gets absurd. But the being handmaids[72] of the Church brings all right; and the School of St.

Sophia develops even the intellect.' (*The Pillars of the House*, ch. 41, p. 363)

That classical learning was one of the occupations in the satirised School is clear from the reference to the inspecting owl of Athena:

'Hearing them pronounce *vicissim we-kiss-im* in turns, and making a note.' (p. 365)

The School of Athena evidently uses the new pronunciation,[73] whereas St Sophia no doubt adhered firmly to the old anglicised mode and said *'vie-siss-im'*. That is as one might have expected.

---

1 Christopher A. Stray, *Classics Transformed: Schools, Universities, and Society in England, 1830-1860* (Oxford: Clarendon Press, 1998). See especially Part I for the process of change and its social background.

2 For an account of the classical experience of some literary women from Burney to Woolf, and of their creations, see R. Fowler, 'On Not Knowing Greek:' The Classics and the Woman of Letters', *Classical Journal* 78 (1983) pp. 337-49. (Yonge is not among those covered.) An excellent account of the education of women of Yonge's class (based on the Paget family, whose extensive network of connections includes several families known to the Yonges) is provided by M. Jeanne Paterson, *Family, Love and Work in the Lives of Victorian Gentlewomen* (Bloomington: Indiana University Press, 1989) pp. 34-57 (pp. 54-55 on the classics).

3 C. M. Yonge, 'Autobiography', in Christabel R. Coleridge, *Charlotte Mary Yonge: her Life and Letters* (London: Macmillan, 1903) p. 74.

4 *ibid.*, p. 102 (the date is specified on p. 97).

5 *ibid.*, p. 110.

6 *ibid.*, pp. 107-08. Further details of the reading programme which supplemented formal lessons are given in C. M. Yonge, 'A Real Childhood', in *The Woman Reader, 1837-1914*, ed by K. Flint (Oxford: Clarendon Press, 1993) pp. 192-93 (first published in *Mothers in Council* 3 (1893) p. 19 ff.)

7 C. M. Yonge, *Womankind* (London: Mozley and Smith, 1876).

8 *Monthly Packet* [hereafter cited as *MP*], first series, 2 (Dec. 1851) p. 478.

9 *MP*, new [second] series, 8 (1869) pp. 57-61, 170-77, 293-96, 587-92; 9 (1870) pp. 55-62, 401-06; 10 (1870) pp. 203-07.

10 *MP*, new [second] series, 8 (July 1869) p. 58.

11 *MP*, third series, 3 (1882) pp. 1-8, 254-58, 590-95.

12 *MP*, new [fourth] series, 1 (1891) pp. 135-46, 360-74, 581-93; and 2 (1891) pp. 136-45.

13   *MP*, first series, 29 (May 1865) pp. 480-90.

14   Letter from John Keble to Yonge, 30 June 1851, quoted in C. M. Yonge, *Musings over the 'Christian Year' and 'Lyra Innocentium'*, (New York: Appleton, 1871) p. 27. (English edition, Oxford: James Parker, 1871).

15   C. M. Yonge, 'Conversations on the Catechism', *MP*, first series, 2 (1851) pp. 85-103; the quotation is from p. 90.

16   F. Hayllar, 'Studies in the Iliad', *MP*, new [fourth] series, 3 (1892) pp. 459-69, 579-90, 700-10; F. J. Snell, 'Plutarch's Heroes', *MP*, new [fourth] series, 14 (1897) pp. 32-41, 142-51, 270-79, 396-406, 498-507, 642-51.

17   Gerald W. Smith, *MP*, third series, 1-5 (1881-83); fifteen articles appeared at irregular intervals.

18   Stray, *Classics Transformed*, p. 79 n. 113, attributes the preference of women for Greek over Latin to 'its combination of high status, flexibility, and exotic freedom. It offered a realm of individuality beyond the Latinate public male sphere.'

19   [No named author], *Ancient History for Village Schools* (London: Mozley, 1862).

20   *MP*, first series, 24 (Nov. 1862) p. 558.

21   George Rawlinson, *The Five Great Monarchies of the Ancient Eastern World; or, The History, Geography and Antiquities of Chaldaea, Assyria, Babylon, Media, and Persia* (London: Murray, 1862-67).

22   George Rawlinson, *History of Herodotus: A New English Version* (London: Murray, 1858-60).

23   *MP*, first series, 25 (April 1863) p. 448.

24   *MP*, new [second] series, 15 (May 1873) additional pages [7]-[8]; *MP*, new [second] series, 27 (June 1879) pp. 618-20; *MP*, third series, 9 (June 1885) pp. 597-99.

25   The articles appeared at irregular intervals in volumes 4 to 13 (1852-7).

26   *MP*, first series, 4 (Nov. 1852) pp. 385-89; the quotation is from p. 389.

27   *MP*, first series, 7 (May 1854) pp. 342-71; the quotation is from p. 370.

28   *MP*, first series, 21 (Jan. 1861) pp. 94-104.

29   A. Werner, 'A Sketch of B.C. 75', *MP*, third series, 9 (April 1885) pp. 384-92.

30   C. M. Yonge, *History of Christian Names*, new edition, revised (London: Macmillan, 1884) p. viii.

31   C. M. Yonge, *What Books to Lend and What to Give* (Westminster: National Society's Depository, 1887) pp. 68-69.

32   C. M. Yonge, *A Book of Golden Deeds of All Times and All Lands* (London: Macmillan, 1864).

33   C. M. Yonge, *A Book of Worthies Gathered from the Old Histories* (London: Macmillan, 1869).

34   C. M. Yonge, *Aunt Charlotte's Stories of Greek History for the Little Ones* (London: Marcus Ward, 1876); C. M. Yonge, *Aunt Charlotte's Stories of Roman History for the Little Ones* (London: Marcus Ward, 1877).

35   C. M. Yonge, *The Slaves of Sabinus: Jew and Gentile* (Westminster: National Society's Depository, 1890).

36   Yonge states in the Preface [p. v] that 'his history and fate are recorded among those of the martyrs of the Church': this is not evident from Cassius Dio 67.14, but may be implied by Eusebius, *Ekklesiatike Historia* 3.18, and is explicit in Georgius Syncellus, *Ecloga Chronographica* p. 650.

37   This is quoted on the advertisement page 4 of the 1896 reprint of *Slaves of Sabinus*; the *Guardian* is the Church paper of that name, not the current newspaper, which until 1959 was known as the *Manchester Guardian*.

38   *A Modern Telemachus* (1886) is not considered here: despite its title, this novel does not depend closely on an ancient narrative.

39   C. M. Yonge, *My Young Alcides: A Faded Photograph*, 1875 (London: Macmillan, 1889).

40   Clemence E. Schultze, 'Manliness and the Myth of Hercules in Charlotte M. Yonge's *My Young Alcides*', *International Journal of the Classical Tradition* 5 (1999) pp. 383-414.

41   C. M. Yonge, *Love and Life: An Old Story in Eighteenth Century Costume*, 1880 (London: Macmillan, 1906). The first edition does not include the Preface which gives the derivation from Apuleius and explains the allegorical reading.

42   From the account by Miss Elizabeth Wordsworth, later Principal of Lady Margaret Hall, Oxford, of two visits to Charlotte Yonge in 1872 and 1873, reproduced in E. Romanes, *Charlotte Mary Yonge. An Appreciation* (London and Oxford: Mowbray, 1908) pp. 155, 139-40.

43   By changing the word *piscium* to *ovium*, Guy wittily adapts the tag (Horace, *Odes* 1.2.7-9) quoted by Philip so as to refer to the rescued ram – but the metre demands a long O in that position. 'Do anything but take liberties with Horace!' exclaims Philip. (*The Heir of Redclyffe*, 1853, [London: Macmillan, 1889] ch. 4, p. 33). '[. . .] in Victorian society, it was precisely the mastery of quantities which demonstrated the quality of one's culture' (Stray, *Classics Transformed*, p. 77).

44   C. M. Yonge, *The Young Stepmother*, 1861 (London: Macmillan, 1908) ch. 19, p. 233; cf. ch. 19, p. 225.

45   C. M. Yonge, *Beechcroft at Rockstone*, 1888 (London: Macmillan, 1889).

46   C. M. Yonge, *The Castle Builders*, 1854 (London: Innes, 1896).

47   C. M. Yonge, *Heartsease*, 1854 (London: Macmillan, 1888). Cf. Stray, *Classics Transformed*, p. 32, on cultural boundaries: Yonge's lie elsewhere than in the curriculum.

48   *The Young Stepmother*, pp. 221, 225, 230; *Beechcroft at Rockstone*, pp. 71, 79-80, 84-85.

49   C. M. Yonge, *The Three Brides*, 1876 (London: Macmillan, 1889).

50   But see Stray, *Classics Transformed*, p. 60.

51   C. M. Yonge, *The Pillars of the House*, 1873 (London: Macmillan, 1896).

52   C. M. Yonge, *Chantry House*, 1886 (London: Macmillan, 1889).

53   The prevailing ethos of the Kenminster Brownlows' home (largely formed by the mother) sets little value on classical learning even for boys, and regards it as impossible and undesirable that girls should be taught such a defeminising subject as Latin: ch. 10, p. 125, cf. p. 130).

54   C. M. Yonge, *The Daisy Chain*, 1853 (London: Macmillan, 1889) part 1, ch. 16, pp. 139-41; *Magnum Bonum*, ch. 13, pp. 175-76.

55   *The Daisy Chain*, part 1, ch. 8, p. 70; *The Pillars of the House*, vol. 1, ch. 18, p. 314.

56   For example, Maurice Mohun, in *The Two Sides of the Shield*, 1885 (London: Macmillan, 1896) ch. 2, pp. 16-17.

57   This alludes to the 'Homeric question': the dispute over the unity of authorship of the various elements of *Iliad* and *Odyssey*.

58   *The Pillars of the House*, vol. 1, ch. 12, p. 198 and p. 212. In between these two passages lies the episode of Clement's humiliating attempt to present himself as a manly man, the outcome of which has opened his eyes to his tendency towards spiritual pride (p. 207).

59   C. M. Yonge, *Magnum Bonum*, ch. 33, pp. 475, 477, 486-87, 492; ch. 34, p. 500; ch. 37, p. 570.

60   Thus when Albinia Kendal recommends her husband to teach Sophy Sanscrit, she recognises that part of the attraction for the girl will lie in doing something with her father; and that any serious study on a topic that interests her will be of benefit — as Albinia herself had benefited from reading Homer with her brother Maurice (*The Young Stepmother*, ch. 9, p. 109).

61   Claire Breay, 'Women and the Classical Tripos, 1869-1914', in *Classics in 19th and 20th century Cambridge: Curriculum, Culture and Community*, ed. by C. Stray (Cambridge Philological Society, Supplementary volume 24) (Cambridge: Cambridge Philological Society, 1999) pp. 49-70; see pp. 50-54 for a useful survey of the classical curriculum within girls' schools. Gillian Sutherland, 'The Movement for the Higher Education of Women: its Social and Intellectual Context in England, c. 1840-80', in *Politics and Social Change in Modern Britain: Essays Presented to A. F. Thompson*, ed. by P. J. Waller (Brighton: Harvester, 1987) pp. 91-116 (see especially pp. 106-110 on changing attitudes to educational standards).

62   Significantly, Yonge approves of the Cambridge Local Examinations because they 'are conducted in writing, and are not competitive' (*Womankind*, p. 84).

63   For the examination ethos, see Stray, *Classics Transformed*, pp. 49-54.

64   Livy 8.9. Allusions occur in *The Daisy Chain*, part 1, ch. 3, pp. 18-21; part 2, ch. 5, pp. 342-44; ch. 8, pp. 367, 374-75.

65   June Sturrock, *"Heaven and Home": Charlotte M. Yonge's Domestic Fiction and the Victorian Debate over Women* (English Literary Studies Monograph 66) (Victoria, B.C.: University of Victoria, 1995). Sturrock rightly points out that, while Norman and Ethel both in the end abandon their classical studies, Norman's have earned public credit that reflects well both upon himself and his family, as Ethel's never can (pp. 45-46).

66   Luke 14, especially verses 10-11.

67   Ethel refers to progress from the basics of Latin accidence to the high flights of verse composition in one of the more complex classical metres, and the reading of the Greek historian Thucydides, a notoriously difficult stylist.

68   Stray, *Classics Transformed*, pp. 68-74.

69   Valerie Sanders, *Eve's Renegades: Victorian Anti-Feminist Women Novelists* (Basingstoke: Macmillan, 1996) stresses Ethel's difficulty in coming to terms with the limited life she has accepted (pp. 62-64).

70   The potential danger of idealising and idolising persons is something frequently discussed in the correspondence between Yonge and Marianne Dyson. Various terms are used, whose scope seems to be as follows: the German word Bild denotes an ideal or a hero (who, if a living person, is sometimes taken as a guide of conduct); 'pope' definitely refers to a guide; and 'idol' is the object of an excessive attachment: see Coleridge, *Charlotte Mary Yonge*, especially pp. 189-90, but also pp. 160, 175, 179-80, 183, 272.

71   Compare Mrs May's warning to Margaret of the dangers of wanting to be loved best: a form of wanting to be first (*The Daisy Chain*, part 1, ch. 2, p. 16).

72   i.e. *ancillae*.

73   For the pronunciation controversy, see Stray, *Classics Transformed*, pp. 126-32.

MOTHER GOOSE'S BROOD:
SOME FOLLOWERS OF CHARLOTTE
YONGE AND THEIR NOVELS

Julia Courtney

Ho, Goslings of Old England! Ho, fellow-Goslings! hear
The deeds of your great ancestors, and cackle loud and clear!
Then where o'er London's chimneys the Towers of Julius frown,
Where on fair Edin's city the castle looketh down,
Where the great Thames aye wanders beneath old Chelsea's shades,
Where the bright Yealm meanders through Kitley's verdant glades,
Where gown clad scholars slide upon the Itchen's sparkling ice,
Where Devonport's Whig grocers adulterate their spice,
Wherever unfledged Goslings through Goosedom's bounds run loose,
Shall be great glee to all who see the form of Mother Goose.

This anthem to Goosedom was written for the manuscript magazine
The Barnacle, which flourished between 1863 and about 1869.[1] *The
Barnacle* can be described as somewhere between a family magazine
and an in-house version of Charlotte Yonge's *The Monthly Packet*; as for
the Goslings, Christabel Coleridge tells us that in 1859 Yonge's
extended 'cousinhood' included

> several girl cousins growing up, cousins' cousins also and young
> friends. Most of these girls had time on their hands. Education
> was desultory, and High Schools had not been thought of [. . .]
> the young ones needed a spur to their energies [. . .] [it was]
> proposed that they should form a society amongst themselves,

189

setting four questions a month and sending in the answers, the best set to be chosen and to travel round the circle [. . .] I think Charlotte was asked to be Minerva to a set of young owls. She chose to be Mother Goose to a brood of goslings. [2]

The Goslings were, then, again in Christabel Coleridge's words a

group who precisely exemplified [the relation] in which she stood to numberless other girls and young women who only knew her through her writings. The pleasure she took in all that pleased us, the guidance she gave without seeming to preach, the enthusiasm with which we regarded her, also inspired her readers and made them all her life like a circle of friends. [3]

Significantly, several of the Goslings tried their hands (it's tempting to fall into their own relentless punning and refer to their wingtips) at fiction in the manuscript *Barnacle* before graduating to *The Monthly Packet* and subsequently independent publication, so that this group may be seen in the light of Elaine Showalter's comments on the Female Tradition in women's writing. With *A Literature of their Own*, published back in 1977[4] Elaine Showalter herself might be said to have become the Mother Goose of Anglo-American feminist lit. crit; but as more recent studies such as Toril Moi's *Sexual / Textual Politics*[5], and Showalter's continuing inclusion in such teaching classics as Rice and Waugh's *Modern Literary Theory*[6] suggest, her defining concepts hold good for practitioners of this branch of feminist critique. Showalter proposes a 'female literary tradition in the English novel from the generation of the Brontes to the present day, and [. . .] show[s] how the development of this tradition is similar to the development of any literary sub-culture'[7]. She goes on to define stages in this development: the feminine phase from 1840 till 1880 characterised by 'imitation of the prevailing modes of the dominant tradition, and internalisation of its standards of art and social roles'; the feminist phase from 1880 to 1920, characterised by 'protest' and 'advocacy of minority rights'; and lastly the female phase from 1920 to 1960. Showalter does in fact include (sadly inaccurate) material[8] about Charlotte Yonge in *A Literature of Their Own* and it is certainly possible to place Yonge in Showalter's feminine phase; in which case the novels of the adult and emergent Goslings discussed in this essay would fall into the second or feminist phase and might be expected to show significant differences and developments from the work of their mentor.

Ivy Compton Burnett, whose work will be briefly discussed towards the end of this essay, would thus be categorised by Showalter as female, characterised by 'self discovery, a turning inward freed from some of the dependency of opposition, a search for identity'[9]

To return for a moment to Charlotte Yonge herself: it is significant that she rejected the classical title of Minerva in favour of the native fairy-tale persona of Mother Goose. When Charlotte Yonge did adopt a classical soubriquet in *The Monthly Packet* it was to be Arachne of 'Arachne and her Spiders'; Minerva she felt, perhaps, to be pretentious. If so, her strategy was one not uncommon to Victorian women writers such as Christina Rossetti or Mrs Ewing: the folk tale, the nursery rhyme and the fairy story are unthreatening, low status genres unlike the classically derived epic poem and thus particularly suited to a woman's utterance: especially if she wants to hint at anything at all subversive. Traditional portraits of Mother Goose (including one drawn by a Gosling as cover for an 1866 edition of *The Barnacle*) show her wearing a pointed witch's hat and wielding a broomstick; while the High Anglican Charlotte Yonge's form of magic was purely sacramental there is an interesting subtext of female power here.

Not all the Goslings were to follow Mother Goose and become novelists; missionaries, founders and head teachers of girls schools, and a Principal of St. Hugh's College (Annie Moberly) also started as members of the Brood. Similarly, not all the novel-writing friends and colleagues with whom Charlotte Yonge worked on *The Monthly Packet* or corresponded with in later years had been members of the original Gosling Society. But the Gosling Brood can act as a paradigm (as Christabel Coleridge suggested in the passage quoted earlier) for the relationship between Charlotte Yonge and those novelists I have designated her 'Followers'.

These tend to fall into groups which are often interlinked: the cousinhood; colleagues, usually from *The Monthly Packet*; and Charlotte Yonge's Winchester circle. I propose to take an example from each group starting, almost inevitably, with Christabel Rose Coleridge.

I

Christabel Coleridge is rather an equivocal figure for Yonge scholars. We all have to start with her 1903 *Life and Letters* with its increasingly apparent gaps and failings. Of course like any biographer Christabel Coleridge creates or constructs her subject and as Charlotte Yonge herself noted, 'there is a strong Coleridge personality that must show itself in whatever any Coleridge does'.[10] Georgina Battiscombe writes that when Christabel replaced her mentor as editor of *The Monthly Packet* in 1890 'letters on the subject come nearer to peevishness than anything Charlotte ever wrote'.[11] Christabel Coleridge is also held responsible for the conflagration of all Charlotte Yonge's papers after her death in March 1901.

The Yonge and Coleridge families were distantly connected by marriage, while Christabel Rose Coleridge was a direct descendant of the most famous Coleridge of them all, 'Uncle Sam'. In fact for the highly respectable clergymen and lawyers (including a Lord Chief Justice) who made up the Coleridge clan, S. T. Coleridge was something of a problem, to be claimed with pride because of his famed genius but with a slightly embarrassing lifestyle. Christabel was the daughter of S. T. Coleridge's most conventional child, Derwent, brother of the ill-fated Hartley and the enterprising Sara.[12]

Derwent (1800-1888), an Anglican clergyman, had a vigorous career in various London parishes before retiring to Torquay in 1880, where he died in 1888. Christabel moved there when her parents did and continued to live in Torquay until her death in 1921. From her writings (especially her essay collection of 1894, *The Daughters Who Have Not Revolted*) it seems she experienced some conflicts in her role as 'home daughter', but she also joined with a circle of like-minded friends much involved with the social and intellectual life of Torquay; the novelist Mary Cholmondeley was to write of Torquay in the 1880s 'we soon found out that if we were to keep pace with the social life of Torquay we should have no time left for work [. . .] I remember my astonishment when we received twenty four invitations to luncheon in a fortnight. London was nothing to it'.[13]

Less frivolously, Christabel Coleridge was also involved in the Torquay Education Committee, the management of National, secondary and Sunday schools, support for the church, the National Society for Promoting Education among the Poor, the SPCK, the Union of Women Workers and the Girls' Friendly Society.

The Torquay literati included writers Anna Drury, Margaret Roberts and James F. Cobb, as well as Frances Peard, whose work will be discussed later.

In an interview published in the *Torbay Directory* of 8 January 1896, Christabel declared that she had been writing since the age of twelve and story-telling for as long as she could remember: 'my brother assures me that it is fact that at parties the children would leave their games to come and listen to my stories'; she also revealed that it took her up to two years to complete a novel (possibly due to the extensive social life of Torquay!) Despite this Christabel Coleridge was a prolific writer of fiction for both young people and adults, work which her obituarist in the *Torbay Directory* (November 1921) characterized: 'Gentle and placid in character, full of the goodness and sympathy which radiated from the personality of the writer, the works of Miss Coleridge may be described as the link between the Victorian and the modern novel.'

Christabel's first partially extant work *Melicent Wardour, or, a Tale of Old Chelsea*, ran to twenty-six episodes in the manuscript *Barnacle*, but as far as I can discover was never published. Of two other early works, *Lady Betty*, published in 1870, had appeared in the *Barnacle* in 1867; *Giftie the Changeling* appeared in the *Barnacle* and according to a publisher's advertisement (which admittedly are not always reliable) was published by Warne in 1868. This would make *Giftie* her first published novel, although I have been unable to find a copy. All three of these novels illustrate Christabel's penchant for historical fiction ranging across a variety of periods, with *Giftie* perhaps the most interesting (particularly as it was written so early in her career).

Giftie is believed by her family, and the rest of the remote medieval North Country community in which she lives, to be a fairy child left in exchange for a human baby. Treated with fear and suspicion, the child grows up wild and malicious, convinced, especially after a violent thunderstorm breaks out when she ventures into the local church, that she is really an evil being. Only when a young squire, Hugh, joins the household after one of those riding accidents so frequent in historical fiction, is Giftie offered the chance to change: for Hugh sees her simply as an uncouth, shy child whom he teaches to read and encourages to conduct herself in a 'maidenlike' manner. The result is summed up by the sensible servant who asserts that 'elf-child or not, if Giftie conducts herself like a reasonable lassie, she should be treated as one'. Backed by Hugh and the sympathetic servant Kate, Giftie stands up to her father and convinces everyone including the superstitious priest Father Clement, that she is 'a lass like her sisters'. Christabel as a less experienced writer has the occasional problem of mechanics: 'Noble Sir', said Old Goody, 'I have sent a laddie for Father Clement who knows everything and behold, hither he comes', or of exposition, as in the passage where Hugh attempts to convince Giftie's father that infants may be swapped without the aid of magic (as indeed any reader of Victorian popular fiction should know):

> Children are changed now and again, without witchcraft. There was a knight and he did a lady a great wrong and she vowed revenge for his desertion of her. In short she vowed that child of her rival should never sit on his knee or inherit his wealth. So when the Knight's lady bore him a child, this maiden, who was her sister, snatched it secretly away and put another babe in its place. How she meant to manage if the lady had borne eight or ten hearty babes I know not, possibly in her rage she did not reason closely: but she betrayed herself to my father by a sudden chance and when she found herself discovered threw herself into the castle moat and was drowned.

But despite these awkward moments the tale holds the readers' attention by its use of the supernatural and by the perceptiveness with which the author suggests that a child will behave in the way expected of it by adults. It is only when Giftie, 'a not ungraceful figure, yet weird and strange, with her fair shaggy hair and her deep set eyes' decides to 'do her hair and to practice sewing and demean herself silently and quietly' that she is accepted into society as a 'real' woman. The events described take place in Part One of the story and unfortunately the rest is missing from the collection of manuscript *Barnacles;* it is quite possible that the tale of Giftie continued for another twenty or so chapters.

As Christabel's fiction developed, its themes tend to bear out her obituarist's comment, since she advocates adaptation to changing circumstances while preserving the essence of traditional values and timeless ideals. This preoccupation is appreciable in her historical fiction; for example *Minstrel Dick* of 1896[14] finds a new life as a Winchester scholar after the breaking of his boyish treble means that he can no longer earn his living as a singer. More emphatically, her contemporary novels show an awareness of changing social mores (especially in the lives of young women) and an eagerness to analyse this change in terms of individual experience; she has some sympathy with late-nineteenth-century attitudes. Having defended the Modern Girl in the pages of *The Monthly Packet* in 1872 she introduced 'a genuine suburban damsel' in Patience Bridgewater of *Hanbury Mills*.[15] Similarly up to date figures are the high-spirited Diaphenia Villiers (known as Daffodil) in *The Tender Mercies of the Good* and the college-educated sisters Constancy and Florella Vyner in *Waynflete*.[16]

This novel of 1893 follows Christabel's early *Giftie the Changeling* in its handling of the supernatural, which is combined so successfully with a nineteenth-century love story that Charlotte Yonge commended the novel as 'bringing something of the spirit and idea of *Sintram* into modern life'.[17] Thus it bears a complex relationship to Charlotte Yonge's own *Heir of Redclyffe*, heightened by the introduction of 'a slight, fair young man' named Guy, who is haunted (literally) by an evil doppelganger which seeks to reduce him to the drunken, cowardly degradation of his Waynflete ancestors. This family ghost is 'half his double and half his evil genius' and Guy (he is 'made of rather complex stuff') wonders 'If he shot himself, what would happen to his double?'[18] The 'Verena' of *Waynflete* is Florella Vyner, artist sister of the gifted, intelligent but conceited Constancy. Like Charlotte Yonge's Philip and Laura, Constancy and Godfrey (Guy's immature brother) provide a profane parallel to the sacred love of the purer couple Florella and Guy. As 'a helping angel' Florella has 'entered into definite conflict' with the ancient evil and aids Guy in the climatic struggle on the local bridge when he and the village simpleton Jem Outhwaite 'thrawed t'owd gen'lman in to t'water, *not he us*'.[19]

Like *The Heir*, *Waynflete* had no sequel, although to a less ambitious extent Christabel Coleridge followed the elder novelist in tracing her fictional protagonists through more than one novel; she also liked to collaborate with other writers: 'the method has generally been to first discuss the plot and then write the story bit by bit, each undertaking particular characters and correcting each other's work'.[20] Thus *Strolling Players* (1893) written in collaboration with Charlotte Yonge continues the story begun in *Jack O' Lanthorn*, and *Truth With Honour* written in 1890 with Mary Bramston is a sequel to *An English Squire* of 1881.[21]

Jack O' Lanthorn (1889) and *Strolling Players* suggest that Christabel Coleridge had at least a passing interest in Sir Henry Irving, who is mentioned in connection with the theatrical elements present in both novels, and whose striking looks are echoed in the cousins Alaric

Lambourne and Clarence Burnet. The two young men form a close
friendship despite (or perhaps because of) the intense family
disapproval engendered by the class conflicts caused by the marriage of
Alaric's 'gypsy' mother into the wealthy Lambourne clan, owners of
the desirable estate Monks Warren. Rivals for the hand of Cordelia
Worthing, whose statuesque beauty conceals a limited and
commonplace outlook, Alaric and Clarence move to London after a
rift with Alaric's family and become professional actors under the
tutelege of a long lost theatrical uncle. Recalled to the deathbed of
Martin Lambourne, his conscientious if formerly narrow minded
Guardian, Alaric heeds that cleric's parting injunction to be true to
himself; a process involving reconciliation between the two opposing
sides of his volatile nature and a recognition that his misguided,
immature feelings for Cordelia, and his wilder political ideas, have led
him astray. Eventually Alaric returns to Monks Warren, to his proper
station in life and a marriage to his cousin Emily. Clarence, on the
other hand, disappointed in love, embarks on a successful stage career.
It is not until he assists the amateur troupe in *Strolling Players* that he
finds a suitable wife in the talented Juliet Willingham. Alaric and
Emily also make a cameo appearance in the later novel, attesting to
the happiness of their marriage.

According to reviews and advertisements, *An English Squire* is
Christabel Coleridge's best-known adult novel. It concerns the Lester
family, Tractarian country gentry in the best Charlotte Yonge
tradition and headed by the fascinating 'Squire' Alvar Lester and his
saintly half-brother Cheriton. The love affairs of these two and their
stolid, priggish brother Jack form the staple of the novel, although
Cheriton is not happily settled until the sequel *Truth With Honour*.
Another major theme is the struggle of Alvar, who has been brought
up in Spain, to conform to the social stereotype expected of him as an
exemplary English Squire (perhaps reminiscent of Giftie's similar
struggles). Alvar even more than Giftie is a truly romantic figure, handsome, half Spanish, proud, ill at ease in bucolic English surroundings
yet eager to please the English relatives whom he meets only in adult
life. Like Guy of *The Heir of Redclyffe* Alvar was not entirely the
creation of one author: Christabel Coleridge's Preface states

> In bringing this tale in a complete form before the public, I
> should wish it to be understood that it arose out of a series of

conversations with a friend who suggested the character of Alvar Lester, to the original invention of which I can lay no claim whatever. He came to me from his Spanish home, and I have done nothing with him but turn him into an English Squire.

This, together with Christabel Coleridge's other collaborations, for example on the group novels *Astray* and *The Miz Maze*[22] links her to another significant aspect of *fin de siècle* women's writing, that of joint, group or collaborative production.

II

One of Christabel Coleridge's Torquay collaborators also offers an example of Charlotte Yonge's interaction with colleagues and female fellow-writers. Born in Exminster, Devonian Frances Peard had brought her widowed mother to settle in Torquay in 1864 and was thus an established member of the Torquay circle when the Coleridges arrived in 1880. Frances Peard's personal connection with Charlotte Yonge dated from the early 1860s; according to her memorialist she had been earning a living by writing since about 1853 and by 1861 was a regular contributor to Charlotte Yonge's *Monthly Paper of Sunday Teaching*. Letters between the two women date from April 1861 onwards and, again according to Peard's biographer, indicate that 'friendship and mutual attraction ripen[ed] into intimacy'.[23] During the 1860s the friends met regularly in Torquay and Otterbourne; they visited Oxford together in 1865, when Frances Peard noted how popular Yonge novels remained with a new generation of undergraduates. Frances Peard and Charlotte Yonge shared similar religious, political and intellectual interests; both had a keen involvement in their local communities and a general enthusiasm for life. We are told that Frances Peard was 'one of the old school' for whom 'things were either right or wrong' and she found it difficult to tolerate bores [. . .] but her ready humour and wide fields of interest (including lace-making, chess and the study of Braille) made her generally popular.[24] Like Charlotte Yonge she was a dog-lover; both authors created a variety of fictional dogs with Frances Peard naming one of her novels after a poodle (*Cartouche*).

Peard's work featured in *The Monthly Packet* from the late 1860s, both as reviewed and recommended reading for the young and as contributions to the monthly issues. Occasionally she wrote verse but more usually fiction, often with a distinctively continental setting. For example *The Wood-Cart and other Tales from the South of France* reprinted from the *Magazine for the Young* in 1867 and said in the *Monthly Packet* of January 1868 to be 'full of a quaint, bright atmosphere' is a collection of quite short stories evidently aimed at a younger age group than *The Monthly Packet*'s teens and twenties. The *Tales* can be described as 'picturesque' in the sense of visually realised accounts of events set in 'quaint' surroundings and usually concerning humble folk. 'The Riverside' features a family of peasant children living on the banks of the Gave; 'Jacques and His Sister' is a seaside adventure set in Biarritz. 'The Night Journey' describes a French diligence from which the boy hero falls during the odyssey of the title; 'The Fiery Trial' includes plans to kidnap one of Frances Peard's many canine characters, the Gallic LouLou. A dog also plays a part in 'The Mountain Path', set in the Pyrenees. Perhaps the final story is the most delightful. 'Whirligigtwisty' is a very French lizard, 'delicate and refined' distinguished from the rest of her large family by 'a little notch at the end of her tail'. Not content with her mundane brown skin, Whirligigtwisty longs to be a fashionable green and indulges in 'a grand fit of the dismals' until her natural camouflage saves her from a group of boys. Thus 'she found out that things were chosen for her better than she could choose them for herself', a moral repeated at some time by almost every member of the Yonge circle.[25]

Many of the characteristics of Peard's work were already established in *The Wood-Cart*. Twelve months later in January 1869 Charlotte Yonge was reviewing *One Year or the History of Three Homes*, a full length Peard novel published by Warne. This, she said,

> is as charming a book as we ever chanced to meet with. The scene lies first in France and then in England, and the contrast is most brilliantly drawn. Sometimes we are in a curious old lodging house at Dieppe, full of kindly noise and chatter; sometimes in a cool green Devonshire seaside village, in a great silence of reserve. The whole is full of thoughtful teaching, conveyed not directly but by inference, and the characters are all clearly cut, and so individual, that we feel as if each were a near friend or acquaintance. The busy girl with her perpetual 'irons in the fire'; the awkward girl; the shy clever one, who thinks exclusiveness loyalty; and the shuffling younger sister –

all are admirable portraits, as are the bright little shrew of a French heroine, her vagabond artist father, or the fat concierge and his wife. Few stories better repay reading.

This review both indicates where Frances Peard's fiction ran parallel with Yonge's and hints at where it diverged. The following month's *Monthly Packet* (February 1869) brought *The Stilt Walkers*, a strangely powerful story in which Peard's ability to link landscape to action, detected by Charlotte Yonge in her review of *One Year*, was vividly apparent. The rather melodramatic plot concerns the tangled emotions of a small group of intermarried French peasants living miles from any other habitation in a featureless marshy landscape. So waterlogged is the terrain that the inhabitants have to travel about on stilts, and the scene in which a coffin containing the corpse of an elderly peasant is borne off by the men of his family, all walking on stilts, lives in the memory as a grotesquely bizarre image.

If *The Stilt Walkers* is a successful 'long short story', *A Winter Story*, serialised in *The Monthly Packet* in 1875, is a superbly sustained short novel. The story of a boy, Philip Carr, who comes from a restricted town environment to live with his uncle in the West Country, it invites comparison with early Hardy (written about this time and perhaps read by Peard) and with the twentieth-century novelist Mary Webb, a writer perhaps nearer to her standard of ability. *A Winter Story* displays an intensely visual style together with the integration of character and landscape. The boy's growing delight in nature and his developing confidence and optimism are seen against a background of open moorland, sunshine and vernal foliage. His uncle, a remorse-stricken recluse, is equated with the dead season of the title. Where the novel falters is in its failure adequately to explain the causes of the elder hero's depression; after the atmospheric impression of the man's dreary state of mind this inevitably comes as an anti-climax as does his reconciliation with the lost love of his youth.

Unawares, published by Longmans in 1870, shares this reliance on a contrived plot but lives up to its subtitle of 'A Story of an Old French Town' with characteristic use of attractive settings and entertainingly 'foreign' conversations. It is more openly didactic than *A Winter Story* with a twenty-year-old heroine who like so many young women in Yonge circle fiction, is 'unaware' of her true mission in life until tested and enlightened by trial and suffering.

More illuminating is *Scapegrace Dick*, written for the National Society in 1887. This story for older children is set in the Interregnum of the 1650s, often a tricky or unpopular period for staunchly Royalist Tractarian writers. Frances Peard handles the political situation with remarkable tolerance, for admirable and well-intentioned folk are seen supporting both King and Parliament. Dick the boy hero is in fact 'a sturdy Roundhead' (though he later revises his opinion) and Admiral Blake, Cromwell's Naval Commander, is portrayed as a man of dogged, unromantic heroism and integrity. 'Scapegrace Dick' himself owes something to Charles Kingsley in his bone-headedly practical approach to life, yet he is capable of attachment to the Devonshire countryside:

> There never was a boy with less of what might be called sentiment about him, but something he must have had, though it was unlike the rest of him, and had never been suspected, of an artist's pleasure in colour, for as he came along the road he was noticing the rich browns and yellows of the soil, and the fine fulness of the trees, and the coils of white smoke which went up against the grey sky, and the blue of the distance. He used to tell Anthony that he hated the grange, but 'twas no such thing, and as he came upon it now, a low, grey, tenderly tinted house, set in a hollow, the slopes of which were feathered with fine trees, he looked at it almost lovingly. But nothing touched him with the consciousness that he was looking for the last time.[26]

Dick escapes from an unhappy home life by running away to sea, but his naval career is cut short by capture by the Dutch. Thus begins the central section of the book, as the unimpressed Philistine Dick is introduced into the Dutch artistic society of the age of Rembrandt. The great artist himself features in several episodes; there is a sensitive account of his son Titus, a complex character who clearly fascinated Frances Peard; and perhaps rather imaginative descriptions of the working methods of Gerard Dou and Nicholas Maes.

Only a writer dedicated to the practice and theory of painting could have produced *Scapegrace Dick* and in fact Frances Peard was an accomplished if self-taught watercolourist. For many years sketching holidays on the Continent had to satisfy her urge to travel and search for new subjects to paint, and she visited Oberammagau for the Passion Play, as well as Franzenbad and areas of France. She was already sixty when her mother died in 1895, but, unlike Charlotte Yonge who had made her first and only foray to the Continent by the age of fifty, Frances Peard was eager for new experiences. She became an adventurous traveller, happy to try any form of transport: in 1902 she wrote of the motor car, 'Why did I not live fifty years hence, by which time they will be as common as wheelbarrows!'[27] From 1895 she was based in Rome and travelled all over Europe as well as to Algeria, Tunis and Egypt. From 1899 to 1900 she was in India, returning there in 1907 when she also visited Japan, a country which she admired immensely.

Sadly her last years, back in Torquay, were a battle against arthritis, heart disease and finally blindness before she died in 1923 aged 88.

I would argue that Charlotte Yonge appreciated her friend's talents and approved of the uses to which they were devoted; the two women were linked by social, religious and intellectual similarities as well as by personal affection. In very different ways both achieved satisfaction within socially acceptable bounds; Charlotte Yonge as a writer and teacher while, in the next generation Frances Peard, after years as a dutiful home daughter, successful writer and active member of her local community, was able to take on a second persona as the formidable elderly Victorian lady traveller.

Returning to Showalter's analysis, how do Christabel Coleridge and Frances Peard conform to her paradigm of a female literary tradition or subculture and the developing phases of women's writing?

In the context of a female line of wit, the institution of the Gosling Society and its manuscript magazine, and the relationship of the *Barnacle* to *The Monthly Packet*, with their overlapping circles of contributors, is clear evidence. Christabel Coleridge graduated from the Goslings to professional authorship, while Frances Peard became personally integrated into the Gosling circle through professional links with Charlotte Yonge. Collaborative novels, shared discussion of themes and characters, and internal reviewing and recommendation all fit this pattern and are seen in the careers of both writers. Whether the notion of development in Showalter's sense is appropriate is more questionable. Rather, I think, we see Charlotte Yonge's successful exploitation of traditional social and religious mores and boundaries to exercise her talents within the confines of Tractarian 'safety' being challenged and extended: in Christabel Coleridge's case to provide what her obituarist called the 'link between the Victorian and the modern novel' and in Frances Peard's firstly to work towards a version of landscape writing in the genre of Hardy and Mary Webb and secondly, in later life to undertake adventurous journeys of personal fulfilment.

III

The third category of Charlotte Yonge Followers, her Winchester Circle, is a particularly lively group with links to some of the late nineteenth century's most intriguing families: including the brilliant and troubled Bensons. A notable member is Florence Wilford who between 1858 and 1895 produced a varied output covering the hugely popular *A Maiden of Our Own Day* (1862), *Vivia* (1870) and the challenging *Nigel Bartram's Ideal* (1869) in which Marion, the heroine, is the author of a highly successful sensation novel titled *Mark's Dream*. Unfortunately her fiancé Nigel Bartram, a mediocre but high minded journalist and reviewer, stigmatises the novel as 'calculated to do mischief' and has no idea that it issues from the pen of his ideal of meek, subservient womanhood.[28] Also worth further study is Amélie LeRoy, exhibiting painter, author of the *Harum Scarum* series of girls' stories and partner of the High School founder and community leader Anna Bramston.[29]

However this essay will focus briefly on Mary Bramston, like her half-sister Anna a daughter of a Dean of Winchester (Dean John Bramston, appointed in 1872). Mary's integration into the Winchester circle began in 1868 when at the age of twenty-seven she came to the College as house assistant to her brother, John Trant Bramston, known to generations of Wykehamists as 'Trant'. Mary, described as small, lively, short-sighted and with a 'quick, sharp little laugh'[30] was already contributing to *The Monthly Packet* and her first novel, *Cecy's Recollections*, was published in 1870. When Trant married in 1875 Mary was no longer required as his unpaid assistant and moved to Truro in Cornwall to work with the newly appointed Bishop, Edward White Benson; she followed the family to Addington when Benson became Archbishop of Canterbury in 1883 and ran a boarding house connected with the Croydon Girls' High School. About the turn of the century and certainly after Benson's sudden death in 1896 Mary returned to Winchester where she supervised the building of a house near her brother Trant's retirement home, helped her half sister Anna and her partner Amelie LeRoy with their work for the Winchester

Girls High School, was involved in missionary and GFS activities, and pursued her life long interest in theology. In 1906, at the age of sixty-five she was one of the first five women (two of whom were religious sisters) to gain the Anglican Diploma of Student in Theology, a qualification enabling successful candidates to teach the subject and requiring a year's study and an examination. Not surprisingly, on her death in 1912 the *Church Guardian* obituarist described her as 'far beyond the average in intelligence and learning'.

Mary Bramston's literary output was vast and varied. Amongst the most delightful work are the recitation and performance pieces written for GFS and school Entertainments: I have sat in the round Reading Room of the old British Library struggling to contain my laughter when reading these. She also contributed SPCK books such as *Missy and Master* (1881) evidently influenced by the 'theatrical' fiction of Mrs Walton and Hesba Stretton, and a number of works on the theme of education: *Punch, Judy and Toby* (1896) which mentions a South London Polytechnic and Commercial school, and *Barbara's Behaviour* (1907) one of a number of Girls' High School stories.

Her historical fiction (unusually amongst the Yonge circle) displays awareness of the past as distinguishable from the present by differing social mores, thoughts and emotions as well as romantic costumes and settings. *The Banner of St. George*, a full length adult novel published in 1901[31] is an account of the Peasants' Revolt told if not quite from the viewpoint of the peasants at least from that of a sympathetic participant in the rising. The sturdy, independent bourgeoisie emerge as the real heroes rather than the wild-eyed anarchist followers of Jack Straw, but at least organised political action is shown as a valid response to oppression. As an earlier story set in 1303 noted this as a period when 'the renaissance had not yet numbed our sense of form and colour, and England was behind no country in artistic power and design'[32] one may conclude that Mary Bramston was a disciple of Ruskin and Morris.

Her first novel *Cecy's Recollections*[33] is a *Bildungsroman* with a contemporary setting in which the heroine ('not quite five feet when fully grown') relates a series of experiences which include exploiting her musical talents to support a family of two adults and five children almost unaided. This first novel employs motifs derived from contemporary writing including that of Charlotte Yonge but also shows some attributes peculiar to the author. Central ideas include the ability of women to act as breadwinners; the inadvisability of marriage between partners of unequal intellect; and the difficulties a proud, gifted woman is likely to encounter in the marriage market. Overall, as with Charlotte Yonge, the main theme or metaphor is the Christian process of trial and preparation through suffering and endurance, which alone makes the soul fit for ultimate happiness.

These themes are handled with a new maturity in 1889 with Mary Bramston's *tour de force*, hailed by the *Spectator as* 'one of the strongest of recent novels'. This work is entitled *The Apples of Sodom.*[34] Though enlivened by Mary Bramston's characteristically dry humour, *The Apples of Sodom* is an intensely serious attempt to come to terms with the problems of gender identity and relationships in the late 1880s; I think it may have been triggered by a situation known to the Bramston family since it was written at the same time as Esmé Stuart's *Joan Vellacot:* both novels share the motif of the 'eternal triangle' and Mary Bramston's title repeats the final chapter heading of her friend's three-decker work.

The Apples of Sodom is divided into three sections: Leaf, Flower and Fruit, preceded by an introductory chapter which presents the main characters in the setting of Prize Day at a Public School. In view of the novel's slightly ambiguous title, it is somewhat startling to find the sixth form hero, Marcus Brand, nicknamed Brenda and referred to as 'she'. 'When a fellow's got a girl's name, he does get called she', explains a junior boy with undeniable logic.[35] Although this may suggest obvious conclusions about late-nineteenth-century Winchester (the Public School which Mary Bramston knew best), it is soon clear in the context of the novel that any *double entendres* are not intentional . . . at least I think not. Marcus Brand is to encounter many problems but sodomy in the technical sense is not one of them. His school nickname has been mentioned only to aid the suggestion that

> Marcus' nature was essentially a protecting one, as most men's are in whom there is an element of the woman [. . .] not effeminacy, but womanliness.[36]

Marcus the womanly man is balanced by a young woman 'more boyish than girlish' with a significantly androgynous name. Armine Constable (like Barbara Talbot of *Cecy's Recollections*) is a professor's daughter, something of a Zuleika Dobson as the 'most remarkable young lady in Oxbridge'. A satirical slant on the aesthetic fashions of the 1880s describes her collection of old china and peacocks' feathers, her hand-painted doors and window shutters decorated 'effectively with daffodils, bullrushes and cranes' and her talent for the violin: 'it is an affectation of mannishness when a girl plays the violin', comments a critical observer.[37]

Marcus and Armine fall in love: their complementary natures are made for each other – but it is a guilty passion in that the honourable, chivalrous Marcus is already pledged to his childhood sweetheart the pretty but trivial and petty-minded Jenny Fermor. When the inevitable parting comes Armine cannot fall back on family affection as her widower father has remarried, bringing a jealous and uncongenial stepmother into the household which Armine has ruled for so long. Music is her only resource and like Cecy, though for different reasons, she becomes a professional.

Section II, Flower, follows the now married Marcus and Jenny to London. Marcus has been ordained and they have a daughter, Maidie. In order to make ends meet they take a lodger, a young girl pianist named Anstace Fiennes, who has met Armine some years previously and is now destined to bring Marcus and Armine together. As a successful violinist Armine has needed an accompanist since her previous 'humble admirer' ('she fell in love with me at Leipzig' and gave 'unquestioning devotion') had to leave. Anstace is overjoyed to be taken on, as Armine's admirers apparently included 'quite as many of her own sex as the other'. The narrative voice asks:

> What is it about some people which makes them take so many hearts captive? Is it an underlying stratus of unexpressed masculinity in a woman, and of unexpressed femininity in a man, which makes their nature fuller and completer than the average, and puts more strength and flavour into their common actions than ordinary people have, while it by no means detracts from the outside womanliness or manliness which they show to the world?[38]

This passage is the crux of the novel's most dominant theme, that of gender identity. Charlotte Yonge generally left this unexplored (though we may recall Louis' Fitzjocelyn's need for a husband) and it is probably informed by Mary Bramston's own experiences, for example as an intimate of the Benson family.

Anstace, whose feelings for Armine trigger this passage, is soon to become engaged to a young man called George Eden. Armine still loves Marcus; a moment of relief when Maidie is recovered after wandering away culminates in a passionate stolen embrace between the pair. Horrified, Anstace is a witness; she vows to hold Armine to the path of virtue, finding the cost of 'helpfulness' a high one when duty sends her to Italy with Armine rather than to Australia with George. Meanwhile Jenny has been badly injured in an accident. Possibly due to her lack of good breeding, she is 'not the unselfish sufferer whose sick chamber is often the brightest spot in an anxious house';[39] she is aware that her marriage has been less than successful and dies querulous and disillusioned.

Section III, Fruit, works out the consequences of these events. Anstace and George are reunited. Armine and Marcus marry, but 'the perfect bliss Armine expected, does not come'. Maidie is difficult and unattractive, and Marcus, burdened by guilt for the failure of his first marriage, has become stern and joyless. Religious friction is inevitable since Armine is 'practically a pagan', feels no guilt for the past and nurtures worldly ambitions when Marcus' fame as a preacher spreads. A baby is born, but when the child dies Marcus' reaction (judged 'overstrained and morbid' by the omniscient narrator) is that this sorrow is the 'fruit' of his previous sin. Refusing the offer of a fashionable living, he broods over his past failings and present unhappiness until an illness provides him with the excuse to undertake a recuperative voyage to Australia.

There is a shipwreck and Marcus is reported first missing and then dead. In her grief Armine is reconciled with Maidie and via music and poetry, finds comfort in religious faith. At this point Marcus returns and Armine is able to receive her husband with renewed hope for the future; the novel closes with 'Armine becoming year by year a sweeter and tenderer woman'.[40]

Once again, the underlying message concerns the spiritual pilgrimage towards virtuous happiness. Marcus and Armine both make mistakes which must be expiated before they can find peace and spiritual maturity. Like Charlotte Yonge, Mary Bramston writes with a didactic purpose; but her personal preoccupations with, for instance, the problems of marriage and sexual orientation enrich and diversify her constant theme of earthly life as a time of trial and preparation.

Of the three younger novelists described so far, Mary Bramston comes closest to Showalter's feminist phase in her 'advocacy of minority rights and values, including a demand for autonomy'.[41] But because the theme of a Divine purpose worked out by the human protagonist through trial within the sphere of domestic and familial relationships, is common to Yonge, Coleridge, Peard and Bramston, the final section of this essay will present a contrasted reworking of the Tractarian metaphor. This contrast consists in a major twentieth-century novelist who uses and inverts the entire premise of Charlotte Yonge and her followers, and that novelist is Ivy Compton Burnett.

IV

'I have had such an uneventful life that there is little to say', wrote the disingenuous Compton Burnett when asked to provide a biographical outline for the first Penguin edition of her works. Coincidentally Georgina Battiscombe chose *The Story of an Uneventful Life* as the title for her 1943 biography of Charlotte Yonge. In both cases the word 'uneventful' was at once apt and misleading. Certainly neither of these formidable novelists adventured far from home. Perhaps Hove and Braemar Mansions were marginally more cosmopolitan than Otterbourne, but on the other hand Charlotte Yonge's passions for non-professional activities such as botany, shell-collecting, teaching and GFS work seem like giddy diversification compared with Ivy Compton Burnett's limited (if enviable) preoccupation with expensive chocolates and cultivated flowers. 'Events' in both lives were in one sense limited to the deaths of family and friends (more evidently tragic in the Compton Burnett household) and to the acquisition of professional status as working novelists. The less obvious but deeply significant internal events experienced and written about by Charlotte Yonge and Ivy Compton Burnett were the daily happenings of the Victorian family. Having explored this common territory, they were to offer very different maps to their readers. As R. Glynn Grylls famously remarked, 'any [. . .] novel by Miss Compton Burnett [. . .] is about a family whose address is 'Huis Clos'.'[42] The significance of a comparison of the two novelists lies in this difference of view, the contrasting interpretations of apparently similar situations, revealing a dichotomy which presents an opportunity to compare Charlotte Yonge's created world with Ivy Compton Burnett's alternative reality: alternative in that it is based on observation of a rather similar set of circumstances. Elizabeth Bowen noted that both women wrote about the Victorian family:

> the Victorians had no need to look far beyond the family. The family was the circuit: the compulsory closeness of its members to one another, like the voluntary closeness of people making a ring of contact to turn a table, generated something [. . .] The most obvious instance is Charlotte M. Yonge [. . .] Miss Compton Burnett is not merely copying but actually continuing the Victorian novel. She continues it, that is to say, from the inside [. . .][43]

Both novelists stress emotional ties between siblings, and between parents and children rather than between lovers; they have a sympathetic yet unsentimental view of children; single women are given emphasis and validity; human failings are unsparingly exposed; and the main channel of communication with the reader is through conversation. John Ginger notes the centrality of father / daughter relationships, [44] and *A Father and His Fate* features a character tellingly named Verena.

Hilary Spurling in *Ivy When Young* draws frequent comparisons between Ethel May of *The Daisy Chain* and Dolores, eponymous heroine of Ivy Compton Burnett's first novel. The inference is that the young Compton Burnetts would have felt 'the immense influence' of Charlotte Yonge and indeed other sources suggest that few girls growing up at the end of the century would not have read at least some of the better known Yonge novels. Quentin Bell records Vanessa and Virginia Stephen as readers, characteristically noting down the number of deaths per story. 'Ivy when young' was, then, exposed to Charlotte Yonge's fictional world and her own social milieu, though less distinguished than the senior novelist's, was close enough for the two women to be bizarrely connected by the ill-fated psychic Versailles experience of Annie Moberly and Eleanor Jourdain, sister of Ivy Compton Burnett's companion Margaret.

Fourteen years after the publication of *Dolores*, Compton Burnett found her authentic tone in *Pastors and Masters* (1925) and, according to Hilary Spurling, 'from 1925 onwards she narrowed her focus on the self-contained, heavily controlled and monitored, closed society of the High Victorian family'.[45] 'You write of the family as being a destructive unit', said the novelist John Bowen in a 1960 radio interview with Compton Burnett, who answered austerely: 'I write of power being destructive and parents had absolute power over children in those days. One or the other had.'

In thus defining parental power as a destructive force Ivy Compton Burnett offered a complete negation of Charlotte Yonge's entire theological system, a system which she must therefore have perceived with some clarity.

For Charlotte Yonge the Christian family was the type or metaphor of the relationship between God (the Father and father), Mother Church and her faithful obedient children. Authority was a prime concept in Anglican theology, which was striving to vindicate the Church of England's claim to Apostolicity; obedience to parents, like obedience to the visible Church, meant obedience to God.

Further, the family paralleled the Church in being at once a human and a divine institution; a presentation which combined idealisation of the family with a mechanism for accepting its less fortunate aspects. Ivy Compton Burnett made her own use of the Tractarian metaphor. When she rejected the stereotypes of the subservient 'home daughter' and of the believing Anglican she stayed inside the same structure of thought by stressing the paternal role of the deity whose existence she denied. (In the following quotation from *Pastors and Masters* she omits the divine capital.)

'I like him not childless, and grasping and fond of praise. I like the human and family interest', says Bumpus. Emily Herrick adds, 'And he had such a personality [. . .] such a superior, vindictive and over-indulgent one. He is one of the best drawn characters in fiction'.[46]

Helene Cixous posits that

> Paternity, which is a fiction, is fiction passing itself off as truth. Paternity is the lack of being which is called God.[47]

The existence of God is the (often unspoken) reality to which Charlotte Yonge's fiction attests; for Ivy Compton Burnett, as for Cixous, God is the fiction and the so-called fiction of the novel asserts reality. The antithesis between Yonge and Compton Burnett is the contrast between the family as a divine institution, part of an ordered system and a means of salvation, and the family as a human arena for the attempted resolution of power conflicts, with parental authority seen as a force for evil rather than for good. It is the tension between order and chaos; and where Charlotte Yonge, with her high ideals and expectations, was formidable, 'Ivy', as Hilary Spurling remarked, 'was frightening'.

In feminist terms Yonge accepts and Compton Burnett rejects the Lacanian Law of the Father, suggesting that the latter has moved fully into Showalter's female phase. Kathy Justice Gentile says of this movement towards autonomy that 'while Compton Burnett shuns the theological superstructure of the novel, her house of fiction is nevertheless constructed upon a foundation laid by male and female precursors'.[48] I would take issue with the term 'shuns' since in rejecting patriarchy Compton Burnett inverts and reworks rather than discards a theological agenda. And while Compton Burnett may be imprisoned in her house of fiction (with its 'Huis Clos' doorplate) I would free her as a participant in the Yonge Followers' line of wit, testifying to the very existence of that female literary subculture by her inimitable process of subversion and inversion.

Thanks are owed to the Librarian, Lady Margaret Hall, Oxford, for permission to reproduce material from *The Barnacle*.

1   Originals of *The Barnacle* are held in the Library, Lady Margaret Hall, Oxford. For fuller information on the Goslings and the contents of *The Barnacle* see Julia Courtney, 'The Barnacle, a Manuscript Magazine of the 1860s' in Claudia Nelson and Lynne Vallone (ed.), *The Girl's Own: Cultural Histories of the Anglo-American Girl, 1815-1930* (Athens and London: University of Georgia Press, 1994) pp. 71-97.

2   Christabel Rose Coleridge, *Charlotte Mary Yonge: Her Life and Letters* (London: Macmillan, 1903) p. 201.

3   Coleridge, *Charlotte Mary Yonge*, p. 203.

4   Elaine Showalter, *A Literature of Their Own*, 1977 (London: Virago, 1991).

5   Toril Moi, *Sexual / Textual Politics* (London: Routledge, 1985).

6   Philip Rice and Patricia Waugh, *Modern Literary Theory: A Reader* (3rd ed.) (London: Edward Arnold, 1996).

7   Showalter, p. 11.

8   Showalter, p. 137: Mrs Edmund Stone in *The Heir*; p. 328: Yonge described as 'born in Winchester' and daughter 'of a rich clergyman'!

9   Showalter, p. 13.

10   Coleridge, *Charlotte Mary Yonge*, p. 259.

11   Georgina Battiscombe, *Charlotte Mary Yonge. The Story of an Uneventful Life* (London: Constable, 1943) p. 158.

12   For more information on the Coleridges and their relationship with Charlotte Yonge, see Julia Courtney, 'Charlotte M. Yonge: A Novelist and Her Readers', unpublished PhD thesis, University of London, 1990.

13   Mary Cholmondeley, *Under One Roof* (London: John Murray, 1912) p. 115.

14   Christabel Rose Coleridge, *Minstrel Dick* (London: Gardner, Darton and Co., 1896).

15   Christabel Rose Coleridge, *Hanbury Mills* (London: Frederick Warne, 1872).

16   Christabel Rose Coleridge, *The Tender Mercies of the Good* (London: Isbister and Co.,1895) and *Waynflete* (London: A. D. Innes, 1893).

17   C. M. Yonge, 'Introduction' to F. de La Motte Fouqué, *Sintram* (London: Gardner, Darton and Co., 1896) p. xviii.

18   Christabel Rose Coleridge, *Waynflete*, vol. 2, p. 87.

19   Coleridge, *Waynflete*, vol. 2, p. 242.

20   *Torbay Directory* interview, 8 January 1896.

21   *Jack O'Lanthorn* (London: Walter Smith and Innes, 1889); *Truth With Honour* (London: Walter Smith and Innes, 1890); *An English Squire* (London: Sampson Low, 1881).

22   C. M. Yonge and Others, *Astray* (London: Macmillan, 1886) and *The Miz Maze* (London: Macmillan, 1883).

23   Mary J. Harris, *Memoir of Frances Mary Peard* (Torquay: W. H. Smith, 1930) p. 47.

24   Harris, pp. 73, 69.

25   Frances Mary Peard, *The Wood-Cart and Other Tales of the South of France* (London and Oxford: Mozley, 1867) p. 186.

26   Frances Mary Peard, *Scapegrace Dick* (Westminster: The National Society, 1887) p. 9.

27   Harris, p. 23.

28   Florence Wilford, *Nigel Bartram's Ideal* (London: Frederick Warne, 1869).

29   For more on Amélie LeRoy (aka Esmé Stuart) and Anna Bramston, see Julia Courtney, cited in note 12.

30   *The Times* obituary, 10 February 1912.

31   Mary Bramston, *The Banner of St. George* (London: Duckworth, 1901).

32   Mary Bramston, *Prisoners and Pasties* in *The Monthly Packet* Christmas Number 1873, p. 54.

33   Mary Bramston, *Cecy's Recollections* (London: J. Strachan, 1870).

34   Mary Bramston, *The Apples of Sodom* (London: Walter Smith and Innes, 1889).

35   *Apples of Sodom*, vol. 1, p. 4.

36   *Apples of Sodom*, vol. 1, p. 38.

37   *Apples of Sodom*, vol. 1, p. 148.

38   *Apples of Sodom*, vol. 1, p. 238.

39   *Apples of Sodom*, vol. 2, p. 85.

40   *Apples of Sodom*, vol. 2, p. 322.

41   Showalter, p. 13.

42   R. Glynn Grylls, 'Review of *A Father and his Fate*', *Sunday Times* (11 Aug. 1957), in Charles Burkhart, ed., *The Art of Ivy Compton Burnett* (London: Gollancz, 1972) pp. 66-67; passage cited from p. 66.

43   Elizabeth Bowen, 'Review of *Elders and Betters*', *Cornhill Magazine* (1944), in Burkhart, pp. 58-63; passage cited from pp. 59-61.

44   John Ginger, 'Ivy Compton Burnett', *London Magazine* (January 1970), reprinted in Burkhart, pp. 172-184.

45   Hilary Spurling, *Secrets of a Woman's Heart* (London: Hodder and Stoughton, 1984) p. 174.

46   Ivy Compton Burnett, *Pastors and Masters*, 1925 (London: Allison and Busby, 1984) p. 24.

47   Quoted in Kathy Justice Gentile, *Ivy Compton Burnett* (Women Writers series, London: Macmillan, 1991) p. 66.

48   Gentile, p. 18.

A SERMON PREACHED AT S. MATTHEW'S, OTTERBOURNE

IN MEMORIAM C.M.Y. MARCH 31ST, 1901

By the Rev. Canon Moberly, D.D.
Regius Professor of Pastoral Theology
Christ Church, Oxford

"For it is written, Rejoice, thou barren that bearest not; break forth and cry, thou that travailest not; for the desolate hath many more children than she which hath an husband. – Gal. iv.27"

St. Paul is quoting from the 54th chapter of Isaiah. Both the Apostle and the Prophet are speaking of Jerusalem as the fruitful mother of spiritual children. Both are contrasting the literal Jerusalem with the spiritual Jerusalem, and the literal bearing of children in the natural sense, with the real spiritual motherhood, the bearing of children as in God, and to God. And in this contrast both Isaiah and St. Paul are carried away with the thought what a small thing natural motherhood is in comparison with spiritual motherhood. It is not the woman who has borne and bred most children in the flesh, but she who has borne and bred most children in respect of the divine character and the divine spirit: – she is the true mother; hers is the abiding joy of motherhood. "Break forth and cry, thou that travailest not: for the desolate hath many more children than she which hath an husband."

You know well with what thought it is that I venture to begin by striking such a note as this. We, as we look back today, can see that

213

there have been few indeed to whom could so rightly be given the title that Deborah claimed for herself long ago. You remember the verse in the 5th chapter of Judges, "The inhabitants of the villages ceased, they ceased in Israel, until that I, Deborah, arose, that I arose a mother in Israel." A mother in Israel. In Israel, that will mean to us, in the very House or Church of God: and a mother, one, that is, from whom came the spiritual opening of the eyes, the spiritual formation and sustaining of character, of countless children in Christ. Whom can we name, who has been in her time, or for so long a time, more completely all that word "Mother in Israel" really means than Miss Yonge, whom you reverently miss and mourn today: Miss Yonge – without whom there is no one, I suppose, now living who can at all remember the village of Otterbourne?

It is natural to think of her first and most as a teacher of others, so early in life did she begin to teach, and so long has her work as teacher continued without a break. But let me remind you – what we all know quite well – that there is something else which is really from the first, and throughout, the necessary foundation of teaching. She could teach much because she could learn well. Born herself of parents who were simply, strongly, dutifully religious, and the pupil, from early days, and true spiritual daughter, of Mr. Keble, in whom she learned to discern and to love, the truly reflected image of the spirit of his Lord, she learned first to be, in the simplicity of her own soul, that which she could have never rightly taught to others, if she had not first learned and practised it in herself. It was here in Otterbourne, surrounded by all the familiar Otterbourne surroundings; here at the foot of your familiar hill; here with the Itchen and the water-meadows on one side, and Cranbury Park, and the Hursley Woods, and the New Forest country on the other; here within the range, so to speak, of Winchester Cathedral, and College, and St. Cross, and the fresh chalk downs which encircle them; here in the quiet village life, under these skies, amid these trees, and these flowers, and these birds and butterflies and these particular homes and families and traditions; it was here that she learned her lessons from the past and in the present – learned from history alike, and imagination and religious faith, the true meaning of the true service of God and man. Here, and in this House – in this House from the time of its first building under her father's thoughtful and reverent care – here she waited as a dutiful handmaid upon the Lord: here she learned, as in earlier days, when

Mr. Keble prepared her for her confirmation, so throughout the length of a long life, what Christian truth, and Christian faith and Christian life, and Christian hope, and Christian power – in the Sacraments of Christ's Church – really are.

What she learnt, that she taught. She taught it first, and throughout, in the most direct way. It is not for me to stand here and tell you – rather I would ask you to think how much you could tell me, or even tell one another – as to her religious teaching in the Otterbourne School, or in classes of one kind or another, growing out of it. How many years is it since she began teaching in Otterbourne? How many generations of Otterbourne children have learned in their time to associate Scripture lessons, or other forms of religious teaching, with her own peculiar manner and tone of voice? How many generations of Otterbourne children, or those who were Otterbourne children once, could say of her, as St. Paul said of old of Phebe, "our sister," as he calls her, "which is a servant of the Church which is at Cenchrea . . . For she hath been a succourer of many, and of myself also." – Romans xvi.1.

But it is of something much wider than her work in Otterbourne that we are thinking to-day. After all, quiet as her life was, if you look at its outer conditions, it is wonderful really how much that life contained, and how rich its content was. Will anyone say it was a solitary life? Well, Otterbourne, no doubt, is a quiet place, and her home party never was a large one, and it is many, many years since the death of old Mr. Yonge; so many that even among those whose hair is gray, and who feel themselves old men, there will be some whose very memory of him is little more than a dim and childish memory. And it is many years since Mrs. and Miss Yonge left the old home to go to the house in which you have known her so long, and many years, too, since Mrs. Yonge went to her rest. And since then, at least, shall we say that the life has been in the main a solitary one? Surely, if there is an aspect in which this is partly true, it would be much more true to say that her life has been a richly peopled one; peopled more richly by far than the lives of many who are all day long in a hurry and in a crowd. For she from the first was endowed with what men call, not unaptly, the gift of a lively imagination. What is this lively or "life-giving" imagination, this imagination which makes things to be "alive?" What is the meaning of it, and what is its function? Is it a mere delusion; and idle or misleading unreality? It may be so degraded as to become all this. But this is not at all what it properly means. It may be so misused as to be a mere substitute for truth, mystifying and misleading the minds which yield themselves to it, and find that they have been mocked by an empty illusion. But the real work of a lively imagination is not so much to create unrealities, or substitute the untrue for the true. Rather it is to make the truth living and real, as it was not before to the minds of the unimaginative. It is to make remote truths near and present; and dull precepts fascinatingly interesting; and slumbering principles all alert with living power. It is to bring us into near and living contact with all the realities of all the world, however remote from us outwardly, in place, or time, or kind.

Think how imagination gives life to history. We have heard perhaps that William Rufus, the King, when killed in the New Forest, was carried in a cart along the King's Lane, past Silkstede, to be buried in Winchester Cathedral. How much or how little is this, or any other of the historical events connected with Winchester, or its neighbour-hood, *to us?* But only think how these scenes become alive again, as living realities, and the different actors in them become no longer dull names, but living flesh and blood – with all the throb and play of human anxieties and hopes – to the minds of those who have diligence enough to hunt out all such facts as can be known; and imagination enough to put them all together into a single glowing picture or narrative! And in this it is plain that imagination serves not so much to invent fictions as to make truth living and real.

Again, as imagination makes dead scenes out of history live, so think how it also gives life to abstract principles. A precept becomes a parable. A proverb is recognized as the brief summary of a whole chapter of living incident. So every realized principle, or complexity of principles, to her imagination became a story. The story was the illustration of the principle. But the principle, as illustrated in the story, had a power which as an abstract principle it would never have had, to bite upon the imagination, to sink into the hearts, and be fruitful in the characters, of a great variety of readers. As true history, rightly understood, is the illustration of divine principles, and is therefore, when rightly told, an unfolding of something of the Being of God; so also true principles of the Being and government of God may be set forth, with luminous clearness, in what we call fiction. Perhaps everyone who has read any little story of hers, however slight or small, will recognise herein what I say. And this is the principle which underlay the parables of our Lord Jesus Christ Himself. They were

216

Divine truths put as stories. And they are the sanction for ever of fiction as a vehicle of Divine truths.

Perhaps the smallest stories show this most plainly. But this, probably, is the true account, in principle, of all serious fiction. It is not for amusement only; still less for fantastic extravagance; least of all for demoralization, or for self-indulgence, or the pleasure of studying vice. But it is still, really, even in complicated situations, or exceptional trials, a setting forth of essential truth through fiction – a preaching of righteousness and of truth, of God and of faith, under the shifting forms which human experience suggests. And it is all this through the power which belongs to true, life-giving, but religiously disciplined, imagination.

Now in these ways, for at least half a century, Miss Yonge has been helping to teach, by history and by fiction, one generation after another, not only of children in Otterbourne, but of children, and of grown up people, too, throughout the whole length and breadth of the English-speaking world. And because she was always true to herself and to her God, therefore her teaching in these ways, however much it might otherwise amuse or instruct, went always, most of all, to this – to the true building up of moral and of spiritual character. Every writer of fiction, as well as history, must, whether purposely or not, be teaching something, through his fiction, about God and man. He whose fiction contradicts the character of God, is abusing his God-given power of imagination to perplex and mislead the children of God. But he who understands what faith in God means and is true to the faith which he understands, is always, in all that he teaches, performing that truest service to God upon earth – he is helping to build up Divine character, as in himself, so no less truly in others.

"For at least half a century." Truly may she be thought rich in daughters, aye and in sons, who for so many years has borne such a part in the training for God of the characters of English men and women. Truly may she be called "Mother in Israel." And may we not, in all reverence, think of her as meeting in Paradise with many who, though she knew them not here, yet have owed to her, in the wonderful mercy of God, no small part of what they have themselves been enabled to become? And if it be true that English men and women read her work, or care for it, less now than a generation ago – well, I will not accuse my generation; but let them look to it carefully; let them, before they turn lightly from her, inquire first, and be sure that they can find done as well in other ways that priceless work which she, in her way, did for their elders so loyally and so well. In this work she has surely been herself no small part of the history of our country for the last half century, as that history is recorded in the truth of God.

But that work is over now.

It is Palm-Sunday today. We are entering upon the awe of the Holy week. It is by the power of the death which we this week devoutly worship, that she could, or that anyone can, either live or die in Christ. Under the shadow of the Cross we leave her – which is her and our life.

It is just five-and-thirty years since, in the middle of the Holy Week, Mr. Keble was called to his rest. He fell asleep in the middle of the Holy Week, on the 29th of March. On the 29th of March, just before the Holy Week, all that was mortal of her was reverently laid in the grave. Their further, their more blessed, meeting in the Paradise of God, is, as yet, beyond our sight. Yet, not unaptly to us, they seem to meet and to rest together, there where it is fittest for Christian souls to rest – under the shadow of the Cross of Jesus crucified.

BIBLIOGRAPHY

BOOKS BY YONGE CITED IN THIS VOLUME, WITH ORIGINAL PUBLICATION DATES

Abbeychurch; or, Self Control and Self Conceit (London: James Burns; Derby: Henry Mozley, 1844)

The Armourer's Prentices (London: Macmillan, 1884)

Astray: A Tale of a Country Town (London: Hatchards, 1886) [with Mary Bramston, Christabel Coleridge, Esmé Stuart]

Aunt Charlotte's Stories of English History for the Little Ones (London: Marcus Ward, 1873)

Aunt Charlotte's Stories of Greek History for the Little Ones (London: Marcus Ward, 1876)

Aunt Charlotte's Stories of Roman History for the Little Ones (London: Marcus Ward, 1877)

Beechcroft at Rockstone (London: Macmillan, 1888)

A Book of Golden Deeds of All Times and All Lands (London: Macmillan, 1864)

A Book of Worthies Gathered from the Old Histories (London: Macmillan, 1869)

The Caged Lion (London: Macmillan, 1870)

The Carbonels (Westminster: National Society, 1895)

The Castle Builders (London: J. and C. Mozley, 1854)

Chantry House (London: Macmillan, 1886)

The Chaplet of Pearls; or, The White and Black Ribaumont (London: Macmillan, 1868)

The Clever Woman of the Family (London: Macmillan, 1865)

Countess Kate (London: Masters, 1862)

The Cunning Woman's Grandson (Westminster: National Society's Depository, 1889)

The Daisy Chain; or, Aspirations (London: John W. Parker and Son, 1856)

The Danvers Papers (London: Macmillan, 1867)

The Disturbing Element; or, Chronicles of the Blue-bell Society (London: Marcus Ward, 1878)

The Dove in the Eagle's Nest (London: Macmillan, 1866)

Dynevor Terrace; or, The Clue of Life (London: John W. Parker and Son, 1857)

Friarswood Post-Office (London: J. and C. Mozley; Masters, 1860)

Grisly Grisell; or, The Laidly Lady of Whitburn: A Tale of the Wars of the Roses (London: Macmillan, 1893)

Heartsease; or, The Brother's Wife (London: John W. Parker and Son, 1854)

The Heir of Redclyffe (London: John W. Parker and Son, 1853)

Henrietta's Wish; or, Domineering (London: Joseph Masters, 1850)

History of Christian Names, (London: Parker, Son and Bourn, 1863); new edition, revised (London: Macmillan, 1884)

Hopes and Fears; or, Scenes from the Life of a Spinster (London: John W. Parker and Son, 1860)

How to Teach the New Testament (Westminster: National Society's Depository, 1881)

Kenneth; or, The Rear Guard of the Grand Army (Oxford and London: Henry Parker, 1850)

The Lances of Lynwood (London: John W. Parker and Son, 1855)

The Little Duke; or, Richard the Fearless (London: John W. Parker and Son, 1854)

The Long Vacation (London: Macmillan, 1895)

Love and Life: An Old Story in Eighteenth Century Costume (London: Macmillan, 1880)

Magnum Bonum; or, Mother Carey's Brood (London: Macmillan, 1879)

The Miz Maze; or, the Winkworth Puzzle: A Story in Letters, by Nine Authors (London: Macmillan, 1883)

Modern Broods; or, Developments Unlooked For (London: Macmillan, 1900)

A Modern Telemachus (London: Macmillan, 1886)

Musings over the 'Christian Year' and 'Lyra Innocentium' (Oxford and London: James Parker, 1871)

My Young Alcides: A Faded Photograph (London: Macmillan, 1875)

Nuttie's Father (London: Macmillan, 1885)

The Pilgrimage of the Ben Beriah (London: Macmillan, 1897)

The Pillars of the House; or, Under Wode, Under Rode (London: Macmillan, 1873)

The Prince and the Page: A Story of the Last Crusade (London: Macmillan, 1866)

Questions on the Psalms (London: Walter Smith, 1881)

A Reputed Changeling; or, Three Seventh Years Two Centuries Ago (London: Macmillan, 1889)

Scenes and Characters; or, Eighteen Months at Beechcroft (London: James Burns; Derby: Henry Mozley, 1847)

Scripture Readings for Schools and Families with Comments (London: Macmillan, 1871) [followed by second to fifth series in 1872, 1874, 1876 and 1879]

The Slaves of Sabinus: Jew and Gentile (Westminster: National Society's Depository, 1890)

The Stokesley Secret (London: J. and C. Mozley, 1861)

The Story of the Christians and Moors of Spain (London: Macmillan, 1878)

Stray Pearls: Memoirs of Margaret de Ribaumont Viscountess of Bellaise (London: Macmillan, 1883)

Strolling Players: A Harmony of Contrasts (London: Macmillan, 1893) [with C. R. Coleridge]

The Three Brides (London: Macmillan, 1876)

The Trial: More Links of the Daisy Chain (London: Macmillan, 1864)

The Two Guardians; or, Home in this World (London: Joseph Masters, 1852)

Two Penniless Princesses (London: Macmillan, 1891)

The Two Sides of the Shield (London: Macmillan, 1885)

Unknown to History: A Story of the Captivity of Mary of Scotland (London: Macmillan, 1882)

What Books to Lend and What to Give (Westminster: National Society's Depository, 1887)

Womankind (London: Mozley and Smith, 1876) [first published in the *Monthly Packet*, January 1874 to January 1877]

Young Folks' History of England (Boston: Estes and Lauriat, 1879). [USA publication of *Aunt Charlotte's Stories of English History*]

The Young Stepmother; or, A Chronicle of Mistakes (London: Parker, Son and Bourn, 1861)

OTHER WORKS BY YONGE CITED IN THIS VOLUME

'Authorship', *Monthly Packet*, new [fourth] series, 4 (Sept. 1892) pp. 296-303. Reprinted in *A Chaplet for Charlotte Yonge*, pp. 185-92

'Hints on Reading', in *Monthly Packet*, first series, 2 (1851) pp. 322-24

'Introduction' to La Motte Fouqué, F. de. *Sintram* (London: Gardner, Darton, 1896) pp. xiii-xix

'Lifelong Friends', *Monthly Packet*, new [fourth] series, 8 (Dec. 1894) pp. 694-97. Reprinted in *A Chaplet for Charlotte Yonge*, pp. 181-84

'One Story by Two Authors; or, A Tale without a Moral', [with Jean Ingelow]. *Monthly Packet*, first series, 19-22 (1860-61). [The story runs for seventeen chapters, appearing at intervals throughout the two years.]

'A Real Childhood', *Mothers in Council* 3 (1893) p. 19 ff. Reprinted in *The Woman Reader, 1837-1914*, ed by K. Flint (Oxford: Clarendon Press, 1993) pp. 192-93

'Waiting', *Monthly Packet*, first series, 23 (1862) pp. 462-71

PERIODICALS EDITED BY YONGE

The Monthly Packet of Evening Readings for Younger Members of the English Church (edited by Yonge 1851-93). This ran in six-monthly volumes, and an additional Christmas number was also issued in many years.

First series: 1-30 (January 1851 to December 1865)

New Series: 1-30 (January 1866 to December 1880)

Third Series: 1-20 (January 1881 to December 1890)

New Series: 1-18 (January 1891 to December 1899)

The Monthly Paper of Sunday Teaching (edited by Yonge 1860-75)

Mothers in Council (edited by Yonge 1890-1900)

OTHER NINETEENTH-CENTURY PERIODICALS CITED IN THIS VOLUME

Academy
Athenaeum
Blackwood's Magazine
Christian Remembrancer
Church Guardian
Church Times
Churchman's Companion
Daily Telegraph
Dublin Review
Eclectic Magazine
Edinburgh Review
Fortnightly Review
Fraser's Magazine
Gentleman's Magazine

Guardian
Girl's Realm Annual
Household Words
Literary Churchman
Literary Gazette
Littell's Living Age
London Quarterly Review
Magazine for the Young
Modern Review
Murray's Magazine: A Home and Colonial Periodical for the General Public
Nation
National Review
Nineteenth Century
North American Review
North British Review
Penny Post
Prospective Review
Quarterly Review
Reader
Saturday Review
Spectator
Times

NINETEENTH-CENTURY NOVELS CITED IN THIS VOLUME

BRAMSTON, Mary. *The Apples of Sodom* (London: Walter Smith and Innes, 1889)
— *The Banner of St. George* (London: Duckworth, 1901)
— *Barbara's Behaviour* (London, 1907)
— *Cecy's Recollections* (London: J. Strachan, 1870)
— *Missy and Master* (London, 1881)
— *Punch, Judy and Toby* (London, 1896)
CHOLMONDELEY, Mary. *Under One Roof* (London: John Murray, 1912)
COLERIDGE, Christabel Rose. *An English Squire* (London: Sampson Low, 1881)
— *Giftie the Changeling* (London: Warne, 1868) [from publisher's advertisement]
— *Hanbury Mills* (London: Frederick Warne, 1872)
— *Jack O'Lanthorn* (London: Walter Smith and Innes, 1889)
— *Lady Betty* (London, 1870)
— *Minstrel Dick* (London: Gardner, Darton, 1896)
— *The Tender Mercies of the Good* (London: Isbister, 1895)
— *Truth With Honour* (London: Walter Smith and Innes, 1890) [with M. Bramston]
— *Waynflete* (London: A. D. Innes, 1893)
KINGSLEY, Charles. *Hypatia* (London: John W. Parker and Son, 1853)

LA MOTTE FOUQUÉ, F. DE. *Sintram and his Companions; and Undine* (London: Gardner, Darton and Co., 1896)

NEWMAN, John Henry. *Callista* (London: Burns and Oates, 1855)

PEARD, Frances Mary. *One Year; or, The History of Three Homes* (London: Warne, 1869)

— *Scapegrace Dick* (Westminster: Westminster: National Society's Depository, 1887)

— *Unawares: A Story of an Old French Town* (London: Longman, 1870)

— *The Wood-Cart; and Other Tales of the South of France* (London and Oxford: Mozley, 1867)

READE, Charles. *The Cloister and the Hearth* (London, 1861)

STUART, Esmé. *Joan Vellacot* (London: Richard Bentley and Son, 1889)

WILFORD, Florence. *A Maiden of Our Own Day* (London, 1862)

— *Nigel Bartram's Ideal* (London: Frederick Warne, 1869)

— *Vivia: A Modern Story* (London, 1870)

OTHER WORKS

Ancient History for Village Schools (London: Mozley, 1862)

ASHTON, Rosemary. *George Eliot: A Life* (London: Penguin, 1997)

BAILIN, Miriam. *The Sickroom in Victorian Fiction: The Art of Being Ill* (New York: Cambridge University Press, 1994)

BAKER, Joseph. *The Novel and the Oxford Movement* (Princeton: Princeton University Press, 1932)

BARCZEWSKI, Stephanie L. *Myth and National Identity in Nineteenth Century Britain* (Oxford: Oxford University Press, 2000)

BARING-GOULD, Sabine. 'The Three Crowns', *The Silver Store*, 1868 (London: Skeffington, 1898)

BATTISCOMBE, Georgina. *Charlotte Mary Yonge: The Story of an Uneventful Life* (London: Constable, 1943)

— *John Keble: A Study in Limitations* (New York: Knopf, 1963)

BREAY, Claire. 'Women and the classical tripos, 1869-1914', in *Classics in 19th and 20th Century Cambridge: Curriculum, Culture and Community*, (Cambridge Philological Society, Supplementary volume 24), ed. C. Stray (Cambridge: Cambridge Philological Society, 1999) pp. 49-70

BRIGDEN, Susan. *London and the Reformation* (Oxford: Clarendon Press, 1989)

BROOK, Barbara. *Elizabeth Garrett Anderson, "A Thoroughly Ordinary Woman"* (Aldeburgh: Aldeburgh Bookshop, 1997)

BROOKS, Peter. *Body Work: Objects of Desire in Modern Narrative* (Cambridge, MA: Harvard University Press, 1993)

BURKHART, Charles (ed.). *The Art of Ivy Compton Burnett* (London: Gollancz, 1972)

BUTLER, A. J. (ed.). *Life and Letters of William J. Butler* (London: Macmillan, 1897)

CHADWICK, Owen. *The Victorian Church* (London: A. C. Black, 1970)

A Chaplet for Charlotte Yonge, ed. Georgina Battiscombe and Marghanita Laski (London: Cresset Press, 1965)

COLERIDGE, Christabel Rose. *Charlotte Mary Yonge: Her Life and Letters* (London: Macmillan, 1903)

—— *The Daughters Who Have Not Revolted* (London, 1894)

COLERIDGE, J. T. *Memoir of the Rev. John Keble* (Oxford: James Parker, 1869)

COMPTON BURNETT, Ivy. *A Father and his Fate* (London: Gollancz, 1957)

—— *Pastors and Masters*, 1925 (London: Allison and Busby, 1984)

COOPER, Lettice. 'Charlotte Yonge, Dramatic Novelist', in *A Chaplet for Charlotte Yonge*, ed. Georgina Battiscombe and Marghanita Laski (London: Cresset Press, 1965) pp. 31-40

COURTNEY, Julia. 'The Barnacle, a Manuscript Magazine of the 1860s', in *The Girl's Own: Cultural Histories of the Anglo-American Girl, 1815-1930*, ed. Claudia Nelson and Lynne Vallone (Athens and London: University of Georgia Press, 1994) pp. 71-97.

—— 'Charlotte M. Yonge: A Novelist and Her Readers', unpublished PhD thesis, University of London, 1990

DENNIS, Barbara. *Charlotte Yonge (1823-1901), Novelist of the Oxford Movement: A Literature of Victorian Culture and Society* (Lampeter: Edwin Mellen, 1992)

DRAZIN, Philip J. 'Publications about Charlotte Yonge and her Works', from *Charlotte Yonge: A Bibliography* (1999). [The last version of the late Professor Philip Drazin's (unpublished) bibliography dates to 2001.]

DUNLAP, Barbara. 'Reading Charlotte Yonge into the Novels of Barbara Pym', in *"All This Reading": The Literary World of Barbara Pym*, ed. Frauke Elisabeth Lenckos and Ellen J. Miller (Madison, NJ: Fairleigh Dickinson University Press, 2003) pp. 179-93

FAIRFAX-LUCY, Alice. 'The Other Miss Yonge', in *A Chaplet for Charlotte Yonge*, ed. Georgina Battiscombe and Marghanita Laski (London: Cresset Press, 1965) pp. 90-97

FASICK, Laura. *Vessels of Meaning: Women's Bodies, Gender Norms and Class Bias from Richardson to Lawrence* (DeKalb, IL: Northern Illinois University Press, 1997)

FFOULKES, Charles. *The Armourer and his Craft* (London: Benjamin Blom, 1912)

FLINT, K. (ed.) *The Woman Reader, 1837-1914* (Oxford: Clarendon Press, 1993)

FOWLER, R. ' 'On Not Knowing Greek:' The Classics and the Woman of Letters', *Classical Journal* 78 (1983) pp. 337-49

FROUDE, James Anthony. 'The Oxford Counter-Reformation', *Short Studies on Great Subjects* (4th Series) (London: Longmans, Green, 1883)

GENTILE, Kathy Justice. *Ivy Compton Burnett* (Women Writers series) (London: Macmillan, 1991)

GEZARI, Janet. *Charlotte Bronte and Defensive Conduct: The Author and the Body at Risk* (Philadelphia: University of Pennsylvania Press, 1992)

GILBERT, Pamela K. *Disease, Desire and the Body in Victorian Women's Popular Novels* (New York: Cambridge University Press, 1997)

GORE, Charles. (ed.) *Lux Mundi* (London: John Murray, 1890)

HARRIS, Mary J. *Memoir of Frances Mary Peard* (Torquay: W. H. Smith, 1930)

HAYLLAR, F. 'Studies in the Iliad', *Monthly Packet*, new [fourth] series, 3 (1892) pp. 459-69, 579-90, 700-10

HAYTER, Alethea. *Charlotte Yonge.* (Plymouth: Northcote House, 1996)

—— 'The Sanitary Idea and a Victorian Novelist', *History Today* 19 (1969) pp. 840-47

HOLLAND, Henry Scott. *A Bundle of Memories* (London: Wells Gardner, Darton, 1915)

Household Words: A Weekly Journal 1850-1858, conducted by Charles Dickens. A Table of Contributors and their Contributions, based on the "Household Words Office Book" in the Morris L Parrish Collection of Victorian Novels in Princeton University Library, compiled by Anne Lohrli, (Toronto and Buffalo: University of Toronto Press, 1973)

JOHNSON, Maria Poggi. 'The King, the Priest and the Armorer: A Victorian Historical Fantasy of the *Via Media*', *Clio: A Journal of Literature, History and the Philosophy of History* 28.4 (1999) pp. 399-413.

KEBLE, John. *Sermons Academical and Occasional* (Oxford: John Henry Parker, 1847)

LANGBAUER, Laurie. *Novels of Everyday Life: the Series in English Fiction 1850-1930* (Ithaca: Cornell University Press, 1999)

LANGLAND, Elizabeth. *Nobody's Angels: Middle-Class Women and Domestic Ideology in Victorian Culture* (Ithaca: Cornell University Press, 1995)

LASKI, Marghanita. 'Some Chronological Cruces', in *A Chaplet for Charlotte Yonge*, ed. Georgina Battiscombe and Marghanita Laski (London: Cresset Press, 1965) pp. 79-89

MADDEN, Lionel. *J. B. Shorthouse and C. M. Yonge* (unpublished dissertation, University of London, 1964-65)

MERMIN, Dorothy. *Godiva's Ride: Women of Letters in England, 1830-1880* (Bloomington: Indiana University Press, 1993)

MICHIE, Helena. *The Flesh Made Word: Female Figures and Women's Bodies* (New York: Oxford University Press, 1986)

MITCHELL, Sally. *Dinah Mulock Craik* (Boston: Twayne, 1983)

MOI, Toril. *Sexual/Textual Politics: Feminist Literary Theory* (London and New York: Routledge, 1985)

MOOR, John Frewen. *The Birth-Place, Home, Churches, and Other Places Connected with the Author of "The Christian Year", illustrated in Thirty-two Photographs by W. Savage; with Memoir and Notes*. 2nd ed. (Winchester: William Savage; London: James Parker, 1867)

MURDOCH, Iris. *Existentialists and Mystics: Writings on Philosophy and Literature*, ed. P. Conradi, (London: Chatto and Windus, 1997)

NELSON, Claudia. *Invisible Men: Fatherhood in Victorian Periodicals, 1850-1910* (Athens, GA: University of Georgia Press, 1995)

OLLARD, S. L. *A Short History of the Oxford Movement* (London: Mowbray, 1915)

PATERSON, M. Jeanne. *Family, Love and Work in the Lives of Victorian Gentlewomen* (Bloomington: Indiana University Press, 1989)

POWELL, Violet. 'Genealogical Tables for the Linked Novels of Charlotte Yonge, Dramatic Novelist', in *A Chaplet for Charlotte Yonge*, ed. Georgina Battiscombe and Marghanita Laski (London: Cresset Press, 1965) pp. 195-203

RAWLINSON, George. *The Five Great Monarchies of the Ancient Eastern World; or, The History, Geography and Antiquities of Chaldaea, Assyria, Babylon, Media, and Persia* (London: Murray, 1862-67)

— *History of Herodotus: A New English Version* (London: Murray, 1858-60)

RICE, Philip and WAUGH, Patricia. *Modern Literary Theory: A Reader*. 3rd ed. (London: Edward Arnold, 1996)

ROBERTS, David. 'The Social Conscience of the Tory Periodicals' (*Victorian Periodicals Newsletter* 10.3, Sept. 1977) pp. 154-69

ROMANES, Ethel. *Charlotte Mary Yonge: An Appreciation* (Oxford: Mowbray, 1908)

ROWELL, Geoffrey. *The Vision Glorious* (Oxford: Oxford University Press, 1983)

SANDERS, Valerie. *Eve's Renegades: Victorian Anti-Feminist Women Novelists* (Basingstoke and London: Macmillan Press, 1996)

SCHAMA, Simon. 'Heavy Metal,' *New Yorker*, 21 December 1998

SCHULTZE, Clemence E. 'Manliness and the Myth of Hercules in Charlotte M. Yonge's *My Young Alcides*', *International Journal of the Classical Tradition* 5 (1999) pp. 381-414

SHOWALTER, Elaine. A *Literature of Their Own*, 1977 (London: Virago, 1991)

SNELL, F. J. 'Plutarch's Heroes', *Monthly Packet,* new [fourth] series, 14 (1897) pp. 32-41, 142-51, 270-79, 396-406, 498-507, 642-51

SPURLING, Hilary. *Secrets of a Woman's Heart* (London: Hodder and Stoughton, 1984)

SMITH, Gerald W. [various translations from Greek tragedians], *Monthly Packet*, third series, 1-5 (1881-83)

STRAY, Christopher A. *Classics Transformed: Schools, Universities, and Society in England, 1830-1860* (Oxford: Clarendon Press, 1998)

STURROCK, June. *"Heaven and Home": Charlotte M Yonge's Domestic Fiction and the Victorian Debate over Women* (English Literary Studies Monograph 66) (Victoria, B.C.: University of Victoria, 1995)

— 'Sequels, Series, and Sensation Novels: Charlotte Yonge and the Popular Fiction Market of the 1850s and 1860s', in *Part Two: Reflections on the Sequel*, ed. Paul Budra and Betty A. Schellenberg (Toronto: University of Toronto Press, 1998) pp. 102-17

— 'Women, Work and *The Monthly Packet*, 1851-73', *Nineteenth Century Feminisms* 1 (1999) pp. 51-73

SUTHERLAND, Gillian. 'The Movement for the Higher Education of Women: its Social and Intellectual Context in England, c. 1840-80'. in *Politics and Social Change in Modern Britain: Essays Presented to A. F. Thompson*, ed. P. J. Waller (Brighton: Harvester, 1987) pp. 91-116

'SYBIL'. 'The Girlhood of Famous Women: Charlotte M. Yonge', *Girl's Realm Annual* (1899) pp. 1187-92

THOMPSON, Nicola Diane. *Reviewing Sex: Gender and the Reception of Victorian Novels* (Basingstoke: Macmillan, 1996)

VRETTOS, Athena. *Somatic Fiction: Imaging Illness in Victorian Culture* (Stanford: Stanford University Press, 1995)

Wellesley Index to Victorian Periodicals 1824-1900, ed. W. E. Houghton (Toronto: University of Toronto Press, 1966-89) 5 vols

WERNER, A. 'A Sketch of B.C. 75', *Monthly Packet*, third series, 9 (April 1885) pp. 384-92

WOOLF, Virginia. *The Common Reader* (London: Hogarth Press, 1984)

THE CHARLOTTE M. YONGE FELLOWSHIP

The Charlotte M. Yonge Fellowship can be contacted via its website at: www.cmyf.org.uk

INDEX